AF660990

Python Programming

Python Programming

A Comprehensive Approach

Veena Ghuriani
Associate Professor
Department of Computer Science
Maitreyi College, University of Delhi

Akansha Gautam
Assistant Professor
Department of Computer Science
Rajdhani College, University of Delhi

Vaishali Chawla
Assistant Professor
Department of Computer Science
Keshav Mahavidyalaya, University of Delhi

PHI Learning Private Limited
Delhi-110092
2025

In fond memory of ***Shri Asoke K. Ghosh*** *(October 1942 – February 2024), Founder Chairman and Managing Director of PHI Learning, whose vision endlessly inspires.*

The Legacy Continues. . . .

Published by Pushpita Ghosh, PHI Learning Private Limited, Rimjhim House, 111, Patparganj Industrial Estate, Delhi-110092 and Printed by Multi Colour Services, I-45, DLF Industrial Area, Sector-32, Faridabad, Haryana-121003.

₹695.00

PYTHON PROGRAMMING: A Comprehensive Approach
Veena Ghuriani, Akansha Gautam and Vaishali Chawla

© 2025 by PHI Learning Private Limited, Delhi.

All right reserved. This publication is protected by copyright and may not be reproduced, in whole or in part, in any form or by any electronic, mechanical, or other means, now known or hereafter invented, including photocopying, recording, or any information storage and retrieval system, OR to train artificial intelligence systems without permission in writing from the publisher.

ISBN-978-81-19364-09-1 (Print Book)
ISBN-978-81-19364-08-4 (e-Book)

The export rights of the book are vested solely with the publisher.

Contents

Preface

The scientific field has witnessed a rising demand for the Python Programming language in a wide array of applications. In compliance with this, educational institutes all over the country began incorporating Python Programming as a part of their respective curriculum. Not only was Python included in the syllabi of technical courses, but students of non-technical courses are also given the option to learn Python to enhance their skill set. These amendments, naturally, required comprehensive books on Python.

In the past few years, several books on Python have emerged in the market. On careful inspection of the most popularly recommended text on Python, the authors of this book observed that there is still a need for a book that covers it all—from the basics of a computer to the advanced applications of Python Programming. This has been a motivating factor behind the creation of this book.

The authors have thoroughly researched several popularly used resources of Python, and have attempted to bring it all under one umbrella, in a manner as simple as possible. The book has been written keeping in mind the interdisciplinary nature of the changing syllabus. This book is a great choice for learning Python, regardless of the programming experience or level of expertise. It is intended to assist students to build a solid foundation in programming and prepare them for more advanced courses.

Chapter 1 covers the basic fundamentals of computer system, which explains the different components of a computer and also introduces the flowchart and the algorithm which are the basics of programming. Chapters 2 to 5 cover topics starting from installation of Python, concepts of variables, datatypes, operators, control structures, functions and strings. In Chapter 6, the mutable and immutable objects like lists, tuples, sets and dictionary are covered in detail, elaborately explaining the built-in functions associated with each type. Chapter 7 and 8 are devoted to discussion of classes, objects and other concepts of object-oriented programming. Chapter 9 covers the use of files in Python Programming which is significant in real world application where real data is to be analysed. It also discusses exceptions and exception handling.

Chapter 10 covers sorting and searching techniques, selection sort, bubble sort, insertion sort and linear and binary search. Chapter 11 covers the Python modules, NumPy and Pandas, it extensively covers the series and dataframe for organizing data. Chapter 12 covers Data Visualization using the Matplotlib library, it covers various 2D and 3D plots which are used nowadays for representing data. All the chapters have numerous worked programs to enhance the learning process.

As the authors of this book, we sincerely hope that our vision of making the process of learning Python easy and lucid come to fruition.

Veena Ghuriani
Akansha Gautam
Vaishali Chawla

Acknowledgements

A successful project involves the effort of a lot more people than those who are credited. We take this opportunity to express our gratitude to all those who have worked behind the scenes.

Firstly, we would like to thank our families and friends for being a constant source of support as we worked through months in the making of this book. Their love, care, and belief acted like a boost of confidence. Also we thank our colleagues and mentors for guiding us through various stages of the work, as they have been supportive throughout this journey.

Our students have been a great resource for us, who constantly gave their feedback to improve the contents and make the book better than the resources they are currently using. Getting feedback from the target audience during development of this book has definitely been a guiding light.

We also thank the editors and publishers of the book, who guided us through every stage of the publishing process and have gone to lengths to make things convenient for us. The editors and the production team have played a major role in the quick formatting and typesetting. We are grateful to them.

Veena Ghuriani
Akansha Gautam
Vaishali Chawla

0

Computer Fundamentals

Mankind has always thrived to innovate things to make their lives convenient. A calculator was devised to simplify the task of doing computations. As human intelligence and technology evolved with time, a computer was devised. In its initial stages, a computer was not of much use to the common man. It was used majorly for scientific applications. Years later, its design was modified to suit the requirements and usability skills of the common man. Since then, there has been no stoppage in the evolution of computers.

In this chapter, we understand the very basics of a computer, its parts, and its working. We further delve into the process of making a computer program by learning the concept of an algorithm and pseudocode.

0.1 WHAT IS A COMPUTER?

A computer is an electronic machine that runs a set of programs, known as software, to perform computations. A computer is designed to work on information, often taken as input from the user. The software in the computer then performs certain processing on this data and produces a result called output.

Figure 0.1 Desktop Computer System.

0.1.1 Types of Computer and their Parts

It must be noted that there are several forms of a computer. A simple handheld calculator that performs some basic arithmetic is also a computer. Other forms include a desktop computer that is commonly seen in offices. Figure 0.1 shows a common desktop computer. A laptop is a concise form of a desktop, designed for portable use. Further, a wide array of handheld devices such as tablets and smartphones are available in the market. While these types of computers provide a vast array of services, some computers are designed only for specific purposes such as the machine embedded in a microwave or a washing machine.

Irrespective of its size or application, every computer consists of the following basic components:

- **Central Processing Unit (CPU):** It is the brain of the computer and is responsible for all the activities in a computer. A system may have one or more CPUs.
- **Memory:** The main memory of a computer stores programs and data.
- **Input Devices:** They are the hardware devices connected to the computer through which the computer receives user input (Example: Mouse, Keyboard, etc.)
- **Output Devices:** These are used to provide output to the user in the form of display, sound, etc. (Example: screen, speaker, printer, etc.)

In addition to this, a computer may also have some networking devices attached that help connect to a network. Further, storage devices such as magnetic disks may also be present.

0.1.2 Language of a Computer

A computer is an electronic device. It does not understand the language understood by humans. It operates on voltage signals—On/Off, High/Low. Hence, it can be established that a computer understands only 2 types of values. The language of a computer is known as the *Binary Language.* The word "Bi" means 2, denoting the 2 values understood by a computing device. Binary language comprises 2 symbols, represented as 1 and 0.

The smallest unit of information in a computer is known as a *bit*, short for *Binary Digit.* A bit can have 2 values—either 1 or 0. A group of 8 bits is called a *Byte.* Half a byte, i.e., a group of 4 bits is called a *nibble.* The collection of bits and bytes follows a hierarchy that is used to specify the storage capacity of devices.

1 Byte (B)	⇒	8 bits
1 KiloByte (KB)	⇒	1024 Bytes
1 MegaByte (MB)	⇒	1024 KB
1 GigaByte (GB)	⇒	1024 MB
1 TeraByte (TB)	⇒	1024 GB
1 PetaByte (PB)	⇒	1024 TB
1 ExaByte	⇒	1024 PB
1 ZettaByte	⇒	1024 ExaBytes

0.2 ORGANIZATION OF A COMPUTER SYSTEM

Having learned about the basic components of a computer, we shall now understand the interaction among these components. The different parts of a computer communicate, via a *bus system*. As of now, it can be understood as a set of wires and other digital components that help transfer information. The working of a computer system can be understood from Figure 0.2.

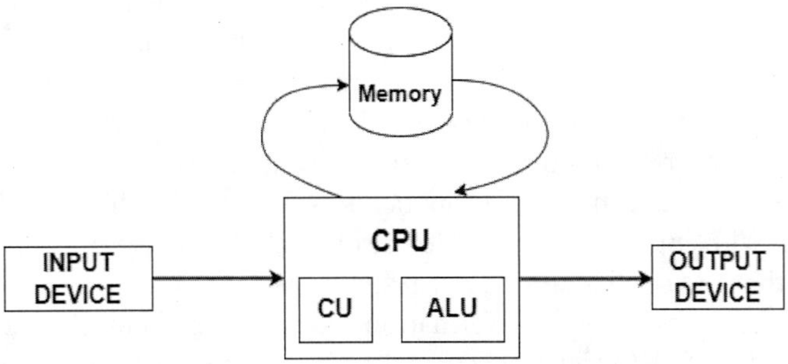

Figure 0.2 Organization of a computer system.

The user is prompted for input that can be in the form of a click, sound, text, or touch. This data is recorded in the corresponding input device and is passed to the CPU for processing. The CPU consists of 2 sub-units: the Control Unit (CU), and the Arithmetic and Logical Unit (ALU). The CU is responsible for handling various control signals whereas the ALU performs necessary computations. The CPU can read and write data from and to the memory, to execute an instruction specified by the user. The result of the execution is then transferred to the output device, to be presented to the user.

0.2.1 Memory Unit

One of the most important parts of any computer system is the memory or storage unit. As implied by the name, this component is in charge of archiving instructional materials, data, and preliminary findings. Other names for this internal storage component include the main memory, primary storage, and random access memory (RAM). The size of the memory unit has a big impact on the computer's speed, power, and overall performance. A computer system has two different types of memory: primary memory and secondary memory. The memory unit primarily stores the information and commands required for processing. It also records the interim results of any calculations or tasks. After processing is complete, the final results are stored in the memory unit rather than being transferred to an output device so the user can view them. The memory unit is in charge of keeping data and, if necessary, transmitting it to other parts of the computer. Its function as a bridge between the input and output devices allows for the uninterrupted transmission of all inputs and outputs.

In conclusion, the memory or storage unit is a crucial component of every computer system. Its functions are essential to the computer's overall performance, and its size greatly affects the speed and power of the machine.

0.2.2 Control Unit

The control unit is another crucial component of a computer system, responsible for managing and directing the operations of all other parts. Despite its name, the control unit does not engage in data processing operations. Instead, it uses electrical signals to instruct the computer system on how to execute already stored instructions. The major job of the control unit is to keep the information flowing through the processor. By reading instructions from the memory unit, decoding them, and then executing them, it accomplishes this. In a sense, the control unit serves as the conductor of the computer orchestra, making sure all of the instruments are playing in unison.

The control unit's main responsibilities include managing all of the computer's components, interpreting input from the memory unit, and coordinating the transmission of data and instructions between various computer components. Additionally, the control unit is responsible for communicating with input and output devices to transfer data or results from memory. It's important to note that the control unit is not responsible for processing or storing data. Instead, it focuses on managing the flow of information and ensuring that all parts of the computer work together seamlessly. Without the control unit, a computer system would be unable to function effectively.

0.2.3 Arithmetic Logic Unit (ALU)

The Arithmetic Logic Unit (ALU) is responsible for performing both arithmetic and logical functions. It is divided into two subsections, namely the Arithmetic Section and the Logic Section. Basic arithmetic operations like addition, subtraction, multiplication, and division are handled by the Arithmetic Section. The ALU performs these precise computations necessary for carrying out complex calculations. Additionally, the ALU can perform more complex operations by making repetitive use of the basic arithmetic functions. On the other hand, the Logic Section is responsible for performing logical operations such as selecting, comparing, matching, and merging data. These operations are essential for decision-making processes and data manipulation. The ALU executes these functions with accuracy and speed.

It is significant to remember that a CPU may contain numerous ALUs. These parts can be used to track timers that assist computer system operation. Overall, the ALU is an essential component of a computer system that enables it to do challenging calculations and logical processes quickly and efficiently.

0.3 COMPUTER MEMORY

The digital equivalent of the human brain is computer memory. It acts as a repository for the data, knowledge, and instructions needed for processing. This data storage device is an essential part of any computer system because it is in charge of storing both input and output.

In the world of computing, there are two main types of memory: *Primary and Secondary*. Primary memory, also referred to as main or temporary memory, is an internal component of the computer that stores data and instructions currently in use by the system or CPU. This type of memory is considered volatile, meaning that it loses all data when power is switched off. On the other hand, secondary memory, also known as external or auxiliary or permanent memory, is a crucial component of any computer system. Its main purpose is to permanently store various programmes and data, guaranteeing that information is kept even if the power is turned off. Non-volatile memory is a term used to describe a form of memory that permanently stores data without the need for a continuous power supply.

0.3.1 Primary Memory

Primary memory is of two types: *RAM and ROM.* Any computer system needs random access memory (RAM), which is a critical component. RAM, as its name implies, is a form of memory that enables random access, making it possible to swiftly and effectively access any piece of data kept within. Since RAM is in charge of storing and retrieving data that is currently being used by the system, it is frequently referred to as the main memory of a computer system. The fact that RAM is only a transient memory should be noted. This means that whenever the computer's power source is turned off, all information that was saved there would be gone. As a result, RAM is frequently utilised to store data that is only needed temporarily.

A sort of permanent memory known as read-only memory (ROM) keeps its data even when the power is turned off. The maker of the computer write the contents of ROM during the manufacturing process; the computer is unable to overwrite this data. Because of this, it qualifies as non-volatile memory. Three different ROM memory types exist:

- **Programmable Read-Only Memory (PROM):** This type of memory allows for the one-time writing and repeated reading of data. The stored data cannot be modified once the chip has been programmed.
- **Erasable Programmable Read-Only Memory (EPROM):** The data previously recorded in this type of memory can be erased in order to programme it. By shining ultraviolet light on the chip, it is possible to remove the data from an EPROM.
- **Electrically Erasable Programmable Read-Only Memory (EEPROM):** In just milliseconds, unique electrical waves can programme and erase this sort of memory. It is possible to delete only one byte of data or the complete contents of the device.

Some characteristics of the main memory include:

- Main memory is a semiconductor memory that is faster than secondary memory.
- It is typically a volatile memory, meaning that it requires a constant power supply to retain data.
- As the primary memory of the computer, it is an essential component that cannot be overlooked. Without it, a computer system would be unable to function.

0.3.2 Secondary Memory/Storage Unit

The storage unit is a component of the computer system that is used to store data and processing-related instructions. A storage device is an essential part of the hardware of a computer that saves the data and information required to process the results of computations. Without a storage device, a computer couldn't run or even turn on. Alternatively, a storage device could be thought of as a piece of hardware that is used to transfer, store, or extract data files. It can also permanently and temporarily store information or data.

Magnetic disc drives, optical disc drives (CD and DVD), and USB flash drives are the three main categories of storage devices. Let's understand them in detail.

Disks

A magnetic disk, shown in Figure 0.3, is a type of secondary memory that utilizes a flat disc coated with a magnetic material to store information. This technology is commonly used to house a variety of programs and files. The polarization of the data is represented as 1 for one direction and 0 for the other. While magnetic disks are less expensive than RAM and can store vast amounts of data, their data access rate is slower than main memory due to their secondary nature. However, magnetic disks offer the convenience of easy data modification and deletion, as well as the ability to access data randomly. In general, magnetic discs are a dependable and affordable option for data storage of huge volumes. They are a useful resource for both individuals and corporations because of their accessibility and adaptability.

Figure 0.3 A magnetic disk.

Optical Disc Drives

Compared to magnetic memory, optical memory is a relatively new and promising secondary storage medium. It can store large amounts of data in limited space, making it a high-capacity random medium. A revolving disc covered in a thin, highly reflective metal or other material makes up an optical-disk storage system. Because data on the disc is recorded and read using laser beam technology, optical discs are also known as laser discs or optical laser discs. A dependable and effective alternative for high-capacity secondary storage, optical memory has revolutionized how we store and retrieve data. It has developed into a crucial part of contemporary computing systems because of its cutting-edge technology and small size. Compact Disk (CD) and Digital Versatile Disk (DVD) are types of optical disks. Figure 0.4 represents a CD.

Figure 0.4 Optical disk.

USB Flash Drives

A USB flash drive is a compact and reliable device that serves the purpose of data storage. It is equipped with a flash memory and an integrated Universal Serial Bus (USB) interface, making it easily accessible and compatible with most devices. These drives are designed to be both removable and rewritable, allowing for convenient and efficient data transfer. Figure 0.5 is a USB drive also commonly known as Pen Drive.

In terms of physical attributes, USB flash drives are compact and strong, which makes them perfect for regular usage. It's interesting to note that the speed of operation increases with storage capacity. This is because they are mechanically sturdy and devoid of any moving elements that could break or malfunction.

The ability of USB flash drives to draw power from the object to which they are connected—typically a computer—via the USB connector is one of their most practical characteristics. This makes them a convenient and effective option for data storage because it eliminates the need for additional power sources or wires.

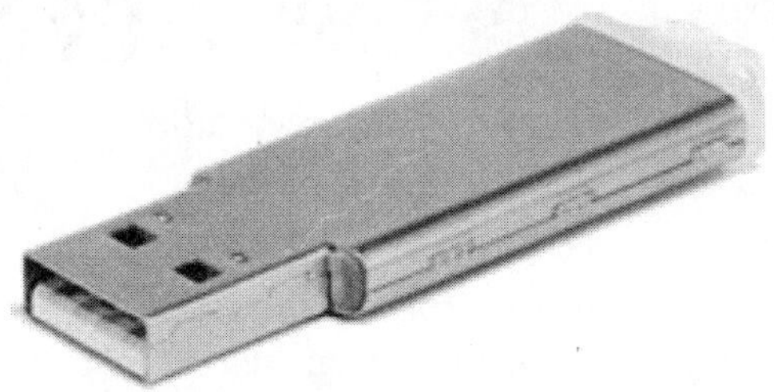

Figure 0.5 Pen Drive, a USB device.

0.4 INPUT–OUTPUT DEVICES

The user communicates with the computer system with the help of input and output devices. The input device is used to give data to the computer for processing and the output devices display the results of processing. The data can be numeric, textual, image, audio or video type. There are different input and output devices to handle different types of data. Keyboard, mouse, joystick, scanner, microphone (mic), web camera, touch screens are some of the input devices. Monitor, printer, plotter, speaker, headphone, projector are examples of output devices. We will discuss the most common ones used in this section.

0.4.1 Input Devices

Keyboard

The keyboard is used to input the numeric and textual information by typing. It is similar to a typewriter and has several keys for typing numbers, alphabets, punctuation marks, etc. A simple keyboard is shown in Figure 0.6. Besides, there are special keys:

- **Function Keys:** These keys are located on the topmost row of the keyboard. There are 12 function keys, F1, F2, F3, F4, F5, F6, F7, F8, F9, F10, F11, F12. These keys have specific functions, like F1 is for help, F2 is for saving, etc.

- **Control Keys:** They include shift, ctrl, alt keys, which are used in combination with other keys to perform designated functions, for example ctrl + c is used for copy function.
- **Formatting Keys:** These include caps lock, space bar, tab, pg up, pg dn, backspace, home, end, delete, arrow keys, etc.

Figure 0.6 A keyboard.

Mouse

Mouse is a pointing device used to interact with the *GUI* (*Graphical User Interface*). It is used to move the mouse pointer (cursor) on the screen, select options/objects and click on them. A mouse with left button and right button is shown in Figure 0.7.

Figure 0.7 A mouse.

0.4.2 Output Devices

Monitor

Monitor is a standard output device to display text, images, videos, graphics generated by the computer. The earlier monitor used the Cathode Ray tube (CRT) technology and the present monitors are flat screen monitors using the Liquid Crystal Display (LCD), Light Emitting Diode (LED), and plasma technology. Figure 0.8 is a flat screen monitor.

Figure 0.8 A monitor.

Printer

Printer is an output device that generates the hard copy output. There are black and white and color printers. Printers are also categorized as impact printers (dot matrix printer, daisy wheel printer) and non-impact printers (inkjet printer, thermal printer, and laser printer). The printing quality of non-impact printers is higher than that of impact printers. Figure 0.9 is a non-impact printer.

Figure 0.9 A printer.

Plotter

Plotter is an output device used to print graphical output. It uses multi-coloured pens to create graphs, charts, drawings, maps, etc. It is suitable for architectural drawings and CAD applications. There are different types of plotters: drum plotter, flatbed plotter, pen plotter, thermal plotter and many more. Figure 0.10 is a drum plotter.

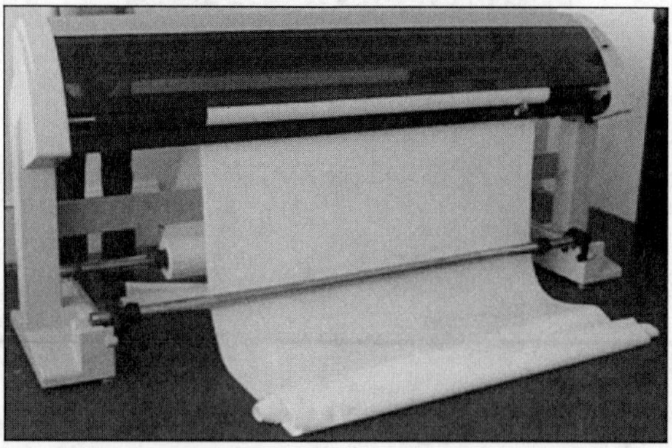

Figure 0.10 A plotter.

0.5 ALGORITHM AND FLOWCHART

0.5.1 Algorithm

An algorithm is a set of instructions to solve a problem. It takes a specific set of inputs and generates the results in a finite time. The instructions should be simple, precise, easy to understand, lead to the solution and executed in finite time. For example:

Algorithm 1: Algorithm to add two numbers

1. Start
2. Input two numbers, n1 and n2
3. Add n1 and n2, result = n1 + n2
4. Print result
5. Stop

As can be seen in Algorithm 1, the instructions are written in simple English and do not follow the syntax of any programming language. A few more examples of algorithms are given below.

Algorithm 2: Algorithm to find maximum of two numbers

```
1. Start
2. Input two numbers, a and b
3. If ( a > b )
      Print "a is maximum"
   else
      Print "b is maximum"
4. Stop
```

Algoritm 2 shows how to find maximum of two numbers. Let a and b be the two numbers, in order to find maximum, a and b are to be compared.

Algorithm 3: Algorithm to check whether a number is prime or not

1. Start
2. Input a number, num
3. Initialize flag = 1 and i = 2
4. Repeat until i <= num / 2
   (a) Calculate remainder r of num / i
   (b) If remainder r = 0
         flag = 0
         Go to step 5
   (c) i = i + 1
5. If flag = 0
      Print num is not prime
   Else
      Print num is prime
6. Stop

Algorithm 3 checks whether a number is prime or not. Let num be the number, in order to see if a number is composite or prime, it has to be divided by numbers in the range 2 to num/2, if num is divisible by any one of these numbers, it is not prime.

Algorithm 4: Algorithm to calculate factorial of a number

1. Start
2. Input a number, num
3. Initialize fact = 1 and i = 1
4. Repeat until i <= num
   (a) fact = fact * i
   (b) i = i + 1
5. Print fact
6. Stop

Algorithm 4 calculates the factorial of a number, say num. The factorial of num is 1*2*3*4* .....*num–1*num. A loop is created from 1 to num and multiplied one by one in order to calculate factorial.

0.5.2 Flowchart

A flowchart is a pictorial representation of the sequence of steps for solving a problem. It uses standardized symbols to represent the steps. The symbols used in a flowchart are shown in Figure 0.11.

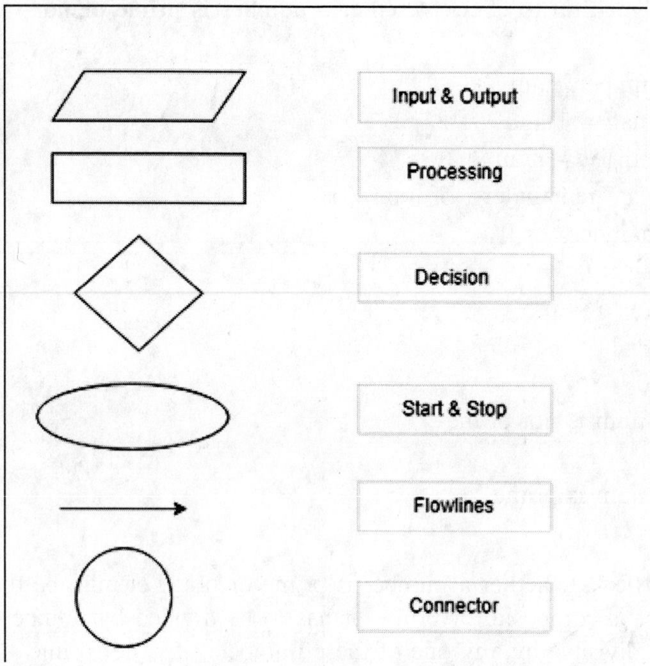

Figure 0.11 Symbols of flowchart.

Let us now see the flowcharts for the algorithms stated in section 0.5.1. Figures 0.12 to 0.15 are flowcharts of the algorithms given above.

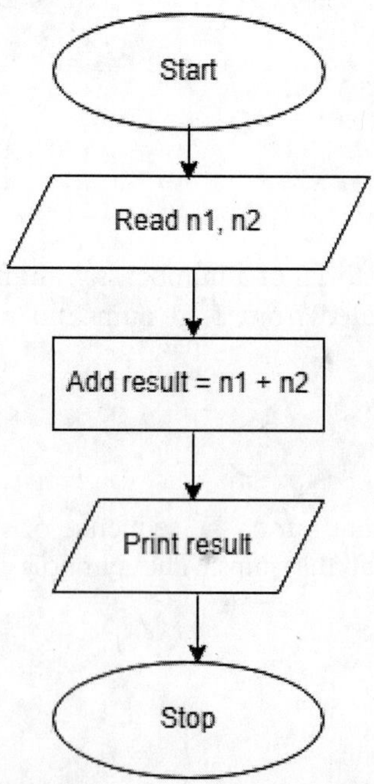

Figure 0.12 Flowchart to add two numbers.

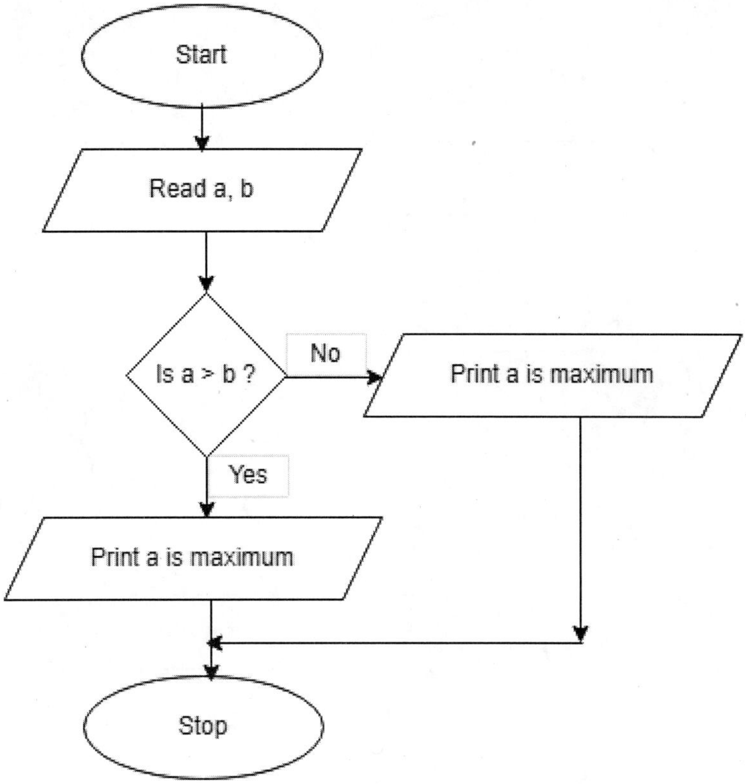

Figure 0.13 Flowchart to find the maximum of two numbers.

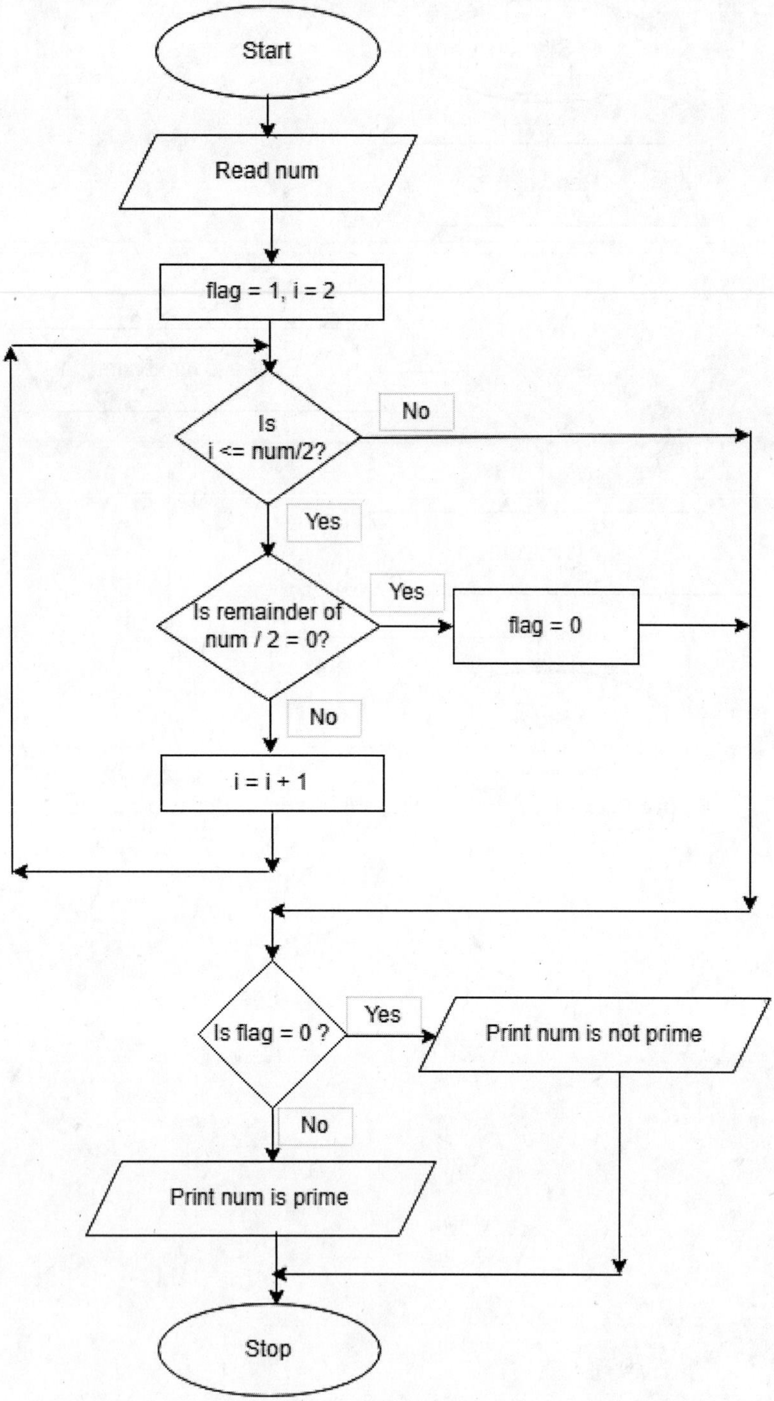

Figure 0.14 Flowchart to check whether a number is prime.

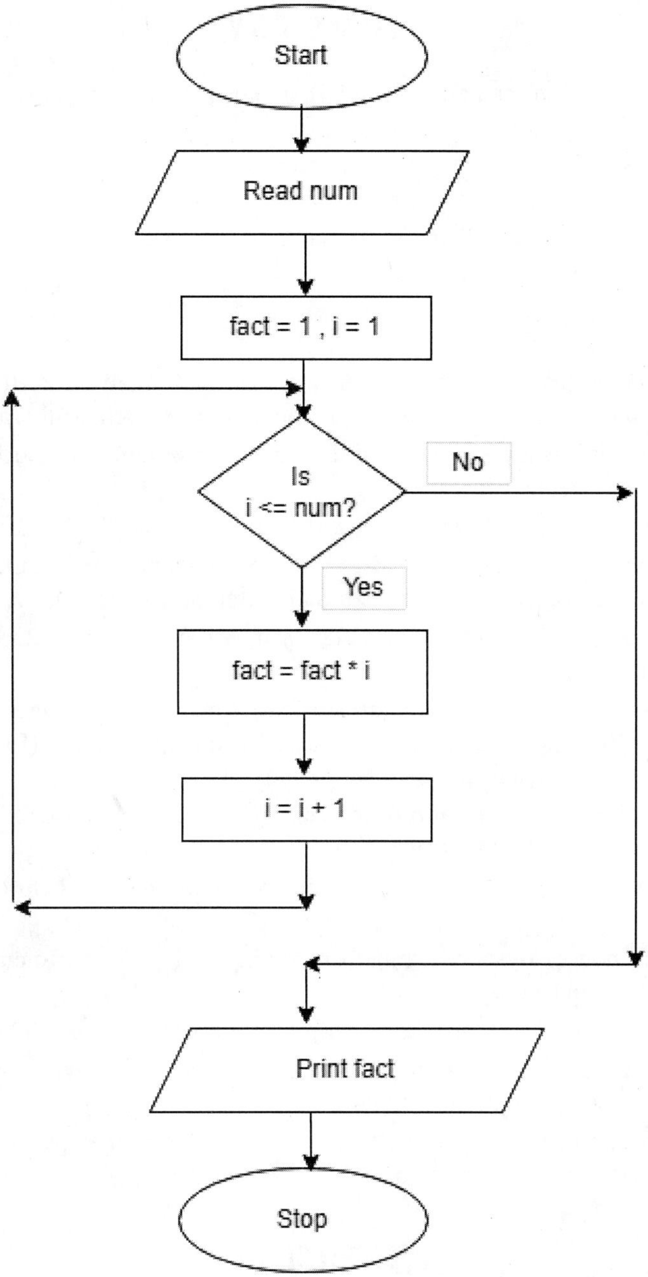

Figure 0.15 Flowchart to compute the factorial of a number.

SUMMARY

- A computer is an electronic machine that runs a set of programs, known as software, to perform computations.
- The smallest unit of information in a computer is known as a *bit*, short for *Binary Digit*. A bit can have 2 values—either 1 or 0. A group of 8 bits is called a *Byte*.
- The Central Processing Unit (CPU) consists of 2 sub-units: the Control Unit (CU), and the Arithmetic and Logical Unit (ALU).
- The CU is responsible for handling various control signals whereas the ALU performs necessary computations.
- Computer memory is the digital equivalent of the human brain. It serves as a storage unit for data, information, and instructions that are essential for processing.
- The storage unit is a component of the computer system that is used to store the data and processing-related instructions.
- Primary and Secondary are two main types of memory:

  Primary memory, also referred to as main or temporary or volatile memory, whereas Secondary memory is known as external or temporary or non-volatile memory.
- Primary memory is of two types: Random Access Memory (RAM) and Read-Only Memory (ROM).
- ROM memory is further categorized into three types: Programmable Read-Only Memory (PROM), Erasable Programmable Read Only Memory (EPROM), Electrically Erasable Programmable Read-Only Memory (EEPROM).
- Magnetic disc drives, optical disc drives (CD and DVD), and USB flash drives are the three main categories of storage devices.
- The user communicates with the computer system with the help of input and output devices.
- Keyboard, mouse, joystick, scanner, microphone (mic), web camera, touch screens are some of the input devices.
- Monitor, printer, plotter, speaker, headphone, projector are examples of output devices.
- An algorithm is a set of instructions to solve a problem. It takes a specific set of inputs and generates the results in a finite time.
- Flowchart is a pictorial representation of the sequence of steps for solving a problem. It uses standardized symbols to represent the steps.

EXERCISES

0.1 Write short notes on

(a) Control Unit

(b) ALU

0.2 Differentiate between Printers and Plotters.

0.3 What do you understand from a computer memory? What tiny data chunk can a computer store? How many bytes make up one gigabyte?

0.4 What are a computer system's components? To demonstrate the fundamental structure of a computer and to describe the purposes of its many components, draw a block diagram.

0.5 Differentiate between RAM and ROM.

0.6 Describe any two input devices.

0.7 Describe any two soft copy output devices.

0.8 What is a flash memory? What are the features of flash memory?

0.9 Differentiate between an algorithm and a flowchart.

0.10 Draw a flowchart to find the LCM of three numbers.

1

Introduction to Python Programming

Communication is a vital component of nature. A pair of communicating entities must have at least one language that they both understand. We, as humans, use language to communicate and in case two people don't understand each other's language, they need an intermediary.

With time, the interaction or communication between humans and machines has also increased. But it must be understood that humans and machines cannot interact directly. Hence, humans need some language to specify their instructions to the machine. This task looks very convenient superficially, with the advent of voice assistants. However, at the lowest or basic level, these instructions are programmed in a specific language. These languages are known as High level programming languages. A high level language resembles a human readable language, such as English. Programmers use a high level language to specify instructions and they are converted internally to machine readable format.

Python, over the years, has become a widely used and highly demanded programming language. In this chapter, we will focus on some features and applications of Python. We then proceed to discuss some platforms that support working with Python and installation of the same.

1.1 FEATURES OF PYTHON

The demand for Python has escalated swiftly owing to many reasons. Some of the striking features of Python are listed below:

- **High Level Language:** As already stated, Python is a high-level programming language and is user friendly.
- **Easy:** Python is one of the easiest programming languages to learn. As compared to other languages such as C++ or Java, the properties of Python make it very easy to learn and code.

- **Free:** Anyone who wishes to work with Python, can download and install it on their system from python.org. It is freely available.
- **Open Source:** Being open source means that the source code of the software is openly available and users can suggest or add improvements to it. Python is also an open source language.
- **Interpreted:** This feature concerns how a Python program is executed. There is an interpreter that works when a Python program is executed. It runs the program line by line and stops the execution if an error occurs in a line.
- **Portable:** Python is platform independent, i.e., the same code can run on any system with any hardware configuration, provided it has the appropriate Python environment installed. This property makes Python programs easily portable.
- **Loosely Type Checked:** While creating programs, one may require to store data of different types. To store data, we create variables in our program. Python provides flexibility to an extent that a variable that was storing a number earlier, can later be made to store a word. Since Python is not imposing any check on the data type of the variable, it is a loosely type checked language.
- **Case Sensitive:** Python is a case-sensitive language. It means that a value called "StudentNAME" is different from another value called "studentName".
- **Indented:** In almost all of the high level programs, one might need to create separate blocks of code which perform different functions. While some languages make this task possible by using a pair of brackets, in Python the programmer has to maintain the same level of indentation for statements of code that belong to the same block.
- **Object Oriented Language:** Object oriented programming languages provide special data structures and properties that help model real life entities including their attributes and functionalities.
- **Huge Collection of Libraries:** A library is a collection of several Python programs or functions. A programmer can just include a particular library and use the code snippets already defined in it. Python comes with thousands of such libraries each of which has various functions defined, that just need to be invoked to be used. Since Python is open source, programmers over the world have created some programs and they have been added to the tremendous collection of libraries. Figure 1.1 demonstrates the output of the WordCloud library.

It is safe to attribute the rising popularity of Python to the plethora of features and ease of use offered by it. The areas where Python can be or is being used, are elaborated in the subsequent section.

1.2 APPLICATIONS OF PYTHON

The previous section elucidated some striking properties of the Python programming language. These features have largely contributed to the rise in demand and usage of Python in a large number of applications. In this section, we see some application areas which have become highly reliant on Python.

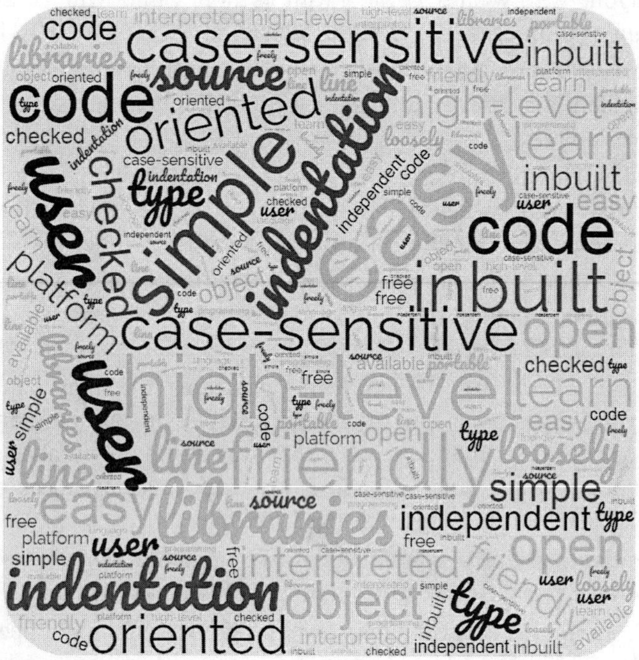

Figure 1.1 A WordCloud depicting some striking features of Python.

- **Scientific Applications:** The dominance of Artificial Intelligence and Machine Learning is directly proportional to the dependency of humans on technology. Applications such as voice recognition, image processing, data analysis, etc. are becoming more prevalent. Python provides several libraries and suitable properties for the implementation of complex machine learning algorithms. Libraries such as *NumPy*, *Sci-Kit Learn*, *Pandas*, *SciPy* provide many built-in functions that implement these algorithms. Further, the *matplotlib* library provides functionalities for data visualization.
- **Web Development:** Many of the popular web development frameworks such as Django, Pyramid, Flask, etc. have Python as their base. They come with standard built-in libraries that support database connectivity, content management and support for internet protocols such as HTTP, SMTP, IMAP, and POP among others. These frameworks are secure and scalable.
- **Desktop GUI Applications:** Desktop applications for any operating system might require an efficient and interactive GUI (Graphical User Interface). Python frameworks such as Tkinter, PyGUI, Kivy, PySide help developers to create interactive GUI-based desktop applications.
- **Image Processing:** Features like face recognition, object detection, pattern recognition, etc. involve a great deal of image processing algorithms. Python simplifies this task by providing libraries such as OpenCV, Pillow which provide implementation for several algorithms. In addition to this, Python is also widely used to create 2D and 3D visualization softwares.

- **Software Development:** The packages and libraries provided by Python aid in the software development process. During this process, Python can provide support at stages like—build, design, testing and management.
- **Game Development:** Python libraries like PySoy and PyGame are the most popular choices for game developers. Python has formed the base for games like Vega Strike, Battlefield 2 and many more.

Some other applications of Python include—Data analytics, Artificial Intelligence, Natural Language Processing and IoT-based application development.

1.3 PYTHON DEVELOPMENT PLATFORMS

The next step in the learning process of Python programming is to look for a suitable environment where one can create and execute Python programs. Programming softwares, that provide a platform for development, are known as Integrated Development Environment or IDE in short. Not only can the programmer write the code in an IDE, but steps like compilation, execution, debugging are also provided there. This section aims to acquaint the reader with some popular Python IDEs.

Table 1.1 Popular Python IDEs and their icons

Development Platform	Icon
PyCharm	
Spyder	
PyScripter	
Python IDLE	
Google Colaboratory	

- **PyCharm:** PyCharm is an IDE created by Jet Brains. It was created using JAVA and Python. PyCharm provides support for compilation, debugging among others. It also provides code completion. Smooth refactoring is another popular feature of an IDE and PyCharm offers that. It even offers support for web development frameworks. PyCharm is available for Windows, Mac and Linux operating systems. The basic version is free however, the professional developer version is paid.
- **Spyder:** Created by a community called the Spyder Project Contributors, Spyder is a Python IDE made by scientists for scientists. It finds great usage in the field of data analytics. The IDE was designed in Python. It provides plug-in components such as Spyder notebook and console and hence, the developer can run the code by cell or by line. Spyder can automatically detect and highlight the variables being used in the environment. Spyder also provides several features such as zoom, export, etc. for working with plots. It comes free of cost for Windows, MacOS, Linux and Qt.
- **PyScripter:** Providing all the necessary and modern Python features, PyScripter is a lightweight package which comes for only Windows operating system. It was created in Delphi, Python, and Object Pascal. It comes with features such as syntax highlighting, unit testing, debugging among several others. However, it may lack support for advanced Python features.
- **IDLE:** Provided by Python developers only, IDLE is one of the simplest, yet the most popular and flexible choice for Python developments. This IDE comes free of cost for operating systems such as Windows, Linux, MacOS, etc. IDLE is easy to install and use and therefore makes an ideal choice for beginners. It accommodates features such as code colorization, error highlighting, undo and smart indentation. It has powerful debugging capabilities, however, it lacks the line numbering feature which is very useful for the process of debugging and testing.
- **Google Colaboratory:** Very similar to IDEs like Jupyter notebook, Google Colaboratory ("Colab" for short) is a product by Google Research. It is a free Python IDE that runs on cloud. It requires no setup or installation. Developers can just login to their Google account and edit, modify and execute their code. Google Colab provides special support for several Python libraries. It is a popular choice for people in the field of Data Science, Machine Learning and allied research. It even provides options to add documentation to the code by using text cells. One can also import datasets from online repositories such as Kaggle. Creating and sharing one's work has been made very easy as it can be done via Google Drive. Colab notebooks can also be published on GitHub.

These are just a few of the plethora of platforms available for Python Development. While each of the above-mentioned IDEs have their plus points, for the sake of simplicity for beginners, in the remainder of this book, all the Python code snippets will be designed and executed in IDLE.

1.4 IDLE INSTALLATION

Let us now start working with Python IDLE on our computer. This is a step-by-step guide to download and install it on our system. It must be noted here that we only need to download and install the desired version of Python; the IDLE environment comes with it. Windows based installation is being covered below.

1.4.1 Downloading Process

- Visit www.python.org in the browser and go to the downloads section as in Figure 1.2.

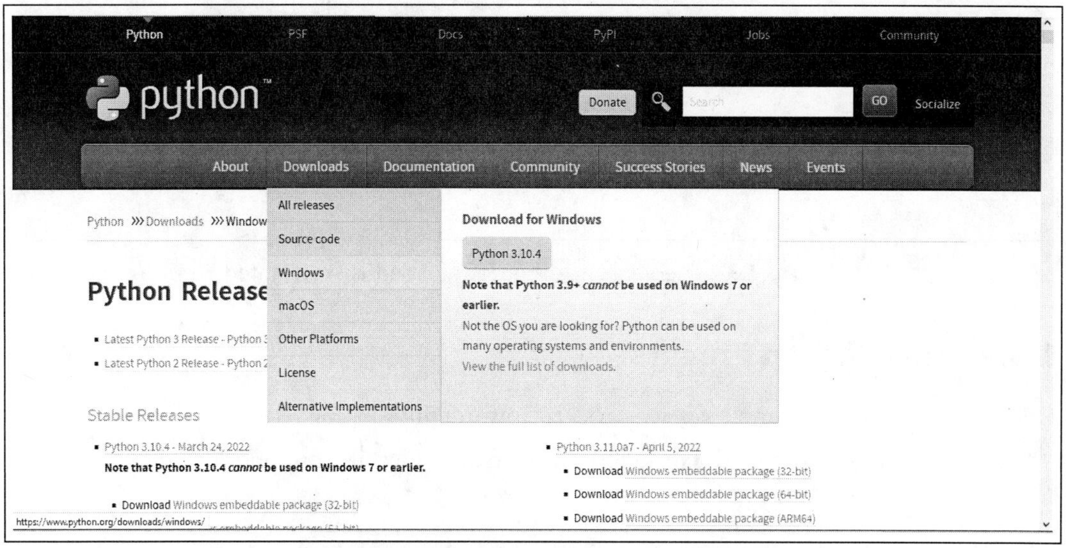

Figure 1.2 Downloads page at www.python.org

- Next step is to select the version to be downloaded. Although the latest versions of Python are available now, we will be using 3.7.4 in the context of this book.
- Before downloading, we must confirm the version compatible with the Windows (32 bit or 64 bit) installed on our computer.

On a 64 bit Windows operating system, the highlighted version in Figure 1.3 is to be downloaded.

- Click on the link and the download should begin.

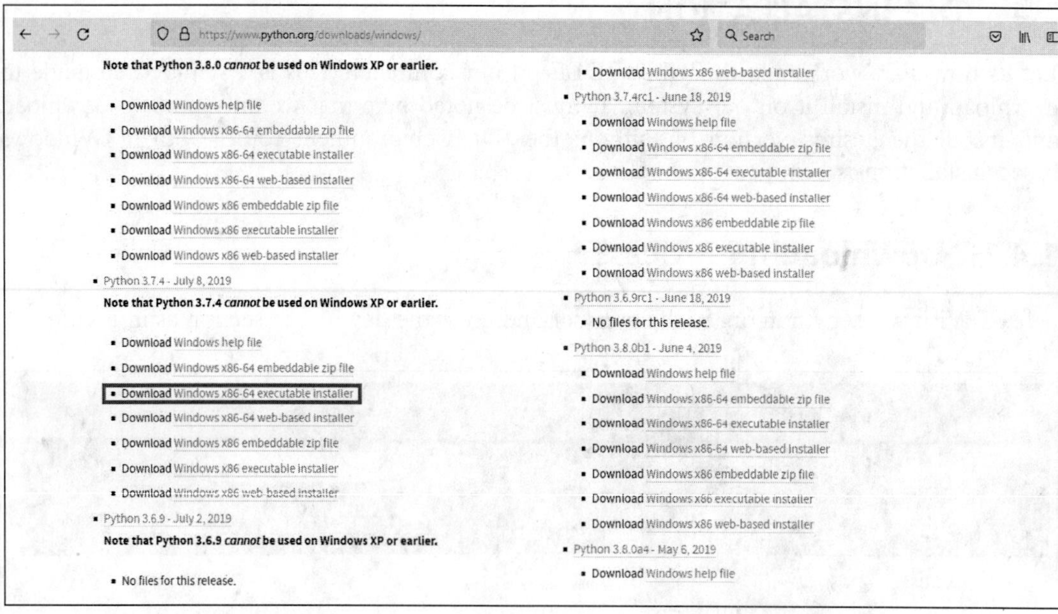

Figure 1.3 The version to be downloaded is highlighted.

1.4.2 Installation Process

Once the download is completed, we proceed towards installation.

- When we click on the executable file, a dialog box like the one in Figure 1.4 should appear. Click on the Run option.

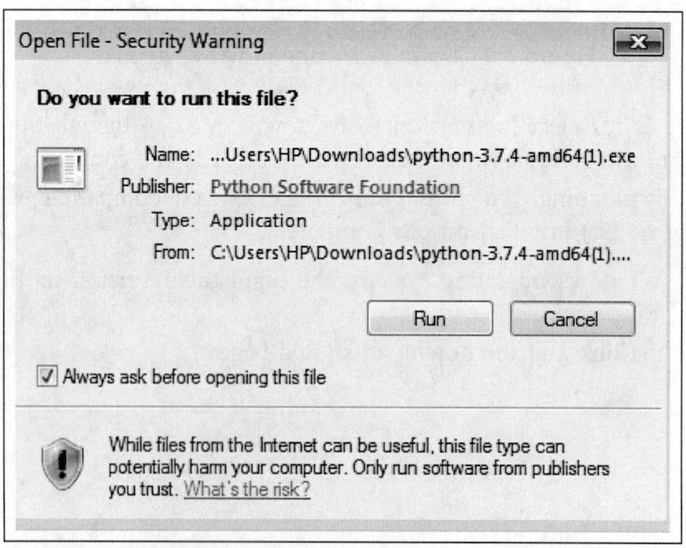

Figure 1.4 Permission dialog box.

- After we run this file, the dialog box in Figure 1.5 comes up. Select the "Install Now" option. Note that it says that IDLE is included.

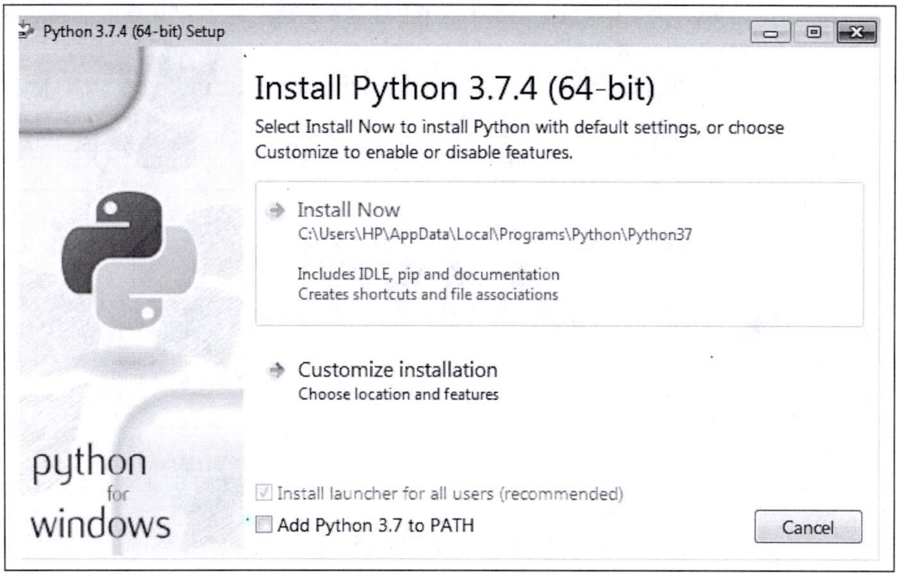

Figure 1.5 IDLE installation setup.

- The setup will execute after this.
- Once the setup is complete, you may have a look at the documentation and other links. Click the close button as shown in Figure 1.6 after this.

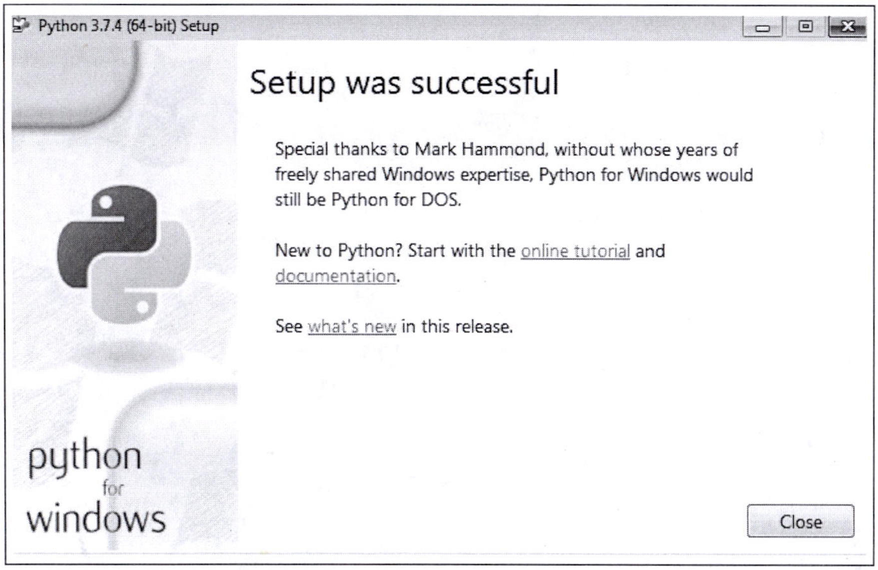

Figure 1.6 IDLE installation complete.

After the installation is completed, you will be able to see the IDLE icon in the start menu.

SUMMARY

- Python is a high-level language that is interpreted, portable and object oriented.
- Python is easy to learn and use, and comes with thousands of libraries.
- Python finds applications in areas such as science and technology, web development, data analysis among many others.
- There are several platforms available for Python development, PyCharm, Spyder, PyScripter, IDLE, Google Colaboratory, etc.

EXERCISES

1.1 Elaborate upon the following terms:
  (a) High level language
  (b) Interpreted language
  (c) Object-oriented language
  (d) Portability
  (e) Loosely Type checked

1.2 Enlist and explain some applications of Python.

2

Python Programming Fundamentals

Python is very simple to use and it is very popular owing to its simple syntax. It is extensively being used by programmers and also by people without any computer background. Python language is very robust and is used in versatile applications like web development, statistical applications, image processing, gaming, natural language processing and many more.

This chapter provides elementary knowledge about programming. We will be covering the building blocks of the programming language like variables, data types, operators and also a simple Python program at the end.

2.1 VARIABLES

A **variable** is a reserved memory location to store values. In other words, a **variable** in a Python program refers to data which is used for processing. A variable can have a short name (like x and y) or a more descriptive name (age, carname, total_volume). For example, the Program 2.1 shows the use of variables *radius* and *area*.

Program 2.1: Program to calculate area of a circle

```
#program to calculate area of a circle
radius=2
area=radius*radius*3.14
print("Area of circle is" ,area)
```

In the Program 2.1 variable `radius` is assigned the value 2, variable `area` is assigned the expression `radius * radius * 3.14`, finally the value assigned to the variable `area` is being printed using the `print` statement.

There are certain rules for naming a Python variable:

- A variable name must start with a *letter* or the *underscore* character.
- A variable name cannot start with a number.
- A variable name can only contain alpha-numeric characters and underscores (a–z, A–Z, 0–9, and _).

- Variable names are case-sensitive (`age`, `Age` and `AGE` are three different variables).
- Variables can be of any length.
- A variable cannot be a keyword.

For example, `area`, `radius`, `roll_no`, `marks1` and `_idno` are *valid* variable names whereas `2A`, `roll no`, `roll-no` and `percent%` are *invalid* variable names.

Python has no command for declaring a variable. A variable is created the moment you first assign a value to it. For example, n=10, will create n of the type integer. Variables do not need to be declared with any particular type and can even change type after they have been set.

2.2 CONSTANTS

A constant is an identifier whose value cannot be changed. The value of a variable may change during the execution of a program, but a constant represents a value that never changes during the program execution. In the Program 2.1, π is a constant. If you use it frequently, you don't want to keep typing its value 3.14159 repeatedly, instead use a descriptive name `PI` for the value. Python does not have a special naming convention for constants, so simply create a variable with the name `PI` for a constant. However, to distinguish between a variable and a constant, use *all capital letters* to name a constant.

Program 2.1: Program to compute area of a circle

```
#program to calculate area of a circle
PI=3.14    # PI is a constant
radius=2
area=radius*radius*PI
print("Area of circle is ",area)
```

The advantage of creating a constant is that, if you have to change the value of the constant (e.g. change the value of `PI` from 3.14159 to 3.14), you have to do it at a single location where it has been defined.

2.3 DATA TYPES

The variables can store different types of data, e.g. numbers, sequence of characters, etc. Since everything in Python programming is an object, data types are classes and variables are instances (objects) of these classes. Python supports many data types, some of them are shown in Table 2.1.

Table 2.1 Data Types in Python

Example	Data type
x = "Hello" / 'Hello'	**str**
x = 20	**int**
x = 20.5	**float**
x = True	**boolean**
x = ["apple", "banana", "cherry"]	**list**

2.3.1 Numeric

Python numbers can be represented as integers, floating point numbers and complex numbers. These are represented as `int`, `float` and `complex` respectively.

```
>>> a=12
>>> b=67.87
>>> print(a,b)
```

The output of the code is given below:

```
12  67.87
```

The code above shows `a` as an integer variable and `b` as a floating point variable. We can use the `type()` function to find which class or datatype the variable belongs to.

2.3.2 Strings

Python strings are sequences of characters. They are enclosed in single/double quotes, multi-line strings are enclosed in triple quotes ''' or """.

```
>>> str1="Welcome"        # String "Welcome" enclosed in double quotes
>>> str2='Students'       # String 'Students' enclosed in single quotes
>>> str3='''This book is on Python. It is a popular programming
         language. This language has several libraries.
         Python is being used in different fields economics,
         engineering, commerce, etc.'''
                          # Multi-line string enclosed in triple quotes
```

2.3.3 Boolean

Python boolean type represents two values `True` or `False`. These values are also called logical values.

```
>>> flag1=True
>>> flag2=False
>>> print(flag1,flag2)
```

The output of the code is given below:

```
True   False
```

2.3.4 List

Python list is an ordered sequence of items. All the items in the list do not have to be of the same type. The list items are enclosed in square brackets [ ] and separated by commas.

```
>>> list1=[12,23,67,55,24]
list2=["Apple","Banana","Kiwi","Grapes","Orange","Pineapple"]
```

```
>>> list1
[12, 23, 67, 55, 24]
>>> list2
['Apple', 'Banana', 'Kiwi', 'Grapes', 'Orange', 'Pineapple']
```

Lists are mutable, which means that the list elements can be altered.

2.3.5 Tuple

Tuples are ordered sequence of items like lists. The difference between lists and tuples is that tuples are immutable, i.e. once created they cannot be changed. It is defined within the () and elements separated by commas.

```
>>> t1=(10,20,30,40,50)
>>> t1
(10, 20, 30, 40, 50)
```

2.3.6 Set

Sets are an unordered collection of items. It cannot have duplicate values. The set is defined within {} and items separated by commas.

Set operations like union, intersection, etc. can be performed on Python sets.

```
>>> set1={11,22,33,44,55,66}
>>> set1
{33, 66, 11, 44, 22, 55}
```

2.3.7 Dictionary

Dictionary is an ordered collection of *key: value* pairs. Dictionaries are used to store huge data and provide fast data retrieval. In Python, dictionary is enclosed within {} in the form of *key: value* pairs, where keys should be immutable data types like strings, numbers, etc. The keys have to be unique.

```
>>> price={"Apple":200,"Banana":80,"Kiwi":100,"Grapes":100}
```

2.4 TYPE CONVERSION

The process of converting one data type into another is called type conversion. Python has in-built functions for converting data from one data type to another. Table 2.2 shows the built-in functions in Python for type conversion.

Table 2.2 Built-in Functions for Type Conversion

Function	Description
int(str)	Converts string to integer
float(str)	Converts string to floating point number
str(val)	Converts value to string
bool(val)	Converts value to a boolean value True or False

2.5 OPERATORS

Operators are symbols used to perform operations on variables and values. In an expression 2 + 3, + is an *operator* and 2 and 3 are *operands*. In general, an *expression* is a valid combination of operands and operators. In Python, all types of data are objects.

Python divides the operators in the following groups:

- Arithmetic operators
- Assignment operators
- Comparison operators
- Logical operators
- Identity operators
- Membership operators
- Bitwise operators

2.5.1 Arithmetic Operators

Arithmetic operators are used with *numeric values* to perform common mathematical operations of addition, subtraction, multiplication, division, exponentiation and modulus. There are two types of numeric data: integers and real numbers. Whole numbers are integers (*int* for short) and real numbers have fractional part. Real numbers are called floating-point numbers (float) in Python.

Table 2.3 Arithmetic Operators

Operator	Name	Example
+	Addition	x+y
–	Subtraction	x–y
*	Multiplication	x*y
/	Division	x/y
%	Modulus	x%y (Calculates the remainder of x/y)
**	Exponentiation	x**y (means x^y)
//	Floor division	x//y (returns the integer part of the result of division)

```
>>> 4+6         #Addition operator
10
>>> 19-2        #Subtraction operator
17
>>> 4*2         #Multiplication operator
8
>>> 6**2        #Exponentiation operator
36
```

The +, – and * are straightforward operators as can be seen in Table 2.3. But, + and – operators can be unary and binary operators. A *unary* operator has only one operand but a *binary* operator has two operands. For example, the operator in –2 is a unary operator to negate the number 2 whereas the operator in 4–3 is a binary operator and is signifying subtraction.

```
>>> 4*(-9)     #-unary operator
-36
```

The / operator for division will always give a float number as result. For example

```
>>> 9/3       #Division results in a floating number
3.0
```

The // operator is a floor division operator and yields an integer result and any fractional part is truncated. For example

```
>>> 9//3     #Floor division results in integer number
3
```

The % operator is called *remainder* or *modulus* operator, it returns the remainder after the division. For example

```
>>> 5%2         #Modulus operator
1
```

2.5.2 Relational Operators

Relational operators are used to compare two values or expressions and yield Boolean values `True` or `False`. The relational operators available in Python are shown in Table 2.4. A relational expression takes the form as

expression1 <relational operator> expression2

The expressions 27 > 20, 27 < 20, 27 == 27 and 27 != 20 will yield `True`, `False`, `True` and `False` respectively.

```
>>> 27<20
False
>>> 27>20
True
>>> 27==27
True
>>> 27!=20
True
```

Table 2.4 Relational Operators

Operator	Operator Name	Example	Description
>	Greater than	x > y	If the value of left operand (x) is greater than the right operand (y) `True` is returned otherwise `False` is returned.
>=	Greater than or equal to	x >= y	If the value of left operand (x) is greater than or is equal to the right operand (y) `True` is returned otherwise `False` is returned.
<	Less than	x < y	If the value of left operand (x) is less than the right operand (y) `True` is returned otherwise `False` is returned.
<=	Less than or equal to	x <= y	If the value of left operand (x) is less than or is equal to the right operand (y) `True` is returned otherwise `False` is returned.
==	Equal to	x == y	If the value of left operand (x) is equal to the right operand (y) `True` is returned otherwise `False` is returned.
!=	Not equal to	x != y	If the value of left operand (x) is not equal to the right operand (y) `True` is returned otherwise `False` is returned.

When the relational operators are applied to the strings, they are compared character by character from left to right, based on their ASCII values. Thus, `'SUPER' > 'CLASS'`, will result in `True` as the ASCII value of 'S' (83) is greater than the ASCII value of 'C' (67). Also, `'class' > 'chess'` will result in `True`, since the first character is identical, the ASCII values of the second characters are compared, the ASCII value of 'l' and 'h' are 108 and 104 respectively, hence the result is `True`.

```
>>> "class">"chess"
True
>>> "SUPER">"CLASS"
True
```

2.5.3 Logical Operators

The logical operators are applied on boolean values to yield `True` or `False`. They are used to combine relational expressions and are written as below:

relational expression1 <logical operator> relational expression2

Table 2.5 Logical Operators

Operator	Example	Description
and	(x > y) and (x > z)	Returns `True` if both the expressions are `True`
or	(x > y) or (x > z)	Returns `True` if any one of the expression is `True`
not	not (a > b)	Reverses the result; if expression is `True` 'not' will return `False` and if expression is `False` 'not' will return `True`

In Table 2.5, the logical operators available in Python are listed. The `and` *operator* returns `True` if both the operands are `True` and returns `False` otherwise. Similarly, `or` operator returns `True`, if either of the operands is `True` and returns `False` otherwise. The `not` is an unary operator, it requires only one operand. It is used for reversing the value of the operand. If the operand is `True`, *not* `True` is `False` and *not* `False` is `True`.

```
>>> (23<20) and (12>10)
False
>>> (23<20) or (12>10)
True
>>> not(23==23)
False
```

While evaluating the expression involving logical operators, both the relational expressions may not be evaluated. For example, in the following expression:

```
(14 < 10) and (2 > 1)
```

The first relational expression `14 < 10` yields `False`, in this case the second expression `2 > 1` is not evaluated, since one of the operand, the first relational expression in this case, has already resulted in `False`, and hence in this situation the complete expression will evaluate to `False`, whatever be the value of the second expression. Python will not evaluate the second expression `2 > 1`. However, had the expression been

```
(14 > 10) and (2 > 1)
```

The first expression `14 > 10` evaluates to `True`, so the second expression `2 >1` will be evaluated to yield the final result of the expression. In this case, since the second expression `2 > 1` evaluates to `True`, the complete expression yields `True`. The result of the complete expression depends on the second expression.

Similarly, in the following expression involving `or` operator

```
(32 > 12) or (23 == 23)
```

The first expression `32 > 12` evaluates to `True` hence we know that the expression will yield `True` whatever the value of the second expression. Python will not evaluate the second expression.

2.5.4 Assignment Operators

Assignment operators are used to assign values to variables. The value of the variable, constant or expression on the right side of the assignment operator is assigned to the variable on the left side. For example

```
>>> a=45
>>> b=t
>>> c=a+10
```

In the first assignment statement, `45` is assigned to the variable `a`. In the second assignment statement, whatever is the value of variable `t` is assigned to variable `b`. In the third assignment statement, the value of the expression `a+10` is assigned to variable `c`. The syntax of the assignment statement is as below:

variable = variable/constant/expression

`+=`, `-=`, `*=`, `/=`, `%=`, `//=`, `**=` are *compound* operators as they combine +, –, *, /, %, // and ** with the assignment operator =. This results in performing the operation with the current value of the variable followed by the assignment to the variable. All the assignment operators are listed in Table 2.6.

Table 2.6 Assignment Operators

Operator	Use	Example	Description
=	`t=4`	t=4	Simple assignment, 4 is assigned to **t**.
+=	`t += 4`	t = t + 4, t = 4 + 4 = 8	Value of **t** is **added** to **4** and then assigned to **t**.
-=	`t -= 4`	t = t - 4, t = 4 - 4 = 0	**4** is subtracted from **t** and then assigned to **t**.
*=	`t *= 4`	t = t * 4, t = 4 * 4 = 16	Value of **t** is **multiplied** to **4** and then assigned to **t**.
/=	`t /= 4`	t = t / 4, t = 4 / 4 = 1.0	Value of **t** is **divided** by **4** and then assigned to **t**.
%=	`t %= 4`	t = t % 4, t = 4 % 4 = 0	Value of **t** **modulus** **4** and then assigned to **t**.
//=	`t //= 4`	t = t // 4, t = 4 // 4 = 1	Floor division of **t** w.r.t **4** is performed and result assigned to **t**.
**=	`t**=4`	t = t ** 4, t = 4 ** 4 = 256	Exponentiation of **t** w.r.t **4** is performed and result assigned to **t**.

2.5.5 Bitwise Operators

Bitwise operators are used to perform operations on binary numbers, i.e. 0 or 1. The integers are converted to binary and then the bitwise operators are performed. Table 2.7 lists the bitwise operators available in Python.

Table 2.7 Bitwise Operators

<table>
<tr><th>Operator</th><th>Name</th><th>Description</th></tr>
<tr><td>&</td><td>Bitwise AND</td><td>Sets output to 1 if both bits are 1</td></tr>
<tr><td>|</td><td>Bitwise OR</td><td>Sets output to 1 if one of two bits is 1</td></tr>
<tr><td>^</td><td>Bitwise XOR</td><td>Sets output to 1 if only one of two bits is 1</td></tr>
<tr><td>~</td><td>Bitwise NOT</td><td>Inverts all the bits</td></tr>
<tr><td><<</td><td>Zero fill left shift</td><td>Shift left by pushing zeros in from the right and let the leftmost bits fall off</td></tr>
<tr><td>>></td><td>Signed right shift</td><td>Shift right by pushing copies of the leftmost bit in from the left, and let the rightmost bits fall off</td></tr>
</table>

Let x and y be two integers represented as `8-bit` binary numbers. If x = 12 and y = 6, Bitwise AND (&) yields 1, if corresponding bits in x and y both are 1 otherwise it yields 0.

```
x & y :  00001100 (12)
         00000110 (6)
         --------
         00000100 (4)
```

Bitwise OR (|) yields 1, if bit in either x or y is 1 otherwise it yields 0.

```
x | y :  00001100 (12)
         00000110 (6)
         --------
         00001110 (14)
```

Bitwise XOR (^) yields 1, if exactly one of the bits in either x or y is 1 otherwise it yields 0.

```
x ^ y :  00001100 (12)
         00000110 (6)
         --------
         00001010 (10)
```

Bitwise Complement (~) is a unary operator, it reverses the bits of a binary number, i.e. converts 0 to 1 and 1 to 0.

~ x : ~ (00001100) will yield 11110011 (–13), which is two's complement of 00001101 (13).

Left Shift `x << y` shifts the binary bits in `x` to the left by `y` places, inserting `y zeros` on the right side. The result of left shift is $x * 2^y$.

`7 << 2` yields 28: 00000111 (7) on performing shift left by 2 places yields 00011100 (28).

Right shift `x >> y` shifts the binary bits in `x` to the right by `y` places. Leftmost `y` bits are filled by the sign bit. The result is $x/2^y$.

`7 >> 2` yields 1: 00000111 (7) on performing shift right by 2 places yields 00000001 (1).

The operations explained above, yield the same results when performed in Python IDLE as shown below:

```
>>> 12&6     #bitwise AND
4
>>> 12|6     #bitwise OR
14
>>> 12^6     #bitwise XOR
10
>>> ~12      #bitwise complement
-13
>>> 7<<2     #Left shift
28
>>> 7>>2     #Right shift
1
```

2.5.6 Precedence of Operators

The precedence of operators guides in which order the operators are executed in an expression. If an expression is having multiple operators, Python executes these operators based on their precedence or priority as given in Table 2.8.

Table 2.8 Precedence of Operators

Order	Operators	Associativity
1	()	
2	**	L - > R
3	+x, −x, ~x (unary)	R -> L
4	*, /, //, %	L - > R
5	+, -	L -> R
6	<< , >>	R -> L
7	&	L -> R
8	^	L -> R
9	|	L -> R
10	<, <=, > , >=, ==, !=	L -> R
11	not	R -> L
12	and	L -> R
13	or	L -> R

Table 2.8 shows the precedence order to solve expressions having arithmetic, relational and logical operators. The order of execution of the operators is decided from Table 2.8. Given an expression: `23 * 2 < 38 + 2.`

The arithmetic operators will be evaluated first as they have higher precedence over the relational operators, it will yield `46 < 40` and then relational operator < will be applied to give `False`. Figure 2.1 shows the steps to evaluate the expression given below:

```
4 ** 2 // 3 + 10 > 7 and 56 < 90
```

Let us evaluate another expression:

```
((8 + 9) > (7 * 10)) and (not (9 > 1) or ((45 + 5) < (9 * 10)))
```

Step 1: `(`**`17 > 70`**`) and (not (True) or (50 < 90))`
Step 2: **`False`** `and (not (True) or (50 < 90))`

Result: `False,` since one of the operands of `and` is `False`, the result will be `False` and there is no need to evaluate the second expression.

We can see in Table 2.8 that more than one operator has the same precedence. When more than one operator has the same precedence, *associativity* helps in deciding their order of execution. The associativity will be *Left –> Right* (*L–>R*) or *Right –> Left* (*R–>L*), i.e. executing the operators of the same precedence from left to right or right to left. If the given expression is

`1**2**3, the result is 1.`

In this expression, there are two ** operators so they will be executed from L–>R, hence first 1**2 is executed and then **3 is applied to the result, which gives the answer 1. Here, first the exponentiation operator to the left is executed as per the associativity.

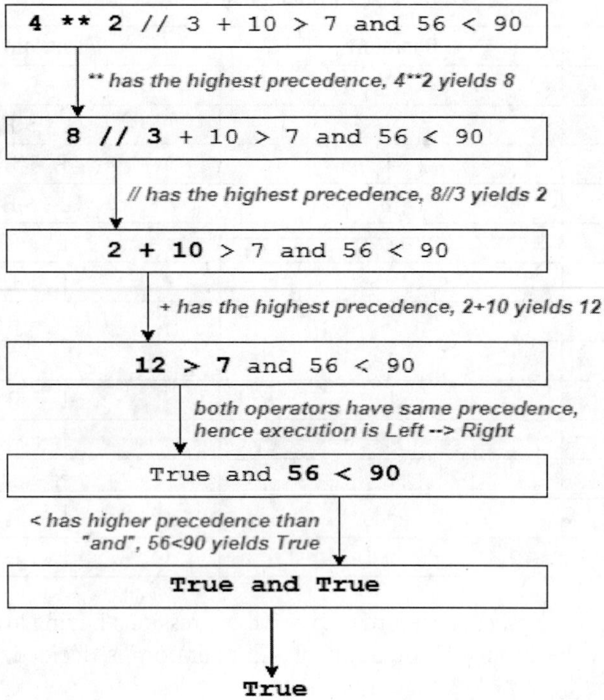

Figure 2.1 Step by step expression evaluation.

Few Python programs are given below.

Program 2.2: Program to calculate percentage of marks

```
marks_obtained = int(input(“Enter the marks obtained: ”))
total_marks = int(input(“Enter the total marks: ”))
percentage = (marks_obtained/total_marks)*100
print(“Percentage =”,percentage)
```

The output of Program 2.2 is shown below:

```
Enter the marks obtained: 75
Enter the total marks: 90
Percentage = 83.33333333333334
```

Program 2.3 depicts the use of Python operators.

Program 2.3: Program to calculate roots of a quadratic equation

```
# Program to find the roots for quadratic equation

a=int(input(“Enter a: ”))
b=int(input(“Enter b: ”))
c=int(input(“Enter c: ”))
```

```
d = b*b - 4 * a * c
root1 = (-b + d ** 0.5)/( 2 * a )
root2 = (-b - d ** 0.5)/( 2 * a )

print("Roots of quadratic equation : ", root1,root2)
```

The output of Program 2.3 is shown below:

```
Enter a: 4
Enter b: 6
Enter c: 2
Roots of quadratic equation : -0.5 -1.0
```

2.6 BUILT-IN FUNCTIONS

Built-in functions are the functions defined in the library of Python. Python provides vast libraries of functions, some of the common functions are shown in Table 2.9.

Table 2.9 Built-in Functions

Function	Description	Example
`abs()`	returns the absolute value of the number	`abs(-7.5)` will return 7.5
`eval()`	evaluates and executes a string expression	`eval('2+3')` will result in 5
`float()`	converts to a floating point number	`float(5)` will return 5.0
`input()`	reads a user input and returns a string	`input("enter a:")`
`int()`	converts to an integer	`int(5.4)` returns 5
`len()`	returns length of a string/object	`len("world")` returns 5
`max()`	returns the largest item in the list	`max(4,2,7,1)` returns 7
`min()`	returns the smallest in the list	`min(4,3,7,1)` returns 1
`pow()`	returns x to the power y	`pow(2,3)` returns 2^3
`print()`	prints to the standard output device	`print(x)` `print("result:", sum)`
`round()`	rounds a number to a specified number of places	`round(77.46876,2)` returns 77.47
`str()`	converts to string	`str(4.6)` return '4.6'
`type()`	returns the data type of the object	x=3 `type(x)` returns integer

2.7 MUTABLE AND IMMUTABLE

"Everything in Python is an Object" Python has a variety of data structures that can be used to represent data and *objects* are abstraction of data.

A first fundamental distinction that Python makes on data is about whether or not the value of an object changes. If the value can change, the object is called **mutable**, while if the value cannot change, the object is called **immutable**.

2.7.1 Mutable Objects

Mutable objects in Python are:

- Lists
- Sets
- Dictionaries

We can add, delete and modify the contents of lists, sets & dictionaries, since they are mutable. In the examples below, the memory location does not change after any kind of update operation. This confirms that lists, sets & dictionaries are mutable objects.

```
>>> list1=["Apple","Kiwi"]
>>> print(id(list1))
2707828251016
>>> list1.append("Banana")
>>> list1
['Apple', 'Kiwi', 'Banana']
>>> print(id(list1))
2707828251016
```

Similarly, it can be shown that sets are mutable.

```
>>> set1={1,2,3,4,5,6}
>>> print(id(set1))
2707831497000
>>> set1.remove(2)
>>> set1
{1, 3, 4, 5, 6}
>>> print(id(set1))
2707831497000
```

Since, the dictionary is also mutable. It can be modified. The example below shows that the `id` of the variable `price` does not change when a new element is added.

```
>>> price={'Apple':200,'Banana':80}
>>> print(id(price))
2707831573144
>>> price['Kiwi']=300
>>> print(price)
{'Apple': 200, 'Banana': 80, 'Kiwi': 300}
>>> print(id(price))
2707831573144
```

2.7.2 Immutable Objects

Immutable objects in Python are:

- Numerals like integers, booleans, floats, complex numbers, and fractions.
- Strings
- Tuples
- Frozen Sets

Since numbers, strings, tuples & frozen sets are immutable, internal state (data) can not be changed. In the examples below, the memory location (address) gets changed as a new object is created at different memory locations whenever an update is done. This confirms that numbers, strings, tuples and frozen sets are immutable.

```
>>> num1=23
>>> print(id(num1))
140725049390016
>>> num1=55
>>> num1
55
>>> print(id(num1))
140725049391040
```

It is observed that when the contents of the numeric variable `num1` are changed, the memory location of `num1` changes, which implies that a new variable has been created at another memory location.

In Python, everything is treated as an object. Every object has these three attributes:

- Identity – refers to the address of the object in the computer's memory.
- Type – refers to the kind of object that is created. For example, integer, list, string, etc.
- Value – refers to the value stored in the object. For exampe, n =10 would hold the integer 10.

While Identity and Type of an object cannot be changed once it is created, values can be changed for *mutable* objects.

2.8 COMMENTS

Proper documentation is essential for a proper understanding of a program. Comments are explanatory remarks added to the program code to increase understanding of the code. These comments help the user understand the various parts of the program, its structure and function. The comments can be written in different parts of the program to increase the readability of the program. Python's interpreter ignores the comments during program execution.

The comments can also be used to ignore some parts of the code while execution, while testing other parts of the program code. This way execution of some parts of the code can be prevented.

2.8.1 Single-line Comments

In Python, we use # to write single line comments. Everything written after # becomes a comment and is not executed by the Python interpreter.

```
a=2
# a=4      single line comment
print("a=", a)
```

The output of the above code is given below:

```
a = 2
```

It can be seen in the above code, first line is an assignment statement and second line is a comment which starts with #, which is followed by an assignment statement. The output obtained of the print statement is 2. Since `a=4` has been made a comment, it is not executed and variable `a` retains the value assigned to it in the first statement.

String literals can also be used to write comments in Python. The string literals which are not assigned are not executed by the interpreter and hence treated as comments. In the above code, the print statement has a string literal "a=", which is treated as a comment. The line enclosed in single/double quotation marks is treated as comment and hence not executed. Single or double quotes can be used for writing a comment, as they are used for string literals.

2.8.2 Multi-line Comments

In a similar way, a multi-line string literal enclosed in triple quotes, is treated as a multi-line comment.

```
'''Program to swap two variables. This is a multi line comment,
enclosed in triple quotes. This will not be executed'''

name="Suraj"
print("Name = ",name)
```

Here in the above code, the multi-line string is not assigned to any variable and hence it is a comment and ignored by the interpreter.

2.9 INDENTATION

In Python, indenting the code is the only way of identifying the different blocks in the program as parentheses are not used to mark the beginning and end of a block. While in other programming languages indentation is done for clarity, but in Python indentation is done for creating blocks. For example:

```
str="BANANA"
count=0
for ch in str: -------------> Block 1: for statement
    if ch=="A":  ------------> Block 2: if statement
        count +=1 -------------> Block 3: inside if statement
print("Number of a\'s in the string: ", count)
```

In the above example, the `if` statement has been indented to represent that it is lying within the `for` statement. Since the `if` statement can also have statements inside it, the statement `count +=1` has been indented. Since, the `print` statement at the end, is not lying within any block, it has not been indented.

While writing a Python program, indentation must be done with care. Incorrect indentation will lead to incorrect results.

2.10 BASIC PYTHON PROGRAM

In order to write a Python program in Python IDLE, click on the *File* Menu —> *New File* Option to create a new file as shown in Figure 2.2.

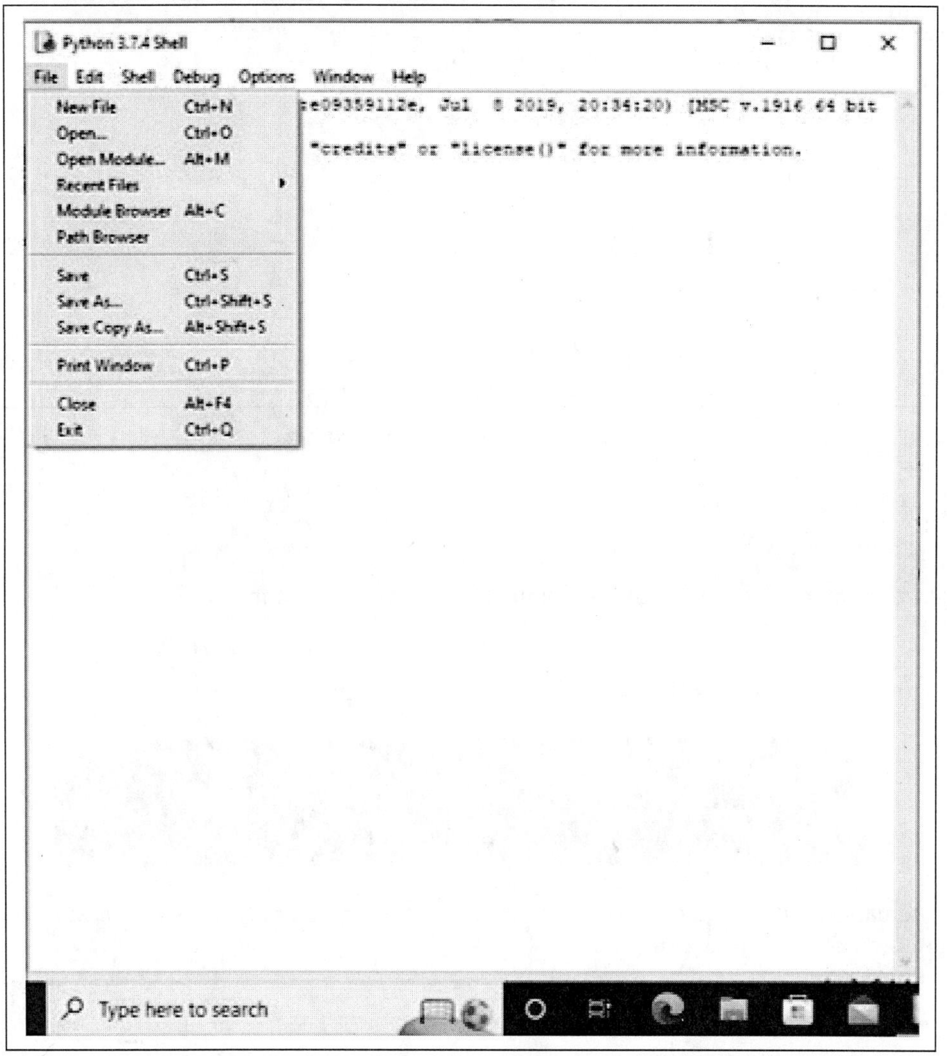

Figure 2.2 New File option in Python IDLE Shell.

This file is called a Python source file or script file. By default, a Python file will have an extension **.py**.

Program 2.4: First.py - Program to print a message

```
# Display a message
print("Welcome")
```

Type Program 2.4 in the Python IDLE as shown in Figure 2.3 and save it with the name *first.py*.

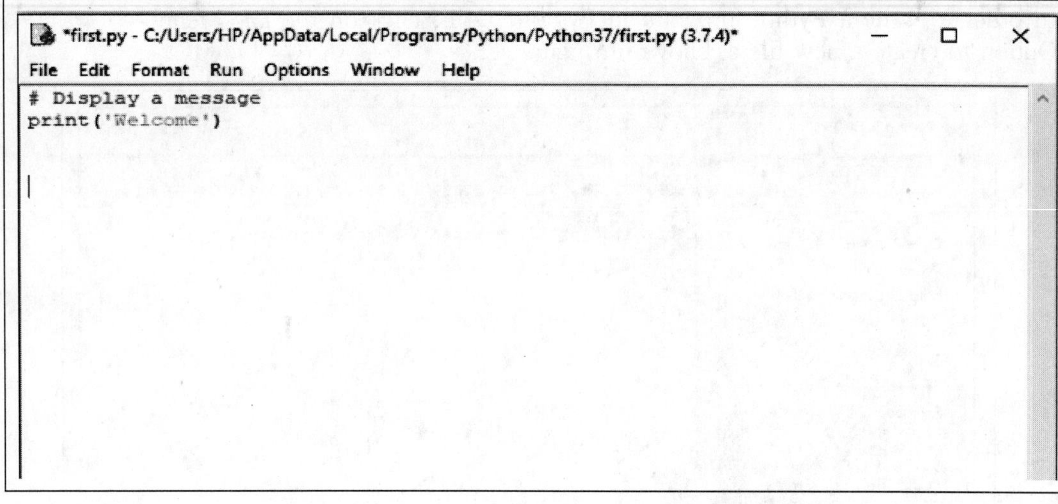

Figure 2.3 First Python Program.

Next, execute a python program using the command prompt by giving the command:

```
python filename.py
```

To run the program *first.py* from the command prompt, the command is

```
python first.py
```

The output of Program 2.4 in the command prompt is shown below:

Alternatively, to execute a Python program in Python IDLE there is a *Run Module* option in the Menu *Run* as shown in Figure 2.4.

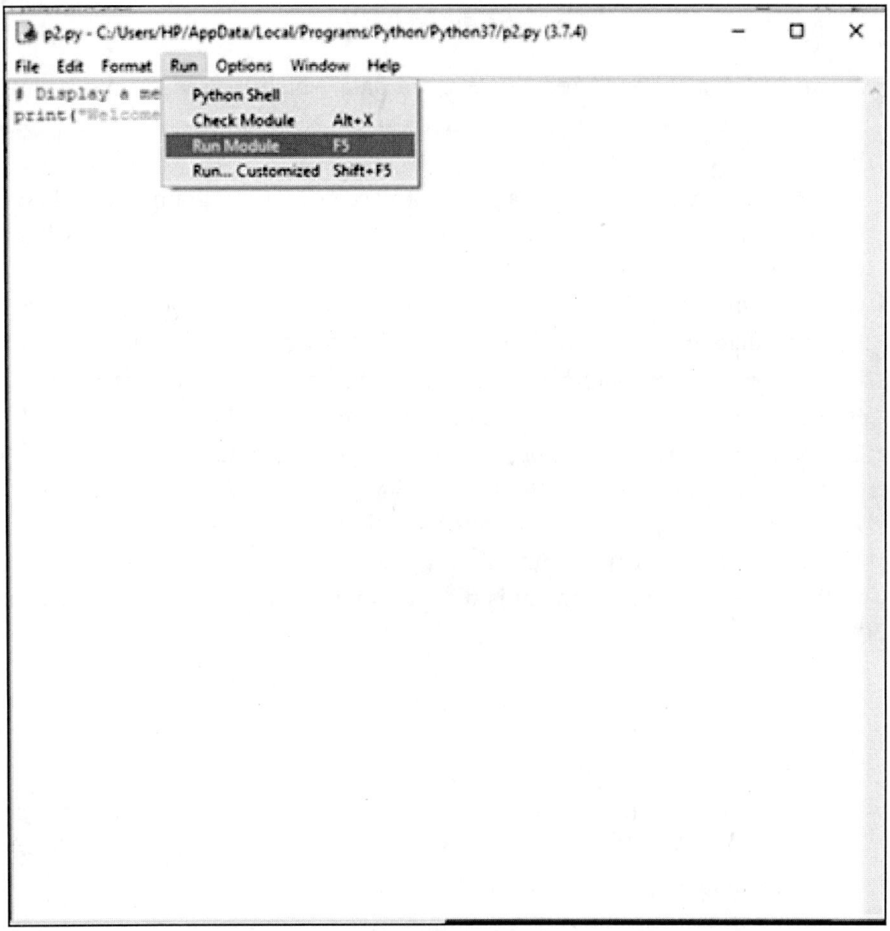

Figure 2.4 Run Menu in Python IDLE Shell.

The output of the Program 2.4 in the shell is shown below:

```
Welcome
```

When a Python program runs from a script file, it is known as running the program in *script mode.* When we type a statement at the prompt >>> in the IDLE shell and execute, it is called *interactive mode.*

SUMMARY

- A variable in a Python program refers to data which is used for processing.
- A constant is an identifier whose value cannot be changed.
- Python is case sensitive.
- Python is an interpreted language, i.e. it executes the program line-by-line.
- Python offers a variety of data types—integer, float, strings, bool, lists, sets, tuples, dictionaries, etc.
- Operators are symbols used to perform operations on variables and values.
- Python offers arithmetic, relational, logical, bitwise and assignment operators.
- Python has built-in functions for changing the data type of the variable.
- Bitwise operators are used to execute on binary digits 0 and 1.
- The object whose value can be changed is called **mutable**, and the object whose value cannot be changed called **immutable**.
- Lists, Sets and Dictionaries are mutable objects.
- Numerals, Strings, Tuples and Frozen Sets are immutable objects.
- In Python, single line comment is written using # and multi-line comments are written using ‘’’.

EXERCISES

2.1 Identify valid and invalid identifiers.

(a) roll-no (b) Roll-no (c) Roll no (d) roll_no
(e) 1roll_no (f) roll_no1 (g) import (h) roll_no.

2.2 Write the following expressions in Python:

(a) $ans = \dfrac{x^2 + y^2}{3x^3 y}$ (b) $eq = 2\left(\dfrac{3}{x} + \dfrac{\sqrt{x}}{10^x}\right)$ (c) $compound = p\left(1 + \dfrac{r}{100}\right)^n$

2.3 Evaluate the following expressions using arithmetic, relational and logical operators:

a = 4, b = 10, c = 15, d = 5

(a) a % b > 2 * d
(b) (c > d) and not (2 * a > b)
(c) not (c == 2 * d + 5) or (b // 4 > c // b)
(d) b + d ** 2 + a – d != 2 * a

2.4 Evaluate the following expressions using assignment and arithmetic operator:

(a) b += b * 5, where b = 10
(b) t *= t – (90 – 2 * t), where t = 20

2.5 Write a logical expression to represent the following:

(a) `marks` are greater than 80 and `attendance` is less than 75
(b) `age` is greater than 50 or `experience` is more than 25
(c) `locatilty` is `rural` and `education` is less than 12 class

2.6 Write a Python program to calculate the age of a person when the birth year is entered as input.

2.7 Write a Python program to convert the time given in seconds to hours, minutes and seconds.

2.8 Write a Python program to calculate the energy using the formula: $E = mc^2$ where **m** is the mass and **c** is the speed.

2.9 Write a python program to calculate the area of a triangle where its three sides s1, s2 and s3 are given using the given formula:

s = (s1 + s2 + s3) / 2
area = √ s (s – s1) (s – s2) (s – s3))

2.10 Write a Python program which converts the temperature entered in Fahrenheit to Celsius.

3

Control Structures

Control flow of any program refers to the order in which the code is being executed. A control structure in programming is a piece of code which decides the flow of a program by examining the values stored in certain variables. Instructions written in a program can be executed in a sequential order, non-sequential order and in a repetitive fashion. Python provides three types of control structures: Sequential Control Structures, Selection or Decision Control Structures and Repetition or Iterative Control Structures. In this chapter, we will study various types of control structures with appropriate examples.

3.1 SEQUENTIAL CONTROL STRUCTURES

Sequential control structures are a set of statements that execute in a sequential or linear order. It is the default mode of execution. Figure 3.1 illustrates the line-by-line implementation of instructions. Let us understand the sequential control flow of a program using an example Program 3.1.

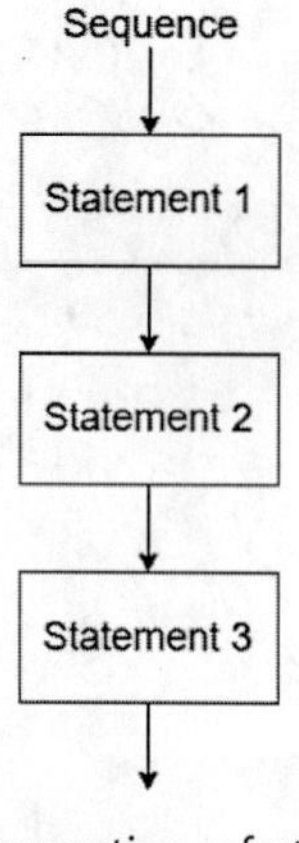

Figure 3.1 Sequential execution of statements of a program.

Program 3.1: Program to show the workflow of a sequential statements

```
#This is a sequential statement
x=50
y=30
z=x-y
print("Subtraction of two numbers is: ",z)
```

The output of Program 3.1 is shown below:

```
>>> #This is a sequential statement
>>> x=50
>>> y=30
>>> z=x-y
>>>print("Subtraction of two numbers is: ",z)
Subtraction of two numbers is: 20
```

In this code snippet, we initialize three variables: `x`, `y`, and `z`. We then use a `print` statement to display the output. This program will be executed line by line, meaning that the code written on line 1 will be executed first, followed by line 2, and so on. However, not all problems can be solved through sequential execution of instructions. In order to solve more complex problems, non-sequential and repetitive executions of the program are necessary. We will explore this concept further in the next section.

3.2 SELECTION OR DECISION CONTROL STRUCTURES

Python programming utilizes selection control structures, which are also referred to as decision control structures or branching structures. These structures allow for the execution of a program based on specific conditions, rather than a line-by-line approach. By testing these conditions and determining whether they are `True` or `False`, the program can execute instructions accordingly. To better understand this process, refer to Figure 3.2 for a visual representation of its functionality.

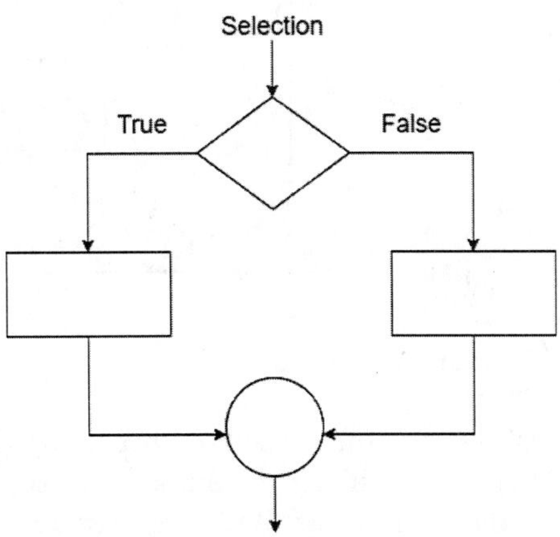

Figure 3.2 Selection or Decision control structure flow.

Decision control structures are categorized into following:

1. Simple if
2. if-else
3. Nested if
4. if-elif-else

Let us understand each category in detail with suitable examples.

3.2.1 Simple if Statements

If there are a set of statements to be executed when a *condition* is `True`, the simple `if` statement is used. The condition is expressed in the form of a relational expression, and only when that condition is met will the corresponding code be implemented. The flow of execution for an `if` statement is illustrated in Figure 3.3. The syntax for an `if` statement is as follows:

```
if condition:
    Sequence of Statements, S1
```

Here, the condition is a relational expression which will return `True` or `False`. For example, `a > b`, `i >= 10`, `n % 2 != 0`, `a + b > c`, `age >= 18`, `str1.isdigit()` and `rollno = = "1001"` are conditions or relational expressions. The `Sequence of Statements, S1,` have to be indented, i.e. shifted right, so that they form a block within the `if` statement. This sequence of statements will be executed when the condition returns `True.` If the condition returns `False,` S1 will not be executed and the control directly goes to the statement following the `if` statement. The user has to take care of indentation while writing the `if` statements of different forms.

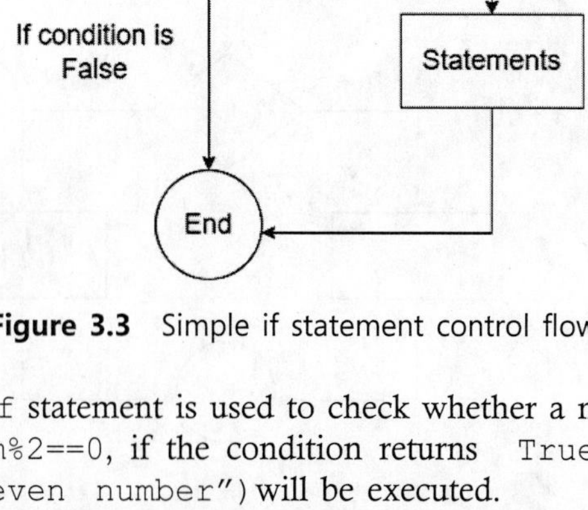

Figure 3.3 Simple if statement control flow.

In Program 3.2, the `if` statement is used to check whether a number is even or not. The condition specified is `num%2==0`, if the condition returns `True`, only then the statement `print("num is an even number")` will be executed.

Program 3.2: Program to demonstrate simple-if statement

```
#This is a simple-if statement
num=20
if num%2==0:
    print("num is an even number")
```

The output of the code is

```
num is an even number
```

As the value of `num` is 20, the condition `num%2==0` evaluates to `True`. Consequently, the `print` statement is executed, producing the output "`num is an even number.`"

Another example, Program 3.3 also uses the simple `if` statement to check whether `num` is positive or not. The condition specified is `num>0`, if the condition returns `True`, the statement `print("num is an even number")` will be executed.

Program 3.3: Program to print "Number is positive" if the number is greater than 0

```
num=10
if num>0:
        print("Number is positive")
```

The output of the code is

```
Number is positive
```

Program 3.3 is designed to evaluate whether a given number is positive or not. In this case, the program has determined that the number stored in the `num` variable is indeed positive, as it is greater than 0. As a result, the program executes the statement within the `if` clause, which confirms the positivity of the number. This simple yet effective program demonstrates the power of conditional statements in programming, and highlights the importance of careful variable assignment and evaluation.

3.2.2 if-else Statements

When we have two sets of statements to execute, depending on a condition, the `if-else` statement is used. This is also a conditional statement. The working of `if-else` structure is depicted in Figure 3.4 with the help of a flowchart.

Syntax of `if-else` statement is as follows:

```
if condition:
   Sequence of Statements, S1
else:
   Sequence of Statements, S2
```

It evaluates the condition and if the condition is `True` it will execute `Sequence of Statements, S1`, but if the condition is `False`, then `Sequence of Statements, S2` is executed. It is to be noted that in no case both S1 and S2 are executed, either S1 or S2 is executed. Both `Sequence of Statements, S1` and `Sequence of Statements, S2` have to be indented, so as to form two separate blocks. Program 3.4 demonstrates the use of `if-else` statement to check whether a number is even or odd.

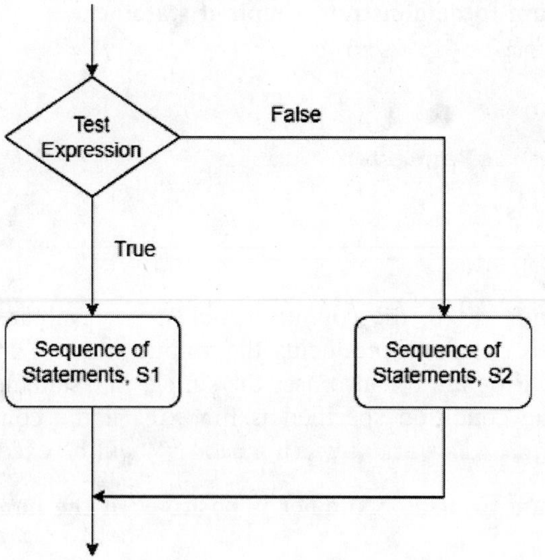

Figure 3.4 If-else statement control flow.

Program 3.4: Program to demonstrate if-else statement

```
#This is if-else statement
num=15
if num%2==0:
   print("num is even")
else:
   print("num is odd")
```

The output of the code is

```
num is odd
```

Program 3.4 assigns the value of 15 to the variable `num`. The expression `num%2 == 0` evaluates to `False` because the remainder of `num` divided by 2 is 1. Consequently, the program executes the statement `print("num is odd")` written inside the `else` clause.

3.2.3 Nested if Statements

Nested `if/if-else` statements are statements inside another `if/if-else` statement block, just like a gift box inside another gift box. Figure 3.5(a) & (b) illustrates the flow of the nested `if/if-else` statements. Lets understand the syntax and execution flow of `nested if` statements.

Syntax1:

```
if condition1:
  if condition 2:
    Sequence of statements, S1
  else:
    Sequence of statements, S2
else:
  Sequence of statements, S3
```

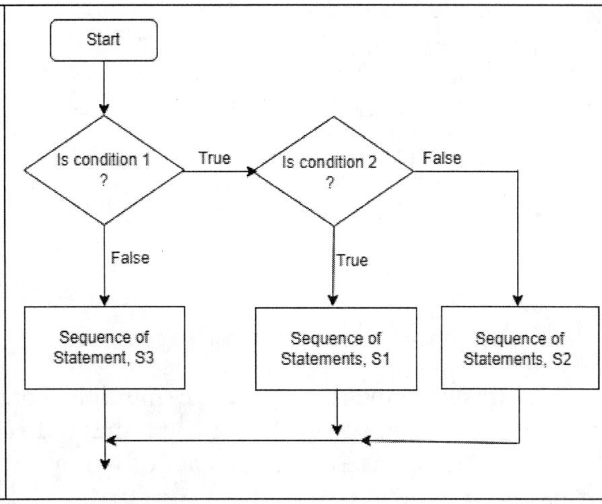

Syntax2:

```
if condition1:
    Sequence of statements, S1
else:
  if condition 2:
    Sequence of statements, S2
  else:
    Sequence of statements, S3
```

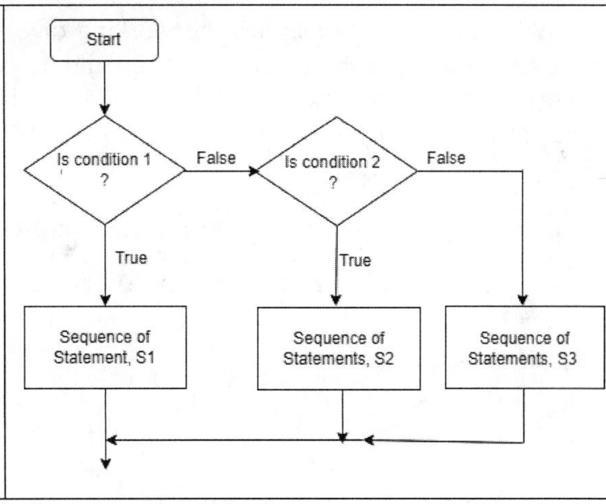

Figure 3.5(a)&(b) Nested if statements.

3.2.4 if-elif-else Statements

The `if-elif-else` statement is an alternative implementation of `nested if` statements. When there are multiple different conditions to be checked and the conditional execution of a separate set of statements based on these conditions, it is convenient to write the `nested if` in the form of `if-elif-else` statement. Unlike the `nested if` where `else` and the following `if` are written separately, in `if-elif-else` they are replaced by writing `elif`. Syntax of `if-elif-else` statements are as follows:

```
if condition 1:
   Sequence of statements, S1
elif condition 2:
   Sequence of statements, S2
elif condition 3:
   Sequence of statements, S3
.
.
.
else:
   Sequence of statements, Sn
```

In this statement , there are multiple conditions, `condition1,` `condition2,` `condition3` and so on. If `condition1` is `True`, `Sequence of statements, S1` is executed, but if it is `False` instead of writing `else` followed by `if` with a `condition`, it has been written as `elif condition`. If `condition 1` is `False`, `condition 2` will be checked, then `condition 3` and so on. If none of the conditions are `True`, the `else` part will be executed.

Program 3.6 demonstrates the working of `if-elif-else` using an example. There are two variables `a` and `b` storing values 20 and 15 respectively. If `a` is equal to `b` then print the message "`Both a and b are equal`", `a` is greater than `b` is written in `elif`, in this case, print the message "`a is greater than b`". If both the above test conditions are `False` then print the message "`a is smaller than b`" which is written in the `else` part.

Program 3.5: Program to demonstrate if-elif-else statement

```
#This is if-elif-else statement
a=20
b=15
if a==b:
   print("Both a and b are equal")
elif a>b:
   print("a is greater than b")
else:
   print("a is smaller than b")
```

The output of the code is

```
a is greater than b
```

When comparing the values stored in variables `a` and `b`, it becomes evident that `a` holds a greater value. As a result, the `elif` block condition evaluates to `True`, triggering the execution of the statement within this block. The output produced by this operation is a clear and concise message: "`a is greater than b`".

Program 3.6: Program to find out largest number among three numbers using nested if statements

```
#This is nested if statement
num1=12
num2=5
num3=15
if num1>num2:
    if num1>num3:
        print("num1 value is largest")
    else:
        print("num3 value is largest")
elif num2>num3:
    print("num2 value is largest")
else:
    print("num3 value is largest")
```

The output of the code is

```
num3 value is largest
```

In the above program, we have initialized three variables with specific values and used conditional statements to determine the largest value. Initially, we check the outer `if` condition to compare `num1` and `num2`. As `num1` is greater than `num2`, we enter the first `if` block. Within this block, we further check if `num1` is greater than `num3`. However, this condition is `False`, and we exit the inner `if` block. We then proceed to the `else` block, where we print the message indicating that `num3` is the largest value.

Program 3.7: Program that prints "Outcome is a prime number" if the user entered 2, 3, 5 and prints "Outcome is not a prime number" if input number is either 1, 4 or 6

```
# Check whether a number is prime or not
num=int(input("Enter any number between 0-6 range:"))
print(num)
if num==2:
    print("Outcome is a prime number")
elif num==3:
    print("Outcome is a prime number")
elif num==5:
    print("Outcome is a prime number")
else:
    print("Outcome is not a prime number")
```

The output of Program 3.7 is shown below:

```
Enter any number between 0-6 range : 4
4
Outcome is not a prime number
```

Table 3.1 summarizes all the types of control structures covered in this section.

Table 3.1 Types of Decision Control Structures

Statement	Description
Simple `if` statement	The simple `if` statement is used to test a condition. If the condition is `True`, a code block written inside the `if` statement is executed.
`if-else` statement	The `if-else` statement is used to test a condition. Based on the condition, if it is `True`, `if` block code is executed, otherwise, `else` block code is executed.
Nested `if` statement	The nested `if` statement allows us to use another `if-else` statement inside an outer `if` statement.
`if-elif-else` statement	The `if-elif-else` statements are used when there are more than one condition to test.

3.3 REPETITION CONTROL STRUCTURES

A repetitive statement is used to repeat a group (block) of programming instructions. This type of control structure is commonly called a *loop*. Whenever we want to repeat a set of lines of code many times, we use repetition control structures. In our day-to-day life, we do a lot of work in a loop like cycling, eating, walking, coding, etc. Similarly, a certain chunk of code may be repeated a given number of times.

Python provides two types of loops:

1. `for` loop
2. `while` loop

3.3.1 for Loop

The `for` loop is used to repeat or iterate over a set of statements for a fixed number of times. Using a `for` loop, we can traverse a list, array, string or any other iterable objects. The loop continues to execute until we reach the last element of the sequence. Let us learn the syntax of `for` loop.

```
for iterator_variable in sequence:
    Statement(s)
```

The statements to be repeated in the `for` loop are written with indentation, this creates a block. Figure 3.6 illustrates the workflow of a `for` loop.

Let us learn the loop using an example. Suppose we want to print the first 10 natural numbers using a `for` loop. First, we will use a built-in function named `range()` inside the loop which generates integers between the specified range as shown in Program 3.8.

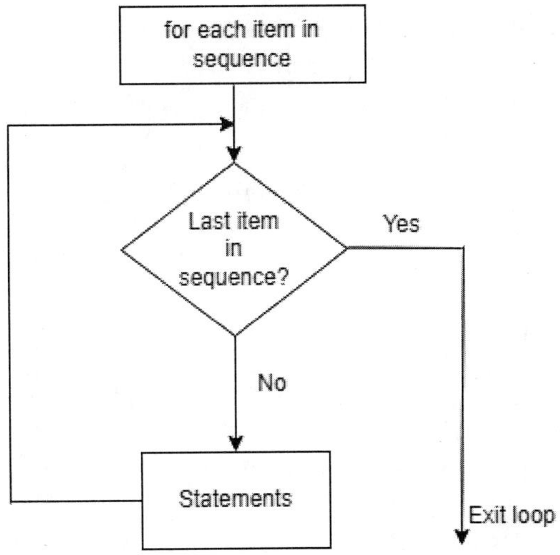

Figure 3.6 Illustration of a for loop control flow.

Program 3.8: Program to demonstrate for loop

```
#This is for loop
for i in range(1, 11):
    print(i)
```

The `range(1, 11)` function generates the numbers starting from 1 to 10. Variable `i` takes up the values generated by the `range()` function one by one in separate iteration and prints them as shown below:

```
1
2
3
4
5
6
7
8
9
10
```

The range () function:

It is used to generate a range of numbers. The syntax of the `range()` function is defined as `range(start, stop, step)`, it generates integers starting from `start` to `stop-1` in steps of `step`. It is optional to provide a `start` argument, the default `start` value is 0, i.e, zero. The `stop` is also an integer which specifies the ending argument. It is mandatory to provide a `stop` value. The `step` value denotes the difference between consecutive pairs of generated integers. By default, `step` size is +1, i.e., one. The `range()` function generates integers from `start` to `stop-1` in step size of `step`. If the numbers are required to be more or less than 1 unit apart, then the step size is explicitly mentioned. Let us understand the `range()` function using some basic examples.

If `range(0,6)` is given, it will generate numbers from 0 to 5.

If `range(1, 12)` is written, this function will generate numbers from 1 to 11 sequentially.

If we write `range(12)`, the default value of start is 0, it will produce a sequence of numbers from 0 till 11.

If we write a range`(1,12,2)`, it will generate numbers from 1 till 11 with a step size of 2 i.e. 1, 3, 5, 7, 9, 11.

If we mention range(10, 0, –2), it will generate numbers from 10 to 1 in reverse order, i.e. 10, 8, 6, 4, 2.

Next, we develop a program to generate terms of fibonacci series in Program 3.9. The fibonacci series has the following terms: 0, 1, 1, 2, 3, 5, 8, 13, 21, 34, ...

In this series 0 and 1 are the initial terms provided and the rest of the terms are generated by adding the previous two terms. The user provides the input `n`, the number of terms of fibonacci series to be generated. 0 and 1 are set as initial values in variables `f` and `s`. The value of `n` is compared to `0`, if it is less than or equal to 0, the value of `f` is printed. Otherwise, the series of terms are generated using the `for` loop. The loop generates the remaining n–2 terms of the series, as the `range(2, n)` generates integers from 2 to n–1.

Program 3.9: Program to generate n terms of fibonacci sequence

```
n=int(input("Enter the number of terms: "))
f=0
s=1
if n<=0:
    print("The Fibonacci series is ",f)
else:
    print(f,s,end=" ")
    for x in range(2,n):
        next_term = f+s
        print(next_term,end=" ")
        f=s
        s=next_term
```

The output of Program 3.9 is shown below:

```
Enter the number of terms: 5
0 1 1 2 3
```

3.3.2 while Loop

In Python, `while` loops are used to execute a block of statements repeatedly till a specified condition is `True`. When the given condition becomes `False`, the loop is terminated and the control goes to the statement written immediately next to the `while` loop. This loop is generally used, when it is not known how many times the loop will be iterating. The syntax of the `while` loop is as follows:

```
while expression:
  Statement(s)
```

Figure 3.7 illustrates a flowchart showing the working of a while loop.

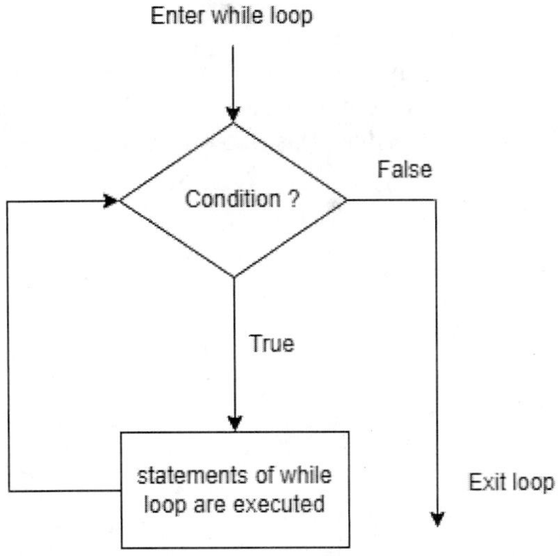

Figure 3.7 Flowchart of a while loop.

Let us learn about the while loop using an example. Suppose you are playing a game. Your scores keep on incrementing by 1 until you reach the score point 50. In this case, there is a continuous incrementation of a number until a given condition is met. Here, a `while` loop comes into picture. Program 3.10 demonstrates the above example

Program 3.10: Program to demonstrate the while loop

```
#Illustration of a while loop
player_score = 0
while player_score < 10:
  player_score+=1  #shorthand notation
print(player_score)
```

The output of the code is

```
10
```

The Program 3.10 initializes the `player_score` to 0. A while loop is then implemented to check if the `player_score` is less than 10, and if so, it increments the `player_score`. This process continues until the `player_score` reaches 10 or higher.

In the above code, we have used shorthand notation which helps in writing the logic with less number of code lines. Next example demonstrates the use of a `while` loop to generate a range of natural numbers.

Program 3.11: Program that will print all the natural numbers from the range 3011 to 3021 (including both 3011 and 3021) using a while loop.

```
# All Natural Numbers from 3011 - 3021 using while loop
num = 3011
while(num <= 3021):
    print(num)
    num = num + 1
```

As can be seen from the Program 3.11, the variable num is initialized to 3011 and the condition of the while loop checks whether `num <= 3021,` if the condition is `True`, it increments `num` inside the loop and prints is as shown below:

```
3011
3012
3013
3014
3015
3016
3017
3018
3019
3020
3021
```

Next example is to check whether a given number is palindrome or not. A palindrome is either a number or a string which remains the same even if it is inverted. For example, 141, 1331, 82728 are some palindrome numbers. MOM, DAD, RADAR, LEVEL, REFER are some palindrome strings. Program 3.12 checks whether a number is palindrome or not.

Program 3.12: Program to check whether the given number is a palindrome or not using a while loop

```
num = int(input("Enter a value:"))
temp = num
rev = 0
while(num > 0):
    dig = num % 10
    rev = rev * 10 + dig
    num = num // 10
if(temp == rev):
    print("This value is a palindrome number!")
else:
    print("This value is not a palindrome number!")
```

The output given below shows that 121 is a palindrome number.

```
Enter a value: 121
This value is a palindrome number!
```

The reader is encouraged to dry run the above program and understand the output of each statement. On similar lines, we can check if a string is a palindrome or not.

3.3.3 The infinite Loop

An infinite loop is a never-ending loop. It does not have any stopping condition. In other words, in a `while` loop, the condition will always be `True`. In order to break an infinite `while` loop, you have to manually stop it by interrupting the code execution. For instance, the condition `True` is always true and when used in a `while` loop, this creates an infinite loop. The general form of an infinite while loop is as follows:

```
while True:
    Statement(s)
```

Instead of specifying a condition, we have written `True`, which creates an infinite loop, the same has been demonstrated in Program 3.13.

Program 3.13: Program to demonstrate an infinite while loop

```
#Illustration of infinite while loop
counter = 0
while True: #infinite while loop
    counter = counter + 1
```

In the example provided above, the `counter` variable is initially set to 0. The condition within the `while` loop is set to `True`, resulting in an infinite loop. Within the loop, the `counter` variable is incremented by one. This means that the value of the `counter` variable will continue to increase until the program is manually stopped.

3.3.4 Nested Loops

Nested loop is a loop inside another outer loop. Here, loop can be both a `while` loop or a `for` loop. The total number of iterations in nested loops are equivalent to:

Total no. of iterations = No. of iterations in outer loop x No. of iterations in inner loop

In a single iteration of an outer loop, all the iterations of an inner loop are executed before moving to the next outer loop iteration. Nested loops can have only while loops, for loops or even combinations of both the loops. Given below are some general forms of nested loops.

```
for loop:
    #Sequence of Statements, S1
    for loop:
        #Sequence of Statements, S2
    #Sequence of Statements, S3
```

OR

```
while  loop:
   #Sequence of Statements, S1
   while  loop:
      #Sequence of Statements, S2
   #Sequence of Statements, S3
```

OR

```
for loop:
   #Sequence of Statements, S1
   while  loop:
      #Sequence of Statements, S2
   #Sequence of Statements, S3
```

OR

```
while loop:
   #Sequence of Statements, S1
   for  loop:
      #Sequence of Statements, S2
   #Sequence of Statements, S3
```

Let's understand the working of nested loops using Program 3.14.

Program 3.14: Program to print a table of 2 using nested while loops.

```
first_num=2
#outer loop
while first_num <=2:
   sec_num=1
   #inner loop
   while sec_num <=10:
      multiple=first_num*sec_num
      print(first_num, "X" ,sec_num, "=", multiple)
      sec_num=sec_num+1
   print() #prints new empty line
   first_num=first_num+1
```

```
2 x 1 = 2
2 x 2 = 4
2 x 3 = 6
2 x 4 = 8
2 x 5 = 10
2 x 6 = 12
2 x 7 = 14
2 x 8 = 16
2 x 9 = 18
2 x 10 = 20
```

In Program 3.14, we have established two variables: `first_num`, which has been initialized with a value of 2, and `sec_num`, which has been initialized with a value of 1. The outer `while` loop will continue to execute until the value of `first_num` is less than or equal to 2, while the inner `while` loop will execute until the value of `sec_num` is less than or equal to 10. As the outer loop runs, the value of `first_num` will continue to change, while the value of `sec_num` will change according to the inner loop. It is worth noting that a simple `print()` statement can be used to print a new empty line. It is also possible to achieve the same output using nested `for` loops.

3.4 BREAK, CONTINUE AND PASS STATEMENTS

Using loops in Python repeats the tasks in an efficient manner. But sometimes, there may arise a condition where we want to exit the loop abruptly, skip an iteration or ignore a condition. These can be done by loop control statements. Python supports the following control statements:

1. `break` statement
2. `continue` statement
3. `pass` statement

3.4.1 break statement

A finite loop executes for a fixed number of times. To exit a loop before it completes all its iterations, use the `break` keyword. Let's understand how to use a `break` statement.

```
while True:
    Statement(s)
    break
    Statement(s)
#Statement(s) outside loop
```

The flowchart of a loop using `break` statement is given below:

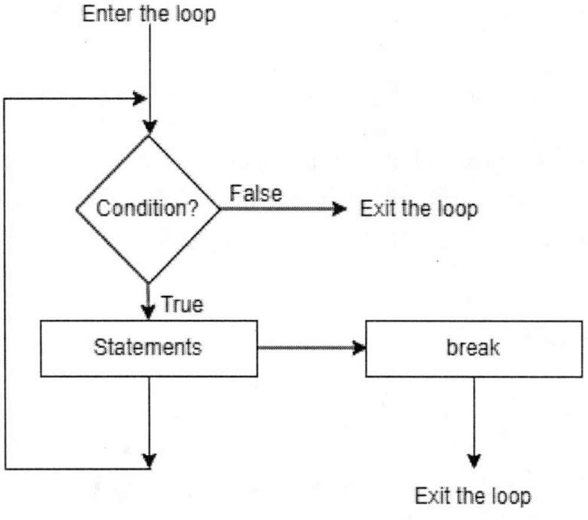

Figure 3.8 Flowchart of a loop with break statement.

The `break` statement transfers the control outside the loop, Program 3.15 demonstrates with an example.

Program 3.15: Program to use break statement with infinite while loop

```
counter = 0
while True:
    counter = counter + 1
    if counter == 2000:
        break
print(counter)
```

The output of the code is

```
2000
```

Program 3.15 increments the `counter` variable until the while loop condition is true, but rest assured that this loop will not run indefinitely. Once the `counter` value reaches 2000, the `break` statement will be executed, causing the loop to terminate. Outside the loop, the `print` statement prints the final value of `counter`. It's worth noting that achieving the same outcome is possible using a `for` loop.

Program 3.16: Program to write a code to calculate the factor value which is initially set to 1 and till 264. Using a while loop, multiply its value every time with 2 and break the while loop when it reaches the final value.**

```
# Break the while loop when factor = 2**64
factor = 1
while factor > 0:
    factor = factor * 2
    if factor == 2 ** 64:
        break
print(factor)
```

The output of the code is

```
18446744073709551616
```

The output displayed above demonstrates that the `while` loop will terminate and the value of the `factor` variable will be printed once it reaches the equivalent of `2**64`. This is achieved through the activation of the `break` statement, which effectively halts the loop.

3.4.2 continue statement

`continue` is also a loop control statement just like the `break` statement. `continue` statement is opposite to that of `break` statement, instead of terminating the loop, it skips to the next iteration of the loop. Figure 3.9 shows flowchart of the `continue` statement inside a loop.

Let us understand the concept of `continue` statement using an example given in Program 3.18. Suppose we want to print numbers from 1 to 10 without printing 6 in it. In this case, we will use the `continue` statement to skip the iteration for 6.

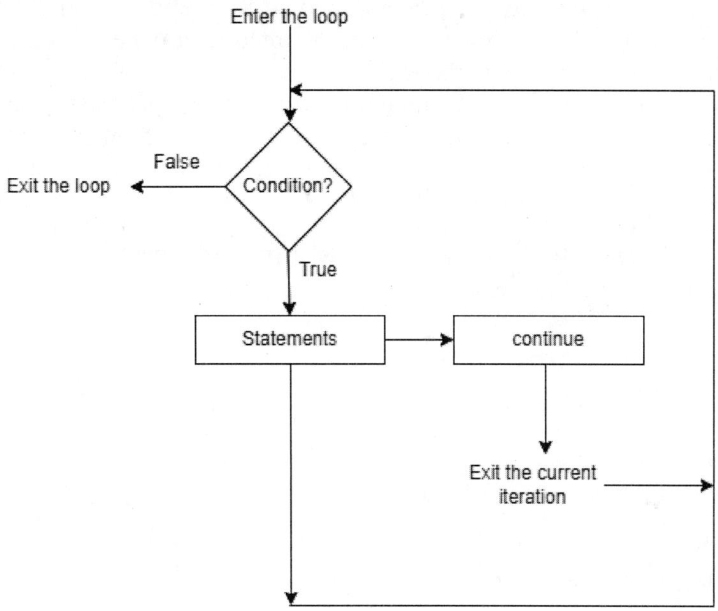

Figure 3.9 Flowchart of a continue Statement.

Program 3.17: Program to demonstrate use of continue statement

```
# loop from 1 to 10
for i in range(1, 11):
   if i == 6: # If i is equals to 6,skip to next iteration
      continue
   else:
      print(i, end = " ")# otherwise print the value of i
```

The output of the code is

```
1 2 3 4 5 7 8 9 10
```

The output of Program 3.17 consists of the numbers 1 through 10, with the exception of 6. This is due to the implementation of a `continue` statement, which instructs the program to skip over the iteration when the value of `i` reaches 6. The program then resumes its execution within the while loop, proceeding to the next iteration.

3.4.3 pass statement

The `pass` statement in Python is used when a statement is required syntactically, but you do not want any command or code to execute. The `pass` statement is a null operation; nothing happens when it executes. So, when to use the `pass` statement? Consider you have an `if-else` control structure with the body left empty. You plan to write the code in the future. The Python interpreter will throw an error if it comes across an empty body. A comment can also be added inside the body of the `if-else` statements, but the interpreter ignores the comment and will throw an error whereas `pass` is not ignored by the interpreter. The `pass` statement can be used inside the body. During execution, the interpreter, when it comes across the `pass` statement, ignores and continues without giving any error.

The `pass` statement can be used with empty functions, empty class, along with `if-else` statements, `for` or `while` loops. Now, let's write a small Python program using `if-else` statements where `num1` and `num2` are two variables. If the value of `num1` is greater than `num2` then `pass` the rest of the code lines.

Program 3.18: Program to demonstrate use of a pass statement

```
# Using pass along with if-else statement
num1 = 30
num2 = 20
if(num1>num2):
   pass
else:
   print("num2>num1")
```

In the above Program 3.18, since the value of `num1` is greater than `num2`, the body of the `if` block is ignored using the `pass` statement.

3.5 ELSE CLAUSE WITH LOOPS

It is possible that the `else` clause can be used after `for` loop and `while` loop. In the case of a `while` loop, if the condition becomes `False`, then the `else` block is executed. Similarly, in case of a `for` loop, when all the iterations of the loop are completed, the `else` block is executed. However, if either a `while` or a `for` loop is terminated by force due to a `break` statement, then the `else` clause is omitted. Let's try to understand this concept using Program 3.19 given below.

Program 3.19: Program to demonstrate the use of else clause along with a while loop

```
num=5
while(num>0):
   print(num)
   num-=1  #using shorthand notation
else:
   print("We have reached till value 0")
```

```
5
4
3
2
1
We have reached till value 0
```

The above Program 3.19 depicts the workflow of a while loop along with the `else` clause. We have initialized the `num` variable value to 5 and started the while loop which will execute till `num` value is greater than 0. The condition written with a `while` loop gets `False` when the value of `num` reaches 0. Loop will get terminated and we will jump directly to the `else` clause and print a message.

Let's use the `else` clause along with a `for` loop using Program 3.20.

Program 3.20: Program to demonstrate else clause with a `for` loop.

```
for i in range(8):
    print(i)
    if i==4:
        break
else:
    print("We have entered else block")
```

```
0
1
2
3
4
```

Program 3.20 above demonstrates the functionality of the `else` clause in conjunction with a `for` loop. The `for` loop will `continue` to iterate until the value of `i` reaches 4. Once the value of 4 is stored in the `i` variable, the loop will be forcefully terminated, and in this case the `else` clause will not be executed.

This program showcases the importance of understanding the behavior of loops and how they interact with conditional statements. By utilizing the `else` clause, we can ensure that our code executes as intended and handles unexpected scenarios appropriately. It is crucial to have a solid grasp of these concepts to write efficient and effective code.

SUMMARY

- Control structures are used to define the order of execution of the statements in a program.
- Sequential control structures are used to execute the program in a linear fashion.
- Selection control structures are used to execute a block of code on the basis of some defined conditions. They are also known as decision or branching control structures.
- Simple `if`, `if-else`, `if-elif-else`, nested `if` statements are examples of selection control structures.
- Simple `if` statement is used when the truth value of a condition is checked. If the condition is `True`, code will be executed.
- While using `If-else` statements, if the condition is `True`, statements in if body will be executed and if the condition is `False`, statements in else body will be executed.

- `If-elif-else` statements are used whenever there are more than one conditions to be tested. If condition1 is `True`, the body will be executed. If it is `False`, the next `elif` condition is checked. We can have as many `elif` blocks as per requirement and conditions given. If none of the conditions is `True`, then the last `else` block will be executed.
- `For` and `while` loop are Repetition structures.
- The `for` loop is used to repeat or iterate over a set of statements for a fixed number of times.
- The `for` loop uses the `range()` function to perform iterations.
- The `range()` function is used to generate a range of numbers.
- The `while` loops are used to execute a block of statements repeatedly till the specified condition remains `True`. When the given condition becomes `False`, the loop ends.
- When the `while` loop condition remains `True` always, it results in an infinite loop.
- Nested loop is a loop inside another outer loop.
- The total number of iterations in nested loops are equivalent to: Total no. of iterations = No. of iterations in outer loop x No. of iterations in inner loop
- In a single iteration of an outer loop, all the iterations of an inner loop are executed in nested loops.
- A `break` statement is used to abruptly terminate a loop.
- The `continue` statement skips a particular iteration.
- `pass` statement is used to ignore a certain block of code without receiving an error.
- `else` clause can be used after `for` loop and `while` loop.

EXERCISES

3.1 Write a program to display the student's name who has received the highest marks in computer science subject among five students. Following are the marks of students:

Student 1: 56

Student 2: 70

Student 3: 89

Student 4: 39

Student 5: 75

3.2 State differences between the `break` and `continue` statements.

3.3 Write the output of the following code snippets:

(a)
```
n= random.random()
print(n)
```

(b)
```
for i in range(0, 5):
    if i==3:
        continue
    else:
        print('i=', i)
```

(c)
```
total=0
for i in range(10, 0, -1):
    total+=1
print(total)
```

(d)
```
a=b=20
x=y=30
if a<100:
    if b>30:
        x+=1
    else:
        y+= 1
print(x)
print(y)
```

3.4 Write a program to display multiplication table of 5 and 6 using both for loop and while loop.

3.5 Print the following patterns using loops:

(a)
```
* * * * *
*       *
*       *
* * * * *
```

(b)
```
$
$ $ $
$ $ $ $ $
$ $ $ $ $ $ $
```

(c)
```
* * * * * *
 * * * *
  * *
   *
```

(d)
```
0 1 2 3 4 5
0 1 2 3 4
0 1 2 3
0 1 2
0 1
0
```

(e)
```
1
12
123
1234
12345
```

3.6 Rewrite the following for loop using while loop:

(a)
```
sum=0
for i in range (1,7,2):
    sum+=i
```
(b)
```
for i in range(1, 20):
    if i%5 == 0:
        print(i)
```

3.7 Write a code using iterative programming/loops that simulates providing the password:

- You have at most three attempts.
- If you provide the right password, the code will print "Welcome in!."
- If you provide the wrong password and it is not the third attempt, the code will print "Wrong password. Please try again." and ask you to enter the password again.
- If your third attempt is not successful, the code will write "You are not allowed to access this computer!" and exit.

Assume that the right password is PyTHon and use the function `input()` for asking the password from the command line.

3.8 Write a program to find the maximum of three numbers using control structures.

3.9 Identify the syntax error in the following code:

```
if(X =Y):
    print('Equal')
else if(x < y):
    print('Smaller')
else;
    print('Larger')
```

3.10 Write a program to find the largest positive factor of a number. Take input from the user.

4

Functions

So far, we have learnt that using different control sequences, data types and operators, one can proceed towards solving a problem using Python programming. A solution is designed, and then it is translated using Python. If the problem requires a simple solution structure, then a basic sequential program might suffice. However, if the problem is a little more complex, then designing a simple program that follows line by line execution might not be an ideal way due to various reasons covered later in this chapter.

A more efficient approach towards solving complex problems would involve dividing a bigger problem into smaller subproblems and then solving each. In some cases, even if the problem is not too complex, the programmer might design the program in such a way that subtasks are performed separately. This approach of dividing the program into smaller chunks that perform separate tasks is called *modularity*. In Python, modularity is achieved using special blocks of code called *functions*.

4.1 INTRODUCTION

A function is a named block of code whose statements are designated to perform a certain task. Functions are used to achieve modularity and reusability in a program. In order to achieve a particular task, as a sub-part of the program, the corresponding function is called using its name and then those statements are executed. A function is to be defined only once. Then it can be called any number of times, from anywhere in the program.

4.1.1 Advantages of Functions

- **Better structure:** Functions provide a better structure to the code. If the program has several hundreds of lines of code, then functions make it more organized and readable.
- **Reusability:** Once defined, a function can be called and used several times. In the absence of a function, if the same task has to be done more than once, the entire code must be written again. This effort is saved by using functions.

- **Teamwork is made easier:** With the use of functions, a bigger problem is divided into smaller independent tasks. This makes it convenient for the work to be divided and managed among teams.
- **Reduced length of code:** Functions allow the programmer to reuse the same code. Thus, the same code need not be written again and again. This leads to a reduction in the number of lines in the code.
- **Easier to debug:** If the same code is written several times in the same program, there might be different errors each time. However, if the code is written at just one place, any errors can be easily detected and corrected.
- **Modification:** Another advantage is that if any modifications are to be made, they are done at just one point and the programmer need not look for repeated occurrences of the same code in the program.

4.2 USER DEFINED FUNCTIONS

There exist two types of functions—*Built-in functions* and *user-defined functions*. Built-in functions are already defined in the standard libraries provided by Python itself. In order to use a built-in function, its corresponding library needs to be imported and the function can be directly called to get the task done. User-defined functions are defined by the programmer to perform any desired task. In this section, we elaborate more about working with user-defined functions.

4.2.1 Syntax of a Function

This section covers the syntax of creating a user defined function. The following syntax is used to define a function.

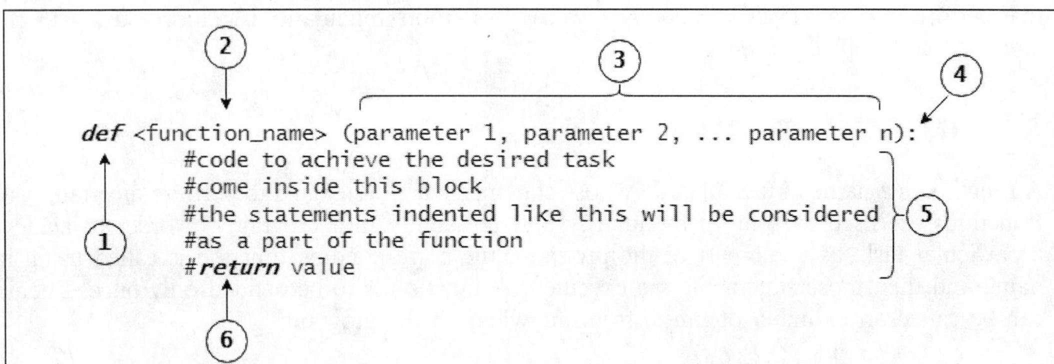

Figure 4.1 Syntax of a function in Python.

The various components of a function as depicted in Figure 4.1 are elaborated below:

1. The `def` keyword is used to define a function. It directs the interpreter that the definition of an entity will come next.
2. Next comes the function name. It is the name by which this block of functions is known. After the function definition, whenever the programmer needs to invoke the

function, it is called by this name. It must be noted here that a function can be named anything the programmer wants, by abiding by the same rules as those for variable naming.

3. After the function name, comes a pair of parentheses. These can be empty or may also contain some values known as parameters. Parameters are values sent as input to the function. Details on this are covered in the next subsection.
4. The parentheses are followed by a semicolon, indicating the beginning of an indented block of instructions from the next line.
   Note that the `def` keyword, function name, parentheses with or without parameter list and the semicolon together comprise the *function header*.
5. A function can have as many statements as needed. All of them follow the same indentation level, thereby making them a block of code. This collection of statements is called the *function body*.
6. A statement beginning with the *return* keyword, followed by some value is called a `return` statement. By making use of the `return` statement, a function can return some value to the place from where it was originally called. Since a function may or may not return a value, the `return` statement is optional.

Let us consider a program that computes the area and perimeter of a circle by taking radius as input from the user. Program 4.1 accomplishes this task in a sequential manner as we have studied till now.

Program 4.1: Program to compute area and perimeter of a circle with radius as input from the user

```
#input radius
r = float(input("Enter radius of the circle : "))
#compute area and perimeter
area = 3.14 * r * r
peri = 2 * 3.14 * r
#print results
print("Area of circle =", area, "sq. units")
print("Perimeter of circle =", peri, "sq. units")
```

Program 4.2 performs the same task as Program 4.1 by using functions, instead of writing all code sequentially.

Program 4.2: Program to compute area and perimeter of circle using functions

```
def circle(radius):
    #compute area and perimeter
    area = 3.14 * radius * radius
    peri = 2 * 3.14 * radius
    #print results
    print("Area of circle =", area, "sq. units")
    print("Perimeter of circle =", peri, "sq. units")
#take input for radius
```

```
r = float(input("Enter radius of circle : "))
#calling function to compute area and perimeter
circle(r)
```

Consider the function in Program 4.2. The function name is `circle` and it has one parameter named `radius`. There are 4 statements and 2 comments in the function body. The output of Program 4.2 is shown below.

```
Enter radius of circle : 4.5
Area of circle = 63.585 sq. units
Perimeter of circle = 28.26 sq. units
```

4.2.2 Arguments v/s Parameters

A function might need some data to perform the desired task, for example, the value of the radius to compute the area and perimeter of a circle. This information is provided to the function at the time of call by passing it as an *argument*, within the pair of parentheses. The value in a function argument is passed to the corresponding *parameter* during the function call. Arguments and parameters may or may not have the same name.

Consider the Program 4.2. First, the user will input the value of radius which will be stored in variable `r`. When a call to the function `circle` is made in the next statement, the variable `r` becomes an argument to the function. Whatever value was stored in `r`, is now passed on to the parameter `radius` in the function `circle`. Figure 4.2 demonstrates the passing of argument to the corresponding function parameter.

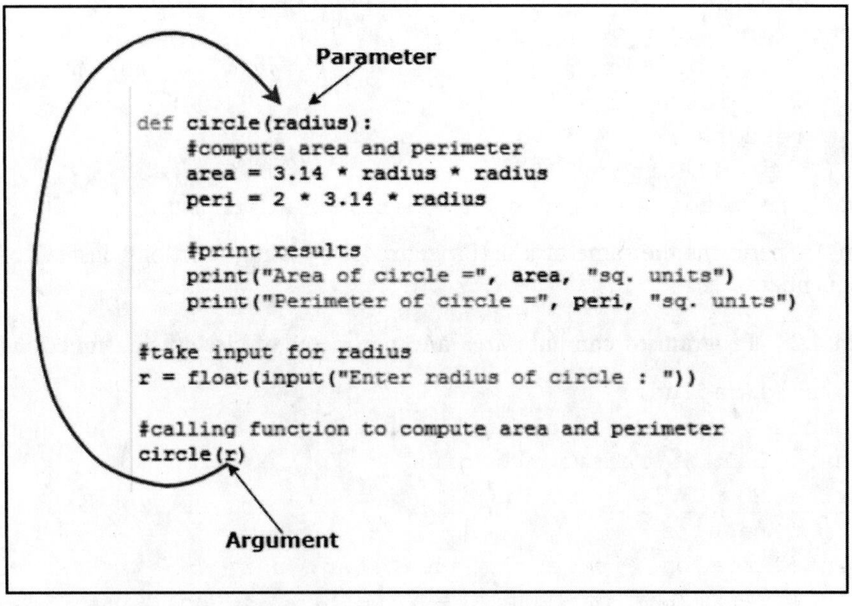

Figure 4.2: Program to demonstrate arguments and parameters.

When a function is called, the interpreter looks for a matching definition of the function having the name and argument list as in the call. Therefore, the number of arguments passed should be the same as the number of parameters specified in the function definition. Their order must also match. If the number and order of arguments does not match with any function, the interpreter will throw an error.

Program 4.3 contains a function that prints string `s1, n1` times and string `s2, n2` times. The first call to this function, `message(str1, str2, 4, 5)` has all arguments in correct order and it produces the desired output. The second call to this function, `message(str1, 4)` does not have the same number of arguments as the parameters, and hence, it leads to an error. What will be the output of a call like, `message("abc", 5, "def", 7)`?

Program 4.3: Function to print messages –s1 and s2; n1 and n2 times respectively.

```
def message(s1, s2, n1, n2):
    print(s1*n1)
    print("First message printed", n1, "times")
    print(s2*n2)
    print("Second message printed", n2, "times")
str1 = "Monday"
str2 = "Sunday"
message(str1, str2, 4, 5)
message(str1, 4)
```

The output of Program 4.3 is shown below:

```
MondayMondayMondayMonday
First message printed 4 times
SundaySundaySundaySundaySunday
Second message printed 5 times
Traceback (most recent call last):
  File "C:\Users\HP\Desktop\Samples\prog3.py", line 13, in <module>
    message, (strl, 4)
TypeError: message() missing 2 required positional arguments: 'n1' and 'n2'
```

It is worth mentioning here that both arguments and parameters point to the same memory location, irrespective of the fact that their names could be different. Their references to memory will become different if the value of the parameter is altered while the function is executing. Let us understand this concept with the help of Program 4.4.

Program 4.4: Program to illustrate the dynamics of memory location of arguments and parameters

```
def function1(x):
    print("Inside function1")
    print("Value of variable x = ", x)
    print("Location of variable x = ", id(x))
    print()

    x = x*10
    print("After modification...")
```

```
    print("Value of variable x = ", x)
    print("Location of variable x = ", id(x))
    print()

n = 60
print("Before function call..")
print("Value of variable, n = ", n)
print("Location of variable n = ", id(n))
print()
print("Call to function1 with n as argument")
function1(n)
print("Outside function...")
print("Value of variable n = ",n)
print("Location of variable n = ",id(n))
```

The output of Program 4.4 is shown below:

```
Before function call..
Value of variable, n = 60
Location of variable n = 8791543937120

Call to function1 with n as argument
Inside function1
Value of variable x = 60
Location of variable x = 8791543937120

After modification ...
Value of variable x = 600
Location of variable x = 50641904

Outside function ...
Value of variable n = 60
Location of variable n = 8791543937120
```

Figure 4.3 pictorially explains the output of Program 4.3. Let us assume that the variable n has a value 60 initially and was at location with id 10201. When function1 is called, the parameter, x gets the same value as n, i.e. 60 and it also refers to the same location as n. After the execution of the statement x=x*10 in function1, the value of variable x changes, however the value of n remains unchanged. This is the reason that x is now allocated a different memory location holding the value 600, and n continues to refer at the same memory location.

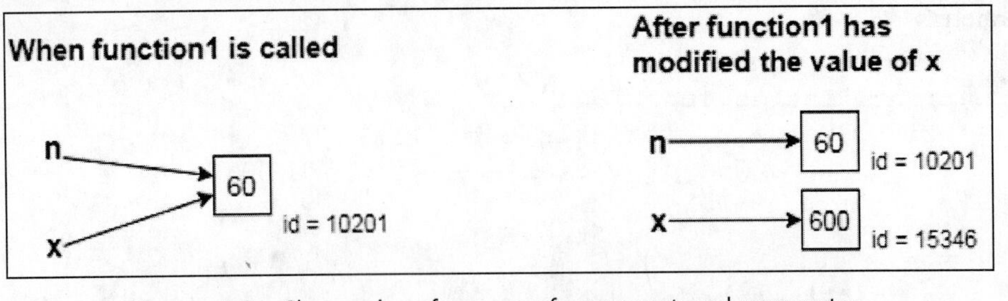

Figure 4.3 Change in references of argument and parameter.

4.3 THE MAIN() FUNCTION

The 'main' function is essentially the starting point of a program. It is also known as the driver function. In several programming languages, it is necessary to have a `main` function. However, a Python program can execute without a `main` function as well. Therefore, the Python interpreter checks whether there is a driver code present or not. This is done by checking the `__name__` variable.

The interpreter assigns a string value to the `__name__` variable depending on the way in which a program is being executed. If a file is imported and is being run, then the `__name__` variable takes the name of that file. However, if the file is being directly executed, then it takes the value `__main__`.

So when we define the `main` function in our program, we must add the following condition:

```
if __name__== "__main__":
  #execute main()
else:
  #display some message, and not execute main()
```

Let us now look at some examples using the `main()` function.

Program 4.5: Program to find out the factorial of a number

```
def factorial(num):
  fac=1
  for i in range(2, num+1):
    fac = fac*i
  print("Factorial of", num, "is", fac)
def main():
  number = int(input("Enter a number:"))
  factorial(number)
if __name__=="__main__":
  main()
```

The output of Program 4.5 is shown below:

```
Enter a number : 6
Factorial of 6 is 720
```

Program 4.6: Program to take string as input and count the number of vowels

```
def vowel_count(message):
  count = 0
  for i in message:
    if i in 'aeiou' or i in 'AEIOU':
      count += 1
  print(message, "contains", count, "vowels")
def main():
```

```
    msg = input("Enter a string:")
    vowel_count(msg)
if __name__=="__main__":
    main()
```

The output of Program 4.6 is shown below:

```
Enter a string:Have A nice dAy!
Have A nice dAy! contains 6 vowels
```

4.4 FRUITFUL AND VOID FUNCTIONS

So far, we have seen the basic syntax of a function, and understood the concept of providing information to the function using arguments. Once the function has done the specified task, there might be a result or a collection of values that the function has computed. If the function returns some value, it is called a *fruitful function*, otherwise it is known as a *void function*. The word "void" means empty. The functions which just complete the said task and do not have to return any value to the place from where it was called are called *void* functions.

A *fruitful* function can either print the result inside its own block, or sometimes, there may be a need to return this value to the place from where the function was called. This can be understood to be similar to a situation where a team leader asks for a monthly expenditure report form a subordinate, the subordinate creates the report and hands it back to the leader. The same purpose is served by using the `return` statement inside a function.

The `return` statement is usually the last statement in a function. The `return` keyword is followed by a value or a variable as shown in Program 4.7. Once the interpreter reaches the `return` statement, the control goes back to the calling statement along with the return value. At the calling statement, a variable is made to store the return value.

Program 4.7: Program to count and return the number of words in a given sentence

```
def count_words(sent):
    spaces = 0
    for i in sent:
        if i==' ':
            spaces += 1
    #assuming that number of words is one more than the number of spaces
    return spaces+1
def main():
    s = input("Enter a sentence:")
    words = count_words(s)
    print("The number of words in this sentence =",words)
if __name__=="__main__":
    main()
```

The output of Program 4.7 is shown below.

```
Enter a sentence: The quick brown fox
The number of words in this sentence = 4
```

A function can also return multiple values using the `return` statement. In that case the `return` keyword is followed by the names of variables to be returned separated by a comma as shown in Program 4.8. The number of variables required to store the returned values at the place of call is the same as the number of values returned by the function.

Another way of returning multiple values is to return them as a tuple, catch them in a tuple and use indexing to access each value.

Program 4.8: Program to compute area and volume of a cube and a sphere

```
def cube(side):
   area = 6*side*side
   vol = side**3
   #returning 2 values separated by comma
   return area, vol
def sphere(radius):
   pi = 3.14
   area = 4*pi*radius*radius
   vol = (4/3)*pi*radius*radius*radius
   #returning 2 values in a tuple
   return (area,vol)
def main():
   s = float(input("Enter the side of cube: "))
   #this function returns 2 values, hence we use 2
   #variables to store the results
   a, v = cube(s)
   print("Area of cube =", a)
   print("Volume of cube =", v)
   r = float(input("Enter the radius of sphere: "))
   #this function returns 2 values in a single tuple
   #hence we use 1 variable to store the result
   result = sphere(r)
   #printing type of this variable
   print("Returned value stored in variable of type :",type(result))
      print("Area of sphere =", result[0])
      print("Volume of sphere =", result[1])
if __name__=="__main__":
      main()
```

The output of Program 4.8 is shown below:

```
Enter the side of cube: 4.5
Area of cube = 121.5
Volume of cube = 91.125
Enter the radius of sphere: 6.75
Returned value stored in variable of type : <class 'tuple'>
Area of sphere = 572.265
Volume of sphere = 1287.59625
```

4.5 FLOW OF CONTROL

Now that we know in detail about the various components of a function, next let's learn the flow of execution, i.e., the order in which statements execute when using functions.

One of the most important facts to be kept in mind is that simply defining a function does not execute it. When the programmer defines a function, the interpreter knows that this block of statements is known by a certain name. Subsequently, after this definition, when a function call is made, the control is transferred to the function body, and execution begins. The code in the function body is executed and lastly, a `return` statement, if any is executed and a value is returned. In case the function is a `void` function, after all statements of the function body have been executed, the control goes back to the statement after the calling statement, without any return value.

```
1 def functionA (x, y):
2       print("Inside the function body")
3       p = x**y
4       return p

5 def main():
6       print("Main function begins")
7       res = functionA(5, 3)
8       print("Result = ", res)

9 if __name__=="__main__":
10      main()
```

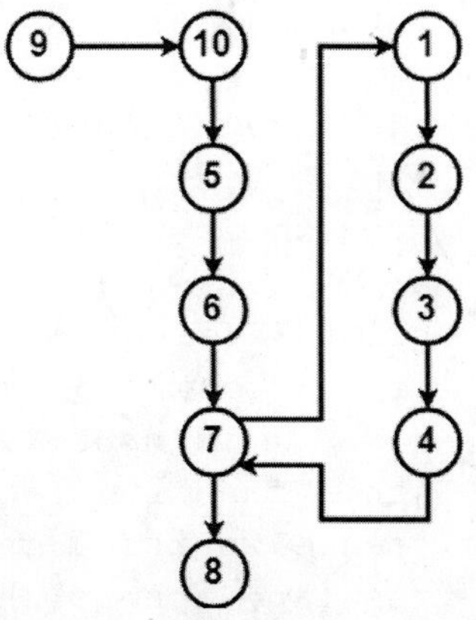

Figure 4.4 Flow of control of a Python program containing functions.

Let us understand the flow of execution of a simple program elaborated in Figure 4.4. The execution of any program begins with the `if __name__`... statement, i.e., line 9. Since, main module is defined, this condition becomes true, and `main` is called in line 10. The control then goes to the `main` function beginning at line 5. The body of `main()` executes. Then at line 7, a function call is encountered, and the control gets transferred to line 1, `functionA`. Line 2, 3, 4 constitute the body of `functionA`. Line 4 is a `return` statement that causes the control to return to the place where the function was called, i.e., line 7. After this the next line, i.e., line 8 gets executed.

4.6 THE GLOBAL KEYWORD

A function is a block of code. The statements inside a function, can only be executed when and if the function is called. This is because the *scope* of those statements is inside the function. We define here the *scope* of a variable as the specific part of code where the variable will be accessible. Every variable used in a program has a well defined scope that can either be *local* or *global*. Figure 4.5 explains the scope of the variables `g` and `x`.

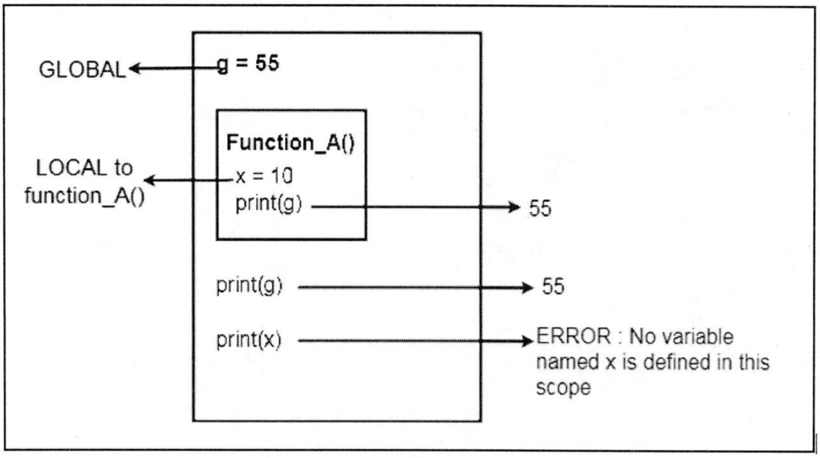

Figure 4.5 Global and local scope.

When a variable is defined within a specific block of code, such as a function, then it is said to be *local* to the function. That variable will not be accessible outside the function. Any modification made to a *local* variable stays within the same scope only. A variable with the same name defined outside the scope, is considered different from the one inside the function.

On the other hand, a variable declared outside any particular block of code, is accessible everywhere in the program; even inside other functions. Such variables are known as *global* variables. Changes made to *global* variables are reflected everywhere in the program. Program 4.9 shows the use of *local* and *global* variables.

Program 4.9: Program to demonstrate local and global variables

```
num = 45
def function_A():
   print("Inside function...")
   a = 2
   print("a=",a)
   print("num=",num)
print("Outside function...")
print("num=",num)
print()
function_A()
print()
```

```
print("After function call...")
num = num*10
print("num after modification=", num)
print("\nTry to access local variable 'a' outside function...")
print(a)
```

The output of Program 4.9 is shown below.

```
Outside function ...
num= 45

Inside function ...
a = 2
num= 45

After function call ...
num after modification= 450

Try to access local variable 'a' outside function ...
Traceback (most recent call last):
  File "C:/Users/HP/Desktop/Samples/prog9.py", line 19, in <module>
    print(a)
NameError: name 'a' is not defined
```

A question that might arise here is that what if a variable inside a function has the same name as the *global* variable? Is the same copy of the *global* variable accessed or not? The answer is NO. It can be well explained with the following statements.

- When a variable with the same name as that of any *global* variable is defined inside a function, it becomes a *local* variable of the function. The *global* variable is neither accessed nor modified by that function.
- If the same copy of the *global* variable is to be used and modified inside a function, then the variable name must be prefixed with the *global* keyword. This indicates to the compiler to use the global copy of that variable.

The above points are illustrated in Program 4.10.

Program 4.10: Program to demonstrate use of *global* keyword

```
num = 50
def modify():
    global num
    num = num*10
print("Before function call...")
print("num = ", num)
print()
modify()
print("After function has executed...")
print("num = ", num)
```

The output of Program 4.10 is given below:

```
Before function call ...
num = 50
After function has executed ...
num = 500
```

The reader is encouraged to modify this program and observe the result if the *global* keyword is not used. How are the variables in the function affected? Are there any errors?

4.7 SPECIAL TYPES OF ARGUMENTS AND PARAMETERS

4.7.1 Keyword Arguments

When arguments are sent as a *parameter* = *value* pair, they are said to be *keyword* arguments, or *kwargs* for short. The syntax for making a call using *keyword* arguments is as follows:

```
function_name(parameter_name = value, parameter_name = value...)
```

As is implicit from the syntax, use of *kwargs* eliminates the need of following the order of arguments at the time of function call. Keyword arguments ensure that the corresponding parameters get the associated values. We demonstrate the use of *kwargs* by Program 4.11.

Program 4.11: Program to count the number of occurrences of a character in a string

```
def counter(string, character):
    count=0
    for x in string:
        if x==character:
            count+=1
    return count
def main():
    s = input("Enter message : ")
    c = input("Enter the character to count occurrence : ")
    n = counter(character=c, string=s)
    print(c, "occurs", n, "times in", s)
if __name__=="__main__":
    main()
```

The output of Program 4.11 is shown below:

```
Enter message : the monkey on the tree
Enter the character to count occurrence : t
t occurs 3 times in the monkey on the tree
```

4.7.2 Default Parameters

It is now known that data can be passed to a function by using arguments. In some cases, it is quite possible that the value for a parameter is set to something default, so that if the user does not supply a value for that parameter, a *default* value may be used. For example, a programmer might want to set the number of subjects for a student to 5, unless mentioned otherwise. This feature is achieved by using *default parameters.* Program 4.12 illustrates the use of *default* parameters within a function.

Program 4.12: Program to create a user defined function to print numbers in a range. It should have parameters begin, end and step

```
def print_numbers(end, begin=0, step=1):
    print()
    print("begin=",begin,"\tend=",end,"\tstep=",step)
    i=begin
    while(i<=end):
        print(i, end="   ")
        i+=step
#call 1
print_numbers(20)
print()
#call 2
print_numbers(20,7,3)
print()
#call 3
print_numbers(20,3)
print()
```

Note that the value for *default* parameter is taken up, only if the corresponding argument is not provided at the time of call. If an argument for that parameter is given, then the *default* value will get overwritten and the corresponding argument value is used.

All *default* parameters in a function must appear towards the right end of the parameter list, i.e., first all parameters that will require a corresponding argument will occur and then the parameters that have a default value, and for whom, the arguments are optional. This is done to avoid any confusion or mismatch at the time of calling. It also ensures appropriate assignment of arguments to parameters. In addition to this, it must be ensured that the arguments are in the same order as the parameters.

In Program 4.12, defining a function like `def print_numbers(begin=0, end, step=1)` will not be allowed. As soon as this is compiled, the interpreter throws an error that "*a non-default argument cannot follow a default argument*".

Now, let us see the results of various types of calls to the function in Program 4.12:

(i) `print_numbers(20)` will cause parameter values to be `end=20, begin=0, step=1`

```
begin= 0        end= 20        step= 1
0  1  2  3  4  5  6  7  8  9  10  11  12  13  14  15  16  17  18  19  20
```

(ii) `print_numbers(20,7,3)` will cause parameter values to be `end=20, begin=7, step=3`

```
begin= 7          end= 20          step= 3
7   10   13   16   19
```

(iii) `print_numbers(20,3)` will make parameter values to be `end=20, begin=3, step=1`

```
begin= 3          end= 20          step= 1
3  4  5  6  7  8  9  10  11  12  13  14  15  16  17  18  19  20
```

One may wonder, what if we wish to skip the values of a few *default* parameters and assign an argument to other default ones? Say, in Program 4.12, what if one wishes to let the `begin` parameter value to be the default 0, and wants the `step` parameter to be 4? This can be done by making the call by using keyword arguments such as— `print_numbers(20, step=4)`.

4.8 ASSERT STATEMENT

The `assert` statement in Python lets the programmer place certain checks or conditions in the code. The syntax for using `assert` statement is

```
assert <condition>
```

The `assert` keyword is followed by the condition to be checked. The code after the `assert` statement executes only if the assertion is `True`. If the assertion is `False` then `AssertionError` is raised and the execution is terminated.

We can also display an assertion error of our own. The syntax is

```
assert <condition>, <error message in a string>
```

Program 4.13: Function to compute the simple interest given principal amount, rate of interest and time period as parameters

```
def simple_interest(p, r, t):
   si = (p*r*t)/100
   amt = p+si
   print("Simple Interest = Rs.", si)
   print("Amount to be paid = Rs.",amt)
def main():
   p = float(input("Enter the principal amount: "))
   r = float(input("Enter the rate of interest: "))
   t = float(input("Enter time period in years : "))
   assert r>0
   assert t>0, "Time period cannot be negative!"
   simple_interest(p,r,t)
if __name__=="__main__":
   main()
```

The output of Program 4.13 is shown below:

```
Enter the principal amount : 500
Enter the rate of interest : 4.5
Enter time period in years : 6
Simple Interest = Rs. 135.0
Amount to be paid = Rs. 635.0
```

```
Enter the principal amount : 500
Enter the rate of interest : -2
Enter time period in years : 6
Traceback (most recent call last):
  File "C:/Users/HP/Desktop/Samples/prog13.py", line 18, in <module>
    main()
  File "C: /Users/HP/Desktop/Samples/prog13.py", line 13, in main
    assert r>0
AssertionError
```

```
Enter the principal amount: 500
Enter the rate of interest: 2.5
Enter time period in years : -8
Traceback (most recent call last) :
  File "C:/Users/HP/Desktop/Samples/prog13.py", line 18, in <module>
    main()
File "C: /Users/HP/Desktop/Simples/prog13.py", line 14, in main
  assert t>0, "Time period cannot be negative!"
AssertionError: Time period cannot be negative!
```

Observe that in Program 4.13, there are 2 `assert` statements. The first one ensures that the rate of interest is positive. There is no custom error message there. However, the next `assert` statement has a custom error message in case the time period entered is negative. The output covers all the cases.

4.9 DOCSTRINGS

When large-scale python applications are designed, it involves a team of people. Thus, in order to make it convenient for other people to understand their code, programmers provide *documentation.* Documentation is a small description about the function. A *docstring* is used to provide documentation about a function in Python. Docstring is the first statement inside the function body. It is enclosed in triple quotation marks, i.e., in a multi-line comment. Generally, a *docstring* contains information about the purpose of the function, input parameters and return value. Providing *docstrings* is a good programming practice. Let us add docstring to the program in Program 4.7 as shown below:

```
def count_words(sent):
    '''
    input parameter : sent, string data type
    return value : number of words, integer
    this function counts the number of spaces in 'sent'
    and returns number of spaces+1
    '''
```

```
    spaces = 0

    for i in sent:
        if i==' ':
            spaces += 1
    #assuming that number of words is one more than the number of spaces
        return spaces+1
def main():
    s = input("Enter a sentence:")
    words = count_words(s)
    print("The number of words in this sentence =",words)
if __name__=="__main__":
    main()
```

4.10 PYTHON LIBRARIES

It has been emphasized several times in this book that one of the most striking features of Python is the presence of thousands of built-in libraries and predefined functions. This section covers some important concepts about the same.

4.10.1 Built-in Functions

A library is a collection of predefined functions. The functions in the libraries are already defined and there is no need for the user to write code for them. In order to use these functions, we need to *import* the library to our program and call the function by its name and appropriate arguments. Without realizing we have used several built-in functions up till this point. Consider the following simple coding statement:

```
username = input("Enter your name:")
```

Here, the `input()` function is being used. It is a built-in function used to take keyboard input from the user. It takes a string as a parameter which is the message to be prompted while taking input. It returns a string which was entered by the user and it is stored in the variable on the left side of the assignment operator (=).

Thousands of such built-in functions are available to make a programmer's life easier! Some of them are summarized in Table 4.1.

Table 4.1 Python Standard Library Built-in Functions

S.No.	Function Name	Parameters	Return Value
1.	`id(x)`	any variable x	the identity (a memory location) of x
	`type(x)`	any variable x	the data type of x
	`len(x)`	a sequence or a dictionary	count of number of elements in x
2.	`str(x), int(x), float(x)` ...	any variable x	variable x, converted to the data type according to the function used
3.	`sum(x)`	x is a sequence of numbers	the sum of all numbers present in x
	`abs(x)`	a numeric value, x	absolute value of x
	`min(x) or max(x)`	a sequence x	the minimum/maximum value in x

4.10.2 The print() Function

We have widely used the `print()` function now. It is used to display some content on the screen as output. It has no return value. Let us understand some special parameters of the `print()` function. The syntax is given below:

```
print(x[,x1,x2…], sep= " ", end= "\n")
```

Let us examine each parameter in detail.

1. The first parameter is the variable that needs to be displayed. It is denoted by `x`. The part in the square bracket is optional. If multiple things need to be printed, then they are mentioned separated by a comma.
2. The second parameter is `sep`. It is short for separator. The programmer can supply any string literal as a separator, depending upon the need. As can be seen, it is a default parameter. By default the separator between multiple values to be printed is a single blank space, i.e., if multiple values are provided to the `print()` function, and no separator is specified at the time of call, then those values will be separated by a blank space.
3. The last parameter is `end`. The string literal in the `end` parameter decides what would be printed after this `print` statement has ended. The `end` parameter has a default value of "\n" which is the newline character. So, if no `end` parameter is provided, then after the `print()` function has displayed the contents of that statement, a *newline* character is printed, or the cursor goes to the next line.

Let us look at some `print()` commands.

```
>>> print("a","b","c", sep=" ** ")
a ** b ** c
>>> print("abc","def", sep=", ", end="END")
abc, defEND
>>> print("abc"+"def"+"mnop", sep=" __ ")
abcdefmnop
```

In the above command, it must be noted that when multiple string arguments are passed by concatenating with the '+' operator, it becomes one string and hence, will not be separated by the `sep` parameter. But in the `print` statement below, the strings are mentioned with a comma as 3 separate values, hence, they are separated by the `sep` parameter specified.

```
>>> print("abc","def","mnop",sep=" __ ")
abc __ def __ mnop
```

4.10.3 Python Modules and Functions

In addition to several built-in functions, Python also consists of several modules. We define a module as a collection of function definitions. In order to use a function, the programmer first needs to import the module and then use the function. The need and advantage of creating modules is similar to that of functions. Modules increase reusability of functions across different programs. They also make the storage of function definitions more organized.

Modules are nothing more than a file containing function definitions saved by the `.py` extension. The `import` keyword is used to link the module to the program. An `import` statement is written as:

```
import <module1>
```

The `import` keyword is followed by the name of the module to be imported. If multiple modules need to be imported, it can be done by appending their names using a comma. Usually, the `import` statement is the first statement in the program. Once imported, the desired function can be called by writing the following statement:

```
module1.functionA()
```

Now, one might wonder that rewriting the name of the module, each time the function is needed, might become cumbersome if the module name is long. To make this convenient, there is a way to access the functions via an alias of the module name. In order to achieve this, the `import` statement must look like:

```
import <long_module_name> as <lmn>
```

Here, `import` and `as` are keywords. After `as`, the programmer writes the short alias by which the module can be accessed. Now, in the program, function call would become:

```
lmn.functionA()
```

Program 4.14: Program to demonstrate use of built in functions and modules

```
import math, random

print(“ceil of 63.78 = ”, math.ceil(63.78))
print(“64 raised to power 12 = ”, math.pow(64,12))
print()
print(“A random number between 0 and 1 = ”, random.random())
print(“Random integer between 17 and 91 = ”, random.randint(17,91))
```

The output of Program 4.14 is given below:

```
ceil of 63.78 = 64
64 raised to power 12 = 4.722366482869645e+21

A random number between 0 and 1 = 0.42201075533513
Random integer between 17 and 91 = 48
```

Program 4.14 demonstrates the use of `math` and `random` modules. It must be noted here that one module may consist of hundreds of functions and the program might need to use just one or two of them. In such a case, it is very ineffective to import the entire module. We can instead import just the required functions by using the `from...import` syntax.

```
from module1 import function1, function2
```

So, the `import` statements in Program 4.14 may be modified to :

```
from math import ceil, pow
from random import random, randint
```

Subsequently, the function calls will be changed to `ceil(63.78)` and `randint(17,91)`.

Now that we know how to use modules, we will discuss some commonly used built-in Python modules and their functions.

math Module

As the name suggests, the math module in Python makes available built-in functions for mathematical purposes. Some of these functions are as follows:

- `math.sin(x)/math.cos(x)/math.tan(x)`: Computes and returns the sine/ cosine/ tangent value of x passed in *radians*.
```
>>> math.cos(math.radians(180))
-1.0
```
- `math.ceil(x)`: returns the rounded up value of passed number, x.
```
>>> math.ceil(107.532)
108
```
- `math.floor(x)`: returns the rounded down value of passed number, *x*.
```
>>> math.floor(107.532)
107
```
- `math.exp(x)`: computes and returns the value of *e* raised to power x.
```
>>> math.exp(5)
148.4131591025766
```
- `math.log10(x)` : computes and returns the value of $log_{10}(x)$
```
>>> math.log10(10)
1.0
```
- `math.pow(x, y)`: returns the value of $(x)^y$
```
>>> math.pow(999, 2)
998001.0
```
- `math.sqrt(x)`: returns the square root of x. If x<0 then a `ValueError` is raised.
```
>>> math.sqrt(144)
12.0
```

random Module

The random module in Python provides some built-in functions that generate random numbers. The usage of the random module is very common in designing games and other useful applications. Some functions of the random module are enlisted below:

- `random.randint(a, b)` : generates an integer k such that $a \le k \le b$.
```
>>> random.randint(9,92)
20
```
- `random.random()` : generates a floating point number between 0 and 1.
```
>>> random.random()
0.48296206328260094
```
- `random.randrange(n)` : generates a random integer between 0 and n–1.
```
>>> random.randrange(5)
2
```

- `random.randrange(start, stop, step)` : generates a random integer in the range specified by `start, stop and step.`
  ```
  >>> random.randrange(4,20,2)
  18
  ```
- `random.choice(x)` : randomly selects and returns any element from the passed sequence, `x.`
  ```
  >>> random.choice([23, 88, 105, 12, 35, 76])
  35
  ```
- `random.shuffle(x)` : shuffles the passed sequence, `x.`
  ```
  >>> x=[23, 88, 105, 12, 35, 76]
  >>> random.shuffle(x)
  >>> x
  [76, 105, 23, 88, 35, 12]
  ```

The `help()` function

Every built-in module in Python has some documentation in it. It is basically a `docstring` added to the beginning of a module. If a user wishes to see the documentation of a module or wants to know what it is about, the `help()` function can be used. In order to see the details of the `math` module, the command would be `help("math")`. The output is shown below:

```
>>> help("math")
Help on built-in module math:

NAME
  math

DESCRIPTION
  This module provides access to the mathematical functions defined
  by the C standard.

FUNCTIONS
  acos(x, /)
    Return the arc cosine (measured in radians) or x.

  acosh(x, /)
    Return the inverse hyperbolic cosine of x.

  asin(x, /)
    Return the arc sine (measured is radius) of x.

  asinh(x, /)
    Return the inverse hyperbolic sine of x.
  atan(x, /)
    Return the arc tangent (measured in radians) of x.

  atan2(y, x, /)
    Return the arc tangent (measured in radians) of y/x.
    Unlike atan(y/x), the signs of both x and y are considered.

  atanh(x, /)
    Return the inverse hyperbolic tangent of x.
  ceil(x, /)
    Return the ceiling of x as an Integral.

    This is the smallest integer >= x.
```

The `help()` command can also be used to display a list of connected Python modules by executing `help("modules")`. One can also import a module and then print its documentation by using the following set of commands.

```
>>> import statistics
>>> print(statistics.__doc__)

Basic statistics module.

This module provides functions for calculating statistics of data, including
averages, variance, and standard deviation.

Calculating averages
--------------------

==================  =============================================
Function            Description
==================  =============================================
mean                Arithmetic mean (average) of data.
harmonic_mean       Harmonic mean of data.
median              Median (middle value) of data.
median_low          Low median of data.
median_high         High median of data.
median_grouped      Median, or 50th percentile, of grouped data.
mode                Mode (most common value) of data.
==================  =============================================
```

4.10.4 User-defined Modules

Python provides built-in functions, yet a programmer can define their own functions called user-defined functions. On similar lines, even though Python provides several built-in modules, we may define our own modules. This section covers the procedure of making user-defined modules.

A user defined module is a Python file (`.py`) which contains the definitions of all the functions that the programmer wants to have in the module. Before the function definitions are written, the programmer may add a `docstring` describing the module. Once its contents are defined, it is saved by the name of this module with *.py* extension. This file is then executed.

When this module needs to be used in a program, its name should be mentioned with the `import` keyword and then it can be used. Make sure that the program where the module is being used, and the module file itself are in the same directory. Program 4.15 demonstrates the use of a user-defined module.

Program 4.15: Program to define a module named "twoD" containing functions to compute the area and perimeter of several two dimensional shapes, and use it in a program

File name: twoD.py

```
'''
Module name : twoD
This module contains functions to find the area and perimeter of
two dimensional shapes.
'''
```

```
def circle(radius):
  p = 2*3.14*radius
  a = 3.14*radius*radius
  return p,a
def square(side):
  p = 4*side
  a = side*side
  return p,a
def rectangle(length, breadth):
  p = 2*(length+breadth)
  a = length*breadth
  return p,a
def triangle(s1, s2, s3):
  p = s1+s2+s3
  s = p/2
  a = (s*(s-s1)*(s-s2)*(s-s3))**0.5
  return p,a
```

Program to use the twoD module:

```
import twoD
def main():
  print()
  print('''Program to demonstrate
  usage of user defined modules''')
  print(twoD.__doc__)
  a = float(input("Enter side 1 of triangle : "))
  b = float(input("Enter side 2 of triangle : "))
  c = float(input("Enter side 3 of triangle : "))

  peri, area = twoD.triangle(a,b,c)
  print("Perimeter of triangle = ", peri)
  print("Area of triangle = ", area)

if __name__=='__main__':
  main()
```

The output of Program 4.15 is shown below:

```
Program to demonstrate
usage of user defined modules

Module name : twoD
This module contains functions to find the
area and perimeter of two dimensional shapes.

Enter side 1 of triangle : 3
Enter side 2 of triangle : 4
Enter side 3 of triangle : 5
Perimeter of triangle = 12.0
Area of triangle = 6.0
```

4.11 RECURSION

Recursion is a very important phenomenon while learning the concept of functions. It becomes very important in implementing certain problems. This section gives a very brief overview of recursion. In simple terms, when a function calls itself, the process is known as *recursion*. The word *recur* means something that happens repeatedly, again and again. Similarly, when a function calls itself, the process repeats itself. There exists a *base condition* in a recursive function, which decides when to stop the recursive calls.

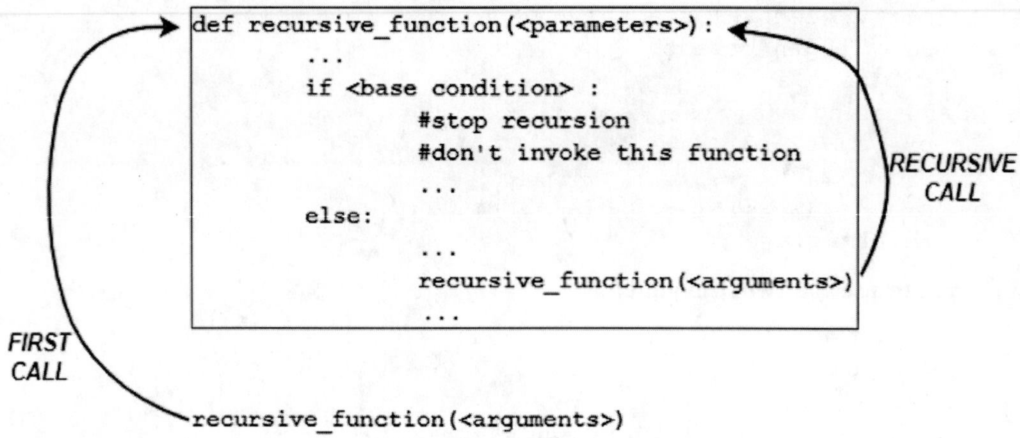

Figure 4.6 General syntax of a recursive function.

Figure 4.6 shows the general syntax of a recursive function. Note that ... in the function denotes zero or more coding statements. The base condition in a recursive function controls when the recursion stops. If it is `True`, the function is not invoked again. However, if it is `False`, the function may be called.

4.11.1 Recursion v/s Iteration

In previous chapters, we have studied the concept of iteration— *for* loop and *while* loop. Most of the tasks can be achieved using any of the two techniques. However, there exist some differences between the two approaches.

- Iteration utilizes the repetition control structure and works till the loop terminates. Recursion, on the other hand, utilizes the selection control structure. It is dependent on the base condition.
- Recursion reduces the size of the code and enhances modularity. Iteration leads to an increase in the lines of code.
- Iteration does not make use of the system stack, recursion uses it to store the state of function calls. Hence, recursion is slower.

It is a point of discussion that if the same problem can be solved using both iteration and recursion, which approach should be used? The execution of recursion requires a lot of memory space for average to large sized problems. However, loops consume a lot of time if the problem size is huge. In some cases iteration may prove a better choice over recursion, or vice versa. Hence, it becomes the responsibility of the programmer to achieve a tradeoff between the time and memory requirements.

4.11.2 Factorial

Computing factorial of a number is a problem that we have covered in the previous sections. Let us now accomplish the same task using recursion and understand its working.

Program 4.16: Compute the factorial of a number using recursion

```
def factorial(number):
    if number==0 or number==1:
        return 1;
    else:
        return number*factorial(number-1)

def main():
    n = int(input("Enter a number : "))
    result = factorial(n)
    print("Factorial of", n, "is", result)

if __name__=="__main__":
    main()
```

In Program 4.5, the program computes the factorial of a number using loops, i.e., iteration. In Program 4.16, we perform the same task using a recursive function. While the structure of the function seems simple to understand, it is the execution and the working that needs to be elaborated. The `factorial()` function is first called from the `main()` function, with a number `n`. Inside the function, it is first checked if the number is 0 or 1, the answer returned is 1, else the statement `number*factorial(number-1)` is executed. This is the part where recursion happens and the same function is now called with a different argument value. A question that arises here is how and when does this recursion stop? For this, a stopping condition is added in the function, which when satisfied, does not call the function again. In this example, the first `if` statement is the stopping condition. Figure 4.6 explains the sequence of calls and computation of result.

4.11.3 Fibonacci Series

Another example that can aid in understanding recursion better is finding the *n*th term of the Fibonacci series. Fibonacci series is a special type of number series where every term is computed as the sum of the previous 2 terms. Program 4.17 computes the term at a particular position in a fibonacci series using recursion. It is encouraged that the reader draws to understand the working of recursive calls in this example, as elaborated in Figure 4.6.

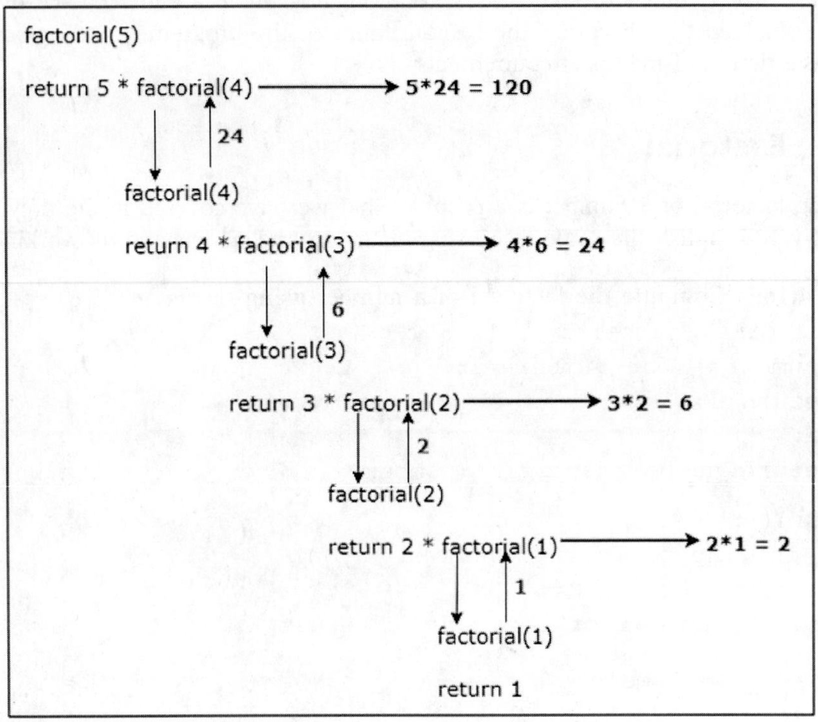

Figure 4.7 Working of the recursive solution to compute factorial of a number.

Program 4.17: Program to compute the *n*th term of fibonacci series

```
def fibo(n):
   if n<=1:
      return n
   else:
      return (fibo(n-1)+fibo(n-2))

def main():
   pos = int(input("Enter the position of term : "))
   term = fibo(pos)
   print("The term in fibonacci series at ", pos, "th position : ", term)

if __name__=="__main__":
   main()
```

The output of Program 4.17 is shown below.

```
Enter the position of term : 6
The term in fibonacci series at 6th position : 8
```

4.11.4 Tower of Hanoi

Another classic problem which is solved easily using recursion is the Tower of Hanoi. It is a popular game that we have played as children. There are 3 rods, each known as an axis sometimes. There are `n` discs placed on one rod, known as source rod, in order, i.e., the largest disc at the bottom, and smallest at the top. The challenge is to transfer these `n` discs to the target rod, using the auxiliary or intermediate rod while following some rules:

- Only one disc can be moved at a time.
- At no stage can a larger disc be placed on a smaller disc.
- Only the topmost disc of a stack may be moved to another stack or an empty rod.

The stepwise solution for 2 discs can be seen in Figure 4.8. Here, A is the source, B is the intermediate, and C is the target rod. The solution can be generalized as follows:

1. Move the top `n-1` discs from source to intermediary.
2. Move the `nth` disc from source to target.
3. Move the `n-1` discs from intermediary to target.

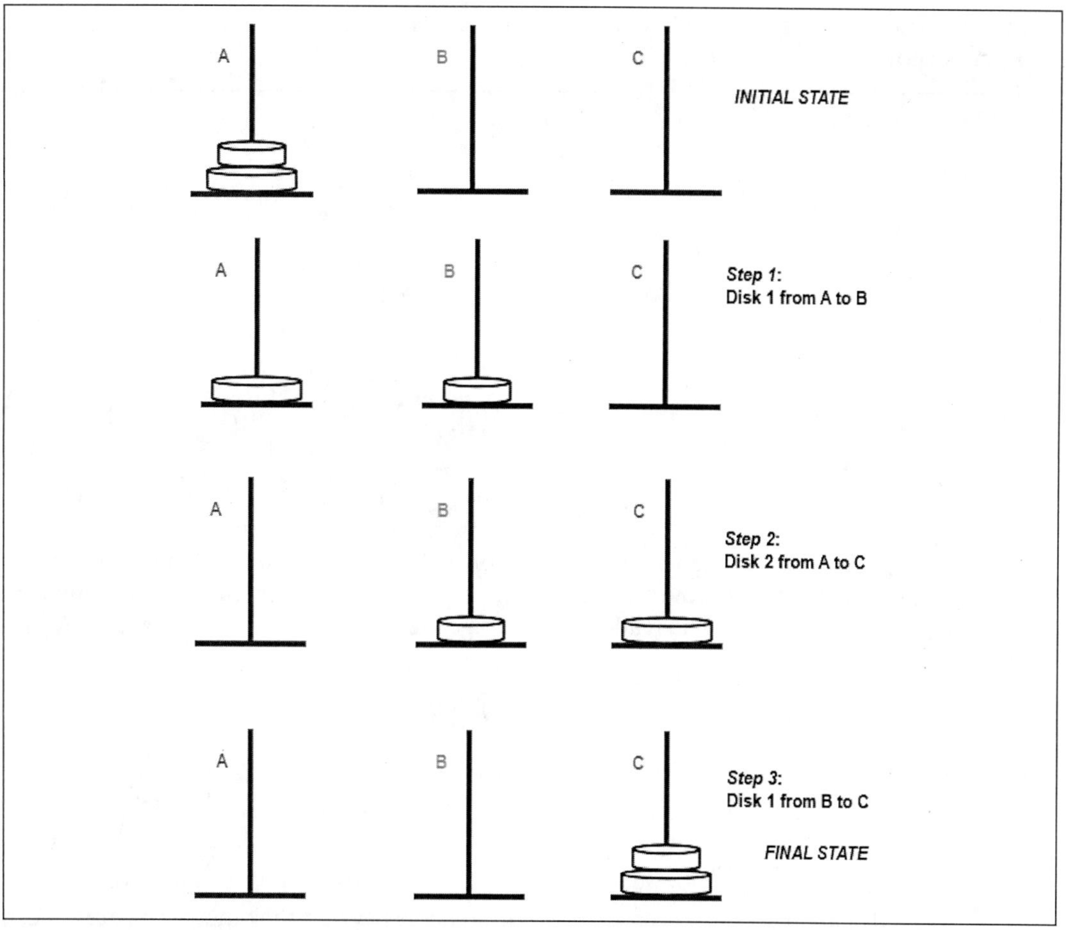

Figure 4.8 Pictorial representation of the solution of 2 disc—Tower of Hanoi problem.

It must be noted here that step 1 and 3 are further solved using these 3 steps as they involve the movement of multiple discs. This is why this solution can be implemented recursively. Program 4.18 shows the recursive code to implement the solution of this task.

Program 4.18 : Program to implement a recursive solution for Tower of Hanoi

```
def hanoi(num_disk, source, dest, mid):
  if num_disk == 0:
    return
  hanoi(num_disk-1, source, mid, dest)
  print("Disk", num_disk, "from", source, "to", dest)
  hanoi(num_disk-1, mid, dest, source)

print("Solution for 2-disk Tower of Hanoi problem :")
hanoi(2, 'A', 'C', 'B')
print("\n\nSolution for 3-disk Tower of Hanoi problem :")
hanoi(3, 'A', 'C', 'B')
```

The Program 4.18 was executed twice—once for 2 discs and another time for 3 discs. The output is shown below:

```
Solution for 2-disk Tower of Hanoi problem :
Disk 1 from A to B
Disk 2 from A to C
Disk 1 from B to C


Solution for 3-disk Tower of Hanoi problem :
Disk 1 from A to C
Disk 2 from A to B
Disk 1 from C to B
Disk 3 from A to C
Disk 1 from B to A
Disk 2 from B to C
Disk 1 from A to C
```

Another general observation is the number of moves. For 2 discs, the number of moves taken is 3, and for 3 discs, 7 moves are made. Thus, in case of n discs, the minimal number of moves required will be 2^n-1. The reader is encouraged to draw the solution for 3 discs by hand.

SUMMARY

- A function is a named block of code. It is created using the *def* keyword.
- Functions are reusable and make the code more organized and readable.
- A function may take some values as input. The values sent during the call are known as arguments and their values are stored in the corresponding parameters.
- Default parameters are used to assign a predefined value to some parameters and the user can skip passing arguments for those parameters.
- Keyword arguments are used to pass arguments as *key=value* pairs.

- The variables declared outside any block of code, are called global variables and the same copy of a global variable is used everywhere in the program.
- A variable declared inside any block of code, is said to be *local* to that block, and this block is called the scope of the local variable. It is accessible only in its scope.
- Docstrings are multi-line comments placed inside a function body and it provides some information about that function.
- Python provides several built-in libraries. In order to use the functions provided in these libraries, they need to be *imported.*
- Python also offers programmers to create user-defined modules.
- When a function calls itself, the process is called recursion.

EXERCISES

4.1 What are the advantages of using functions?

4.2 Differentiate between argument and parameter. Explain using an example when and how the references of argument and parameter change.

4.3 Write short notes on: `global` keyword, `kwargs`.

4.4 What conditions must be considered while using default parameters in a function?

4.5 Differentiate between `random` and `randint`.

4.6 I want to use the `ceil` and `sqrt` functions of the `math` module. Consider the following 2 statements:

- *from math import ceil, sqrt*
- *import math*

Which of these 2 statements is correct? If both are correct then which of this is better and why?

In exercises 4.7–4.10, spot and correct the error(s), if any, and find the output.

4.7
```
n=5
def func(x):
   print("x = ", x)
   n = 35
   print("n = ", n)

print("n = ", n)
n += 10
print("n = ", n)
func(77)
print("n = ", n)
```

4.8
```
def func(a, b, c="hello", d=55):
   print("a = ", a, end="      ")
   print("b = ", b, end="      ")
   print("c = ", c, end="      ")
   print("d = ", d)
```

```
func(3, "alice", 88)
func(33, 66)
func(50, 91, 100, 452)
func(a="peter", b=99, c="Hello")
```

4.9
```
n = 50

def func(a):
    print("Global value of n = ", n)
    print("Value of a = ", a)
    n = n+a
    print(n)

func("60")
```

4.10
```
def even_odd(list1):
    count_ev = count_odd = 0
    ev = odd = []

    for i in list1:
        if i%2 == 0:
            count_ev+=1
            ev += [i]
        else:
            count_odd += 1
            odd += [i]
    return count_odd, count_ev, odd, ev
c1, c2, listO = even_odd([23, 88, 45, 90, 112, 37])
```

4.11 Write a program that accepts numerator and denominator of a fractional number and calls a user defined function `mixedFraction()` when the fraction formed is not a proper fraction. The default value of the denominator is 1.

4.12 Write a function that takes a string as a parameter and converts all consonants in it to uppercase, and returns the count of conversions made, along with the new string.

4.13 Write a function that accepts a number and returns - the number of factors and a list of factors.

4.14 Write a function that accepts a number and checks if it is prime or not. Use this function to print prime numbers between `x` and `y`, where `x` and `y` are taken as input from the user.

4.15 Create a user-defined module called `area_perim`. Define several methods to compute area and perimeter of various 2D and 3D shapes. Use it in another program.

4.16 Write a recursive function called `gcd` to compute the greatest common divisor, GCD of 2 numbers.

4.17 Write a function that accepts numerator and denominator of fraction and computes its lowest form. Use the recursive `gcd` function created in Exercise 4.13.

4.18 Write a program to print first `n` terms of the Fibonacci series, where `n` is taken as input from the user.

5

Strings

In the previous chapters, we have been dealing with numeric data `int`, `float`, etc. and studied the various operations that can be performed on them. In some applications we need to use textual data for name, address, title, etc. which are collections of characters. In Python, string data type represents a collection of characters.

Strings are the objects of the `str` class. Strings are used in input and output. The `input` function is used for reading the string from the keyboard and the `print` function is used for displaying the strings on the monitor.

5.1 INTRODUCTION

A string is a sequence of characters and is enclosed within quotes (single, double, triple). A string spanning multiple lines is enclosed in triple quotation marks. Python treats strings and characters alike and does not have a separate data type for characters.

```
>>> str1="Welcome"      # String "Welcome" enclosed in double quotes
>>> str2='Students'     # String 'Students' enclosed in single quotes

>>> str3='''This book is on Python. It is a popular programming
            language. This language has several libraries. Python is
            being used in different fields economics, engineering,
            commerce, etc.'''
                        # Multi-line string enclosed in triple quotes
```

The above examples show how strings are assigned to variables.

Strings can also be created as objects of `str` class. We can create a string using the constructor of the `str` class.

```
>>> s1=str()             # An empty string object created
>>> s2=str('Welcome')    # String object initialized to "Welcome"
```

A string object is *immutable*, once created its content cannot be changed. This implies that once a string is created, the characters cannot be changed or deleted. But, Python has several operators and built-in functions with which the changed/modified string can be assigned to another string variable.

Python uses one object for strings that have the same content. In the example given below, str1 is assigned "python" and then str2 is assigned str1.

```
>>> str1="python"
>>> str2=str1
>>> str2
'python'
```

Since the content of str1 and str2 is the same, their ids will be the same.

```
>>> id(str1)
2092443979952
>>> id(str2)
2092443979952
```

It can be observed that both the string objects have the same ids, which implies that str2 is the same location as str1.

Python uses *Unicode* to represent the characters internally. Unicode is an international coding standard used to represent characters and symbols from different languages as a unique numeric code that applies across the platforms.

5.2 ACCESSING THE STRING

5.2.1 Indexing

The characters within the strings can be accessed by using a technique called *indexing*. The index refers to the position of the character within the string. Python provides two sets of indexes: positive and negative indices. The indexing of the string str whose value is "Computer" is shown in Figure 5.1.

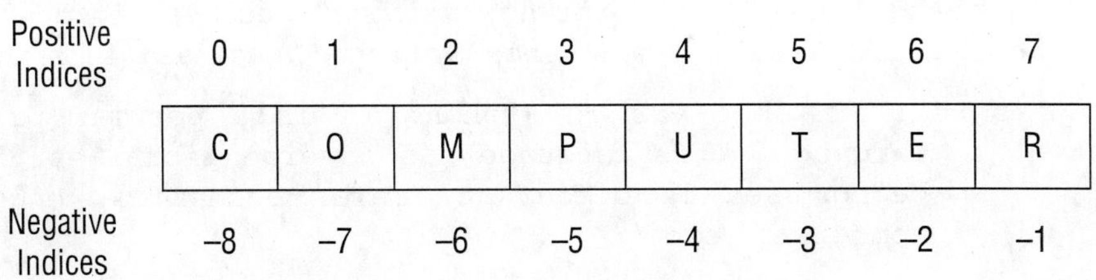

Figure 5.1 Positive and negative indices.

The positive index starts from 0. The index 0 is used to access the first character of the string str, here str[0] refers to the character C. The index is written within the square brackets following the string name. Character P can be accessed by writing str[3]. The positive indices range from 0 to one less than the length of the string. In the above example, the positive indices range from 0 to 7.

```
>>> str[0]
'C'
>>> str[3]
'P'
>>> n=len(str)     # len returns the number of characters in the string
>>> str[n-1]
'R'
```

The negative indices are helpful in accessing the string characters from the end. The negative index –1 refers to the last character of the string. Hence, `str[-1]` refers to the last character R. The negative indices range from –(*length of the string*) to –1. The length of the string is the total number of characters in the string. Since the number of characters in the string `str` is 8, the negative indices range from –8 to –1.

```
>>> str[-1]
'R'
>>> str[-3]
'T'
>>> n=len(str)     # len returns the number of characters in the string
>>> str[-n]
'C'
```

The valid range of positive indices is 0 to one less than the *length* of the string and for negative indices it is –(*length of the string*) to –1. If we try to use an index which is outside the valid range, the Python interpreter will generate an `IndexError` exception as shown in the example below.

```
>>> str[9]
Traceback (most recent call last):
  File "<pyshell#25>", line 1, in <module>
    str[9]
IndexError: string index out of range
Another example:
>>> str[-10]
Traceback (most recent call last):
  File "<pyshell#26>", line 1, in <module>
    str[-10]
IndexError: string index out of range
```

5.2.2 Slicing

Slicing is a technique to refer to a substring in a given string. In order to refer to a substring (*slice*), the range of indices of the substring is to be specified separated by a colon. For example, in order to refer to the substring "COMP" from the string `str` containing "COMPUTER", we will specify the range 0:4.

The slicing sequence start:stop will return the characters from the index start to stop-1. It means that the characters from the index start to index stop-1 are returned (excluding the character at the index stop).

```
>>> str="COMPUTER"
>>> str[0:4]
'COMP'
```

Both start and stop are optional while writing a slice. By default, the start in the slicing is 0 or *–length of the string* and default stop is *length of the string –1* or –1. So, in case if the start or stop index is not given in slicing the default values are taken.

```
>>> str="COMPUTER"
>>> str[0:4]
'COMP'
>>> str="COMPUTER"
>>> str[:4]
'COMP'
>>> str[5:]
'TER'
>>> str[:]
'COMPUTER'
>>> str[:4]+ str[4:]
'COMPUTER'
>>> str[8:]
''
>>> str[:0]
''
```

The start and stop values in a slice can be negative also. The example below shows how the negative start and stop values are used in slicing.

```
>>> str[-5:-1]
'PUTE'
>>> str[-4:]
'UTER'
>>> str[:-6]
'CO'
>>> str[:-4]+ str[-4:]
'COMPUTER'
```

We can also combine positive and negative values in slicing.

```
>>> str[0:-5]
'COM'
>>> str[-7:7]
'OMPUTE'
```

Slice supports a third argument, which is a `step` value. By default, the step value is 1. Using the `step` argument, as `start:stop:step`, we can extract non-consecutive characters from a given string. This way we can extract every `step`th character in the range `start` to `stop-1`.

```
>>> str[0:len(str):2]
'CMUE'
>>> str[-len(str)::3]
'CPE'
```

The concept of slicing can also be applied on other sequence data types like lists, tuples, etc. which we will be discussing in the next chapter.

5.3 OPERATIONS ON STRINGS

5.3.1 Concatenation and Repetition

The most common operations that are performed on a string are concatenation (+) and repetition (*).

The + operator is used to join two or more strings in Python, which is called *concatenation*. There are two strings `str1` is "Hello" and string `str2` is "World", `str1 + str2` will result in "HelloWorld".

```
>>> str1="Hello"
>>> str2="World"
>>> str1+str2
'HelloWorld'
```

The * operator is used to repeat a string given number of times, `str1 * 3` will repeat the string "Hello" 3 times resulting in "HelloHelloHello".

```
>>> str1*3
'HelloHelloHello'
```

5.3.2 Comparison

Strings can be compared using the relational operators discussed in Chapter 2. They are compared character by character starting from the left side, the characters are compared on the basis of the Unicode values of the characters.

```
>>> "CLASS"=="CLASS"
True
>>> "Class"=="class"
False
>>> "Class">"class"
False
>>> "Class"<"class"
True
>>> "Class">"Python"
False
```

Since, string comparison is performed character by character from the left side, if the string value is a number, the results of comparison will be different than the number comparison as can be seen below.

```
>>> "100">"11"
False
```

In the above example, the comparison is being done from the left side, since both the strings have '1' as the first character, comparison proceeds to the second character, comparing '0' > '1' results in False. The comparison terminates here, concluding that "100" is smaller than "11".

The functions `max` and `min` can be used on strings to find the maximum and minimum string value respectively.

```
>>> max("ab","cd","zw","tr","gq")
'zw'
>>> min("ab","cd","zw","tr","gq")
'ab'
```

5.3.3 Membership

Python provides an operator to test whether a substring is present in a given string. The membership operator `in` is used to check if a substring exists in a string or not. The `in` operator returns a boolean value `True` or `False` depending on whether the substring belongs to a given string or not.

```
>>> "HURRAY" in "HELLO WORLD"
False
>>> "Hello" in "Hello World"
True
>>> "Hello" not in "Python Programs"
True
```

The membership operator `in` can be used in the `for` loop to iterate through the characters of a string. The program 5.1 demonstrates counting the character 'a' in a given string.

Program 5.1: To count the occurrences of character "A" in a given string

```
str="BANANA"
count=0
for ch in str:
    if ch=="A":
        count +=1
print("Number of a\'s in the string: ", count)
```

The membership operator can also be used to iterate through a specified range as shown in the example below.

```
for i in range(1,10,2):
    print(i, end=" ")
```

5.3.4 Formatting

Escape Sequences

As we know that the strings are enclosed in single or double quotes, so these quotes cannot be used within a string, this will result in syntax error.

```
>>> str1="He said,"How are you?""
SyntaxError: invalid syntax
```

In order to use single or double quotes within a string, escape sequences are used. An escape sequence begins with a backslash \ and gives a different interpretation to the trailing character. If the string is enclosed in single quotes, then put a backslash before any single quotes within the string. The escape sequence \' represents single quotes and hence single quotes will be permitted within the string. The same thing can be done if the string is enclosed in double quotes, then the escape sequence \" can be used.

```
>>> str1="He said,\"How are you?\""
>>> str1
'He said,"How are you?"'
>>> str1='He said,\'How are you?\''
>>> str1
"He said,'How are you?'"
```

Some of the escape sequences supported by Python are given in Table 5.1.

Table 5.1 Escape Sequences in Python

Escape Sequence	Description
\n	Line Feed
\\	Backslash
\'	Single Quote
\"	Double Quote
\r	Carriage Return
\t	Horizontal Tab
\v	Vertical Tab
\ooo	Octal Value ooo of a character
\xHH	Hexadecimal Value HH of a character

Examples:

```
>>> print("C:\\Program Files\\Google")
C:\Program Files\Google

>>> print("\x48\x45\x58 number")
HEX number
```

```
>>> print("This will be printed\n in two lines")
This will be printed
 in two lines
```

If we wish to ignore the escape sequences mentioned in the string, `r` or `R` should be written before the string, which represents the raw string.

```
>>> print(r"This will be printed\n in two lines")
This will be printed\n in two lines
```

`format()` function

The `format()` function is used for formatting the strings. Placeholders {} can be used to indicate where the values are to be inserted. The value can be integer, float value or strings.

The syntax for formatting is as follows:

```
"String containing placeholders {}".format(value)
```

The examples for using `format()` with strings are given below:

```
>>> print("I am studying {}".format("Python"))
I am studying Python
>>> print("The current year is {}".format(2022))
The current year is 2022
```

We can also use positional or keyword arguments to specify the order of arguments to be placed in the placeholders specified by {}.

```
# Default Arguments
>>> print("I love to eat {},{} and {}.".format("Grapes","Mango","Banana"))
I love to eat Grapes, Mango and Banana.

# Positional Arguments
>>> print("I love to eat {1},{2} and {0}.".format("Grapes","Mango",
"Banana"))
I love to eat Mango, Banana and Grapes.

# Keyword Arguments
>>> print("I love to eat {f3},{f1} and {f2}. ". format (f1="Grapes",
f2= "Mango" , f3="Banana"))
I love to eat Banana, Grapes and Mango.
```

5.4 BUILT-IN STRING FUNCTIONS

`len()` function

This function is used to find the total number of characters in a string as shown in the code below.

```
str="Python for Beginners"
>>> len(str)
20
```

`count()` function

The `count()` function is used to count the occurrences of a character or substring in a string. For example, if we wish to count the number of occurrences of `"l"` in the string `"hello"`, we can write `"hello".count("l")`.The `count()` function can be used to count the vowels and consonants in a string, as shown in Program 5.2.

Program 5.2: Program to count the number of vowels & consonants in a string

```
s1=input("Enter the string: ")
vowels="aeiouAEIOU"
vcount=0
ccount=0
for character in s1:
    if character in vowels:
        vcount += 1
    else:
        ccount += 1
print("The number of vowels : ", vcount)
print("The number of consonants : ",ccount)
```

The above program uses the `in` operator to check the presence of vowels in a given string. The output of Program 5.2 is given below:

```
Enter the string: Programming
The number of vowels : 3
The number of consonants : 8
```

5.4.1 String Testing Functions

Python has many built-in functions for testing the characters of the string. The string testing functions are listed in Table 5.2.

Table 5.2 String Testing Functions

Function Name	Description
`isalnum()`	Returns `True` if the characters in the string are alphanumeric, i.e. alphabets (a–z, A–Z) or numbers (0–9) else `False`
`isalpha()`	Returns `True` if the characters in the string are alphabets (a–z, A–Z)
`isdigit()`	Returns `True` if the characters in the string are numbers (0–9)
`islower()`	Returns `True` if all the characters in the string are lowercase letters

(*Contd.*)

Function Name	Description
isupper()	Returns True if all the characters in the string are uppercase letters
isspace()	Returns True if all the characters in the string are whitespace characters
istitle()	Returns True if the all the words start with uppercase letter and rest are in lowercase letters
isidentifier()	Returns True if the string is a valid identifier
isprintable()	Returns True if all the characters in the string are printable characters. Examples of non printable characters are carriage return, line feed, etc.
isascii()	Returns True if all the characters in the string are ASCII characters

The `islapha()` function checks whether the string has only alphabets or not. For example, the string holding name, cannot have numbers or special characters. So, `islapha()` function can be used to check the validity of the name entered in the string.

```
>>> str1="Python"
>>> str1.isalpha()
True
>>> str2="Python1"
>>> str2.isalpha()
False
```

Similarly, strings holding the address can have alpha numeric characters, i.e., alphabets [a–z] and numbers [0–9] characters. In order to check whether a string is having only alphanumeric characters, `isalnum()` function can be used.

```
>>> str1.isalnum()
True
>>> str2.isalnum()
True
>>> str3="Python#"
>>> str3.isalnum()
False
```

The function `isdigit()` checks whether a string contains only digits/numbers [0–9].

```
>>> str1.isdigit()
False
>>> str4="1234"
>>> str4.isdigit()
True
```

Python has functions for checking the case of a string, `islower()`, `isupper()` and `istitle()` are used for checking for lower, upper and title case respectively.

```
>>> str1.islower()
False
```

```
>>> str5="PYTHON"
>>> str5.isupper()
True
>>> str6="Python Programming"
>>> str6.istitle()
True
```

5.4.2 String Converting Functions

Python provides functions for converting a string in a specified case. It also has functions for replacing a given substring. The built-in functions are given in Table 5.3.

Table 5.3 String Converting Functions

Function Name	Description
`lower()`	Returns a string with all lowercase letters
`upper()`	Returns a string with all uppercase letters
`capitalize()`	Returns a string with first character in uppercase
`title()`	Returns a string with first character of all words in uppercase
`swapcase()`	Returns a string where characters in lowercase are converted to uppercase and those in uppercase are converted to lowercase
`replace(old string, new string)`	Returns a string with all occurrences of the `old string` are replaced with the `new string`
`split(delimiter)`	Divides the string into a list of strings, separated by the `delimiter`.
`join(str1,str2,...)`	Combines the strings

As stated earlier, strings are immutable, hence the original string is not altered. Instead, these functions create new strings. The `lower()`, `upper()`, `title()`, `capitalize()` and `swapcase()` functions ignore the symbols and numbers.

```
>>> str1="python"
>>> str1.upper()
'PYTHON'
>>> str2="PYTHON"
>>> str2.lower()
'python'
>>> str2.swapcase()
'python'
>>> str1="I eat Apples"
>>> str1.replace("Apples","Bananas")
'I eat Bananas'
```

The `split()` function divides the string into a list of strings by separating the substrings at the delimiter specified. Given below is a string `str1`, which has names of cities separated by comma and space. The `split()` function is called with comma and space as delimiter.

```
>>> str1="Delhi, Mumbai, Jaipur, Chennai, Kolkata"
>>> str1.split(", ")
['Delhi', 'Mumbai', 'Jaipur', 'Chennai', 'Kolkata']
```

There is another function `partition()` in Python which splits the string in two parts at the specified delimiter and returns a tuple. The tuple consists of 3 elements: string before delimiter, delimiter and string after delimiter. In the example below, the string is `"Python Programming, Computer Science"` and inorder to split it at comma `(,)` we write the `str1.partition(',')`.

```
>>> str1="Python Programming, Computer Science"
>>> str1.partition(',')
('Python Programming', ',', ' Computer Science')
```

The `join()` function returns the combined string, consisting of all the strings specified in the parameter list separated by the delimiter.

```
>>> ','.join(["RED", "BLUE", "PINK","YELLOW","GREEN"])
'RED,BLUE,PINK,YELLOW,GREEN'
>>> '-'.join(["RED", "BLUE", "PINK","YELLOW","GREEN"])
'RED-BLUE-PINK-YELLOW-GREEN'
```

5.4.3 String Whitespace Stripping Functions

Python provides several functions for removing the whitespace characters from a given string. The whitespace characters are `' '`, `\t`, `\f`, `\r` and `\n`. Table 5.4 shows these functions.

Table 5.4 String Whitespace Stripping Functions

Function Name	Description
`lstrip()`	Returns a string with all the leading whitespace characters removed.
`rstrip()`	Returns a string with all the trailing whitespace characters removed.
`strip()`	Returns a string with all the leading and trailing whitespace characters removed.

The functions `lstrip()`, `rstrip()` and `strip()` are used for removing the white space characters from a string.

```
>>> str1= '   Python    '
>>> str1.lstrip()
'Python    '
>>> str1.rstrip()
'Python'
>>> str1.strip()
'Python'
```

5.4.4 String Searching Functions

Python provides several built-in functions for searching a substring within a given string. Table 5.5 gives a brief description of these functions.

Table 5.5 String Search Functions

Function Name	Description
`index(substring)`	Searches the substring and returns the index of its *first* occurrence and raises an exception, if the string is not present.
`rindex(substring)`	Searches the substring and returns the index of its *last* occurrence and raises an exception, if the string is not present.
`find(substring)`	Searches the substring and returns the index of its *first* occurrence and returns –1, if the string is not present.
`rfind(substring)`	Searches the substring and returns the index of its *last* occurrence and returns –1, if the string is not present.
`endswith(substring)`	Returns `True` if the string is ending with the specified substring, `False` otherwise.
`startswith(substring)`	Returns `True` if the string is beginning with the specified substring, `False` otherwise.

Python has two functions for searching whether a substring is present in a string. The two functions are `index()` and `find()`. The `index()` function returns the position of the first occurrence of the substring inside the string, as can be seen in the example below.

```
>>> str1="Python for Begineer's"
>>> str1.index("for")
7
```

`index()` function searches the substring "for" in the string `"Python for Begineer's"` and return position 7. In the next example, it tries to search for the substring "at" , since it is not present in the string, it returns an exception.

```
>>> sr1.index("at")
Traceback (most recent call last):
  File "<pyshell#37>", line 1, in <module>
    sr1.index("at")
NameError: name 'sr1' is not defined
```

The `find()` function works similar to the `index()` function, except if the substring is not present it returns –1 instead of an exception.

```
>>> str1.find("Python")
0
>>> str1.find("at")
-1
```

The `find()` function returns –1 as “at” is not present in `str1.`

```
>>> str1.startswith("Python")
True
>>> str1.startswith("New")
False
>>> str1.endswith("neer's")
True
>>> str1.endswith("neer")
False
```

We are discussing some programs which use the string functions.

Program 5.3: Program to check whether a password is valid or not. The password has to be of 8 or more characters, contain letters and digits and have 2 or more digits to be a valid password.

```
# Program to check the validity of a password

password = input("Enter the password : ")
count_digits=sum(character.isdigit() for character in password)
if len(password) >= 8 and password.isalnum() and count_digits >= 2:
    print(password + " is valid")
else:
    print(password + " is invalid")
```

The above program uses the `len()` function to count the number of characters in the `password`, `isalnum()` function to check whether the characters are either letters or digits, `isdigit()` function to check whether the character is a digit. The output of Program 5.2 is shown below for two inputs, “Python” and “Program2023”.

```
Enter the password : Python
Python is invalid
```

```
Enter the password : Program2023
Program2023 is invalid
```

The next program checks whether the given string is a palindrome string or not. A palindrome string reads the same from the front and the rear ends. One way is to reverse the given string and compare it with the original string, as is shown in Program 5.2.

Program 5.4: Program to check whether a string is a palindrome or not

```
str1=input("Enter the string : ")
rev_str=str1[::-1]
if (str1 == rev_str):
   print("Palindrome")
else:
   print("Not Palindrome")
```

In order to find the reverse we have used the slice operator, i.e., `str1[::-1]`. We have taken two inputs, the string "Programming" is not a palindrome, since the reverse of it is "gnimmargorP" which is not identical to the original string. The other input is "malayalam" which is a palindrome as its reverse is "malayalam", similar to the original string. The output is shown below:

```
Enter the string : Programming
Not Palindrome
```

```
Enter the string : malayalam
Palindrome
```

SUMMARY

- String is a collection of characters enclosed in single, double or triple quotes.
- Strings are immutable, i.e., they cannot be altered.
- The individual characters in a string can be accessed using indexing.
- Positive indices are used to access elements from the beginning, they range from *0* to one less than the *length of the string.*
- Negative indices are used to access elements from the end, they range from *–1* to – (*length of the string*).
- Slicing is used to access substring from a string by specifying the range as *start:stop*, which returns the characters from index *start* to *stop–1.*
- The string operators are + for concatenation, * for repetition and IN for membership.
- The built-in string functions are given in the table below:

`len()`	Returns the number of characters in a string
`count()`	Returns the count of occurences of a given substring in a string
`isalnum()`	Returns *True* if the characters in the string are alphanumeric, i.e., alphabets (a–z, A–Z) or numbers (0–9) else *False*
`isalpha()`	Returns *True* if the characters in the string are alphabets (a–z, A–Z)
`isdigit()`	Returns *True* if the characters in the string are numbers (0–9)
`islower()`	Returns *True* if all the characters in the string are lowercase letters
`isupper()`	Returns *True* if all the characters in the string are uppercase letters
`isspace()`	Returns *True* if all the characters in the string are whitespace characters
`istitle()`	Returns *True* if all the words start with uppercase letters and rest are in lowercase letters
`isidentifier()`	Returns *True* if the string is a valid identifier
`isprintable()`	Returns *True* if all the characters in the string are printable characters. Examples of non-printable characters are carriage return, line feed, etc.

`isascii()`	Returns *True* if all the characters in the string are ASCII characters
`lower()`	Returns a string with all lowercase letters
`upper()`	Returns a string with all uppercase letters
`capitalize()`	Returns a string with the first character in uppercase
`title()`	Returns a string with the first character of all words in uppercase
`swapcase()`	Returns a string where characters in lowercase are converted to uppercase and those in uppercase are converted to lowercase
`replace(old string, new string)`	Returns a string where all occurrences of the old string are replaced with the new string
`split(delimiter)`	Divides the string into a list of strings, separated by the `delimiter`
`join(str1,str2,...)`	Combines the strings
`lsrip()`	Returns a string with all the leading whitespace characters removed
`rstrip()`	Returns a string with all the trailing whitespace characters removed
`strip()`	Returns a string with all the leading and trailing whitespace characters removed.
`index(substring)`	Searches the substring and returns the index of its *first* occurrence and raises an exception, if the string is not present
`rindex(substring)`	Searches the substring and returns the index of its *last* occurrence and raises an exception, if the string is not present
`find(substring)`	Searches the substring and returns the index of its *first* occurrence and returns –1, if the string is not present
`rfind(substring)`	Searches the substring and returns the index of its *last* occurrence and returns –1, if the string is not present
`endswith(substring)`	Returns *True* if the string is ending with the specified substring, *False* otherwise
`startswith(substring)`	Returns *True* if the string is beginning with the specified substring, *False* otherwise

EXERCISES

5.1 Suppose `str1` and `str2` are two strings as given below:

```
str1 = "python programming"
str2 = "computer fundamentals"
```

What will be the output of the following expressions?

(a) `str1 + str2`
(b) `str2 * 3`
(c) `len(str1)`
(d) `str1 == str2`
(e) `str1[4 : 12]`
(f) `str2[-10 : ]`
(g) `str2[1:-1]`
(h) `str2 > str1`

5.2 Let `str1=" Python "` and `str2=" python "`. Write the code for the following:

(a) Create a new string `str3` that converts `str1` to *uppercase*.
(b) Create a new string `str3` that converts `str1` to *lowercase*.
(c) Create a new string `str3` that trims whitespace characters on both the ends of `str2`.
(d) Create a new string `str3` that combines `str1` and `str2`.
(e) Create a new string that extracts characters from `str1` from index 1 to 5.
(f) Replace 'o' with 'a' in `str1`.
(g) Check whether `str1` is equal to `str2` and assign the result in variable `isEqual`.
(h) Check whether `str2` has a prefix 'ABC' and assign the result in the boolean variable `x`.
(i) Check whether `str1` has a suffix 'XXX' and assign the result in the boolean variable `x`.
(j) Check whether `str2` is *alphanumeric* and assign the result in the boolean variable `x`.
(k) Check whether `str2` is in *lowercase* and assign the result in the boolean variable `x`.

5.3 Write a function that checks whether a string is a valid password, as per the following rules:

(a) Must have at least ten characters.
(b) Must contain only letters and digits.
(c) Must contain at least two digits.

5.4 Write a function that finds the number of occurrences of a specified character in a string using the following header

```
def counter(str,ch):
```

where `ch` is the character to be searched in the string `str`.

5.5 Write a program which counts the number of letters in a given string.

5.6 Write a function that returns the longest common prefix of two strings. For example, the longest common prefix of `'python'` and `'pythagoras'` is `'pyth'`.

5.7 Write a function to count the number of words in a given sentence.

5.8 Write a function to accept a binary number as a string and convert it into a hex number.

5.9 Write a function to check whether a string is a substring of another string without using any built-in function.

5.10 Write a function that accepts a string from the user and checks whether it is in the format `ddd-llll`, where `d` is a digit and `l` is a letter. The function displays 'Valid Number' for a correct input string and 'Invalid Number' for an invalid input.

6

Mutable and Immutable Objects

In Python, every variable denotes an instance of an object. Every object has its own internal state. Some objects allow you to change its internal state or content and some have its internal state or content fixed. Objects whose internal state can be changed are called *mutable objects* while an object which does not allow you to change its state is called an *immutable object*. Some examples of immutable objects include numbers (int, float, boolean), string, sets, tuples. On the other hand, examples of mutable objects include lists, dictionaries. In the previous chapter, we discussed strings which are immutable structures. In this chapter, we will discuss some immutable and mutable structures like lists, sets, tuples, and dictionaries. Refer to the Figure 6.1 and Figure 6.2 given below:

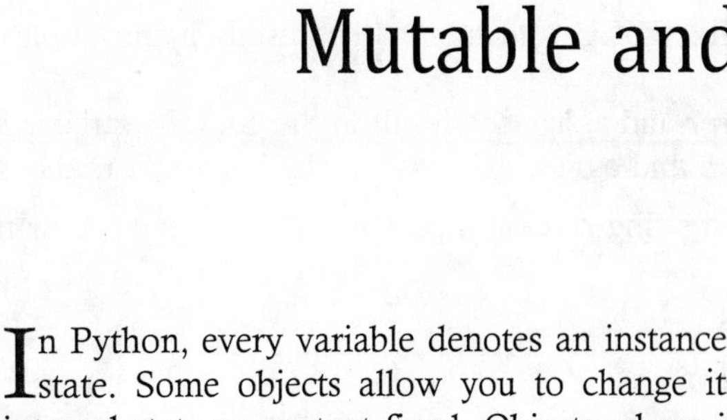

Figure 6.1 Classification of Immutable objects.

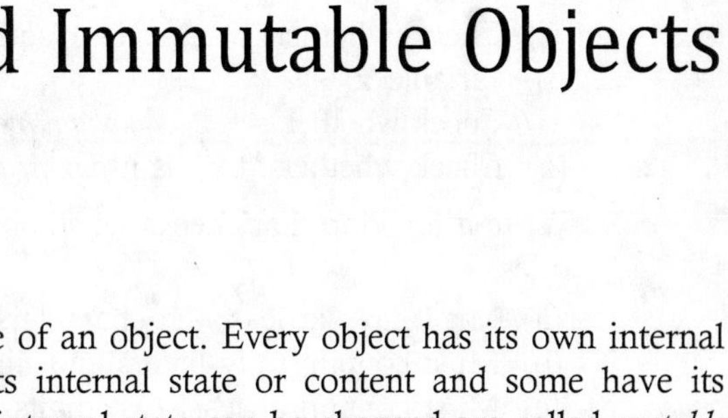

Figure 6.2 Classification of Mutable objects.

6.1 LISTS

A list in Python allows us to store an ordered sequence of values. These values can be of any type, including *strings, integers, floats,* or even other lists. To create a list, simply enclose your values in square brackets and separate them with commas. Before diving into lists, it's important to understand the concept of data structures in Python. While a single variable can store one value at a time, there are often situations where multiple values need to be stored together as a cohesive unit. This is where data structures come in.

Data structures are used to organize and store multiple values within a single variable. By doing so, these values can be easily accessed and modified as needed. Lists are just one example of a data structure in Python, but they are incredibly versatile and useful in a wide range of applications.

A list is one of the data structures that is capable of storing multiple values at a time. Let's understand how a list is created. Given below is an empty list.

```
>>>fruits=[]
>>>print("Empty list ", fruits)
Empty list []
```

As discussed above, elements of a list are separated by comma and arranged in a sequence where the first element has index 0. In the example given below, fruits is a list having four items.

```
>>>fruits=["apple", "orange", "mango", "guava"]
>>>print(fruits)
['apple', 'orange', 'mango', 'guava']
```

We can also check the type of the fruits variable using a type() function. It will return <class list> as an output as shown below:

```
>>>print(type(fruits))

<class 'list'>
```

list()

There is also a built-in list() function that converts any object like set, tuple, and strings into a set. Let's see an example given below using the list() function.

```
>>>my_str="Programming Using Python"

>>>converted_list=list(my_str)

>>>print(converted_list)

['P', 'r', 'o', 'g', 'r', 'a', 'm', 'm', 'i', 'n', 'g', ' ', 'U',
's', 'i', 'n', 'g', ' ', 'P', 'y', 't', 'h', 'o', 'n']
```

Heterogeneous list

A list is not a homogeneous data structure, that is it may store values that belong to different data types. Let's understand it using the following example:

```
details=["Sita", "D-55, Civil Lines, Delhi-110009", 9812345467]
```

If a user wants to enter a list or tuple as an input, it is possible to pass the entire list using the input() function. eval() function is used to transform raw string into a list or tuple. Tuples are explained further in this chapter. Refer to the example given below.

```
>>>details=eval(input("Enter details of Sita: "))
>>>print(details)
("Sita", "D-55, Civil Lines, Delhi-110009", 9812345467)
```

The output above is in the form of a tuple. Tuples are explained further in this chapter.

There are many operations that can be applied to lists to produce the required output. Table 6.1 summarizes some basic operations that can be performed on a Python list.

Table 6.1 Summary of Operations on List

Operation	Description
Repetition Operator *	Replicates the list given number of times.
Concatenation Operator +	Concatenates multiple lists.
Function `len()`	Returns the length of a given list.
Function `min()`	Returns the minimum element from a given list.
Function `max()`	Returns the maximum element from a given list.
Function `sum()`	Computes the sum of all elements of a list, provided they are numeric.
Indexing	Indexing helps in retrieving the element present at a given index.
Slicing Syntax: `start:end:inc`	Slicing is a technique that helps in producing a sublist or a new list from a given existing list.
Membership operator `in`	It returns `True` if an item is present in a given list.
Membership operator `not in`	It returns `False` if an item is present in a given list, otherwise `True`.

6.1.1 Operations on Lists

Repetition Operator *

Repetition operator is denoted using asterisk `(*)` symbol. The `*` operator is used usually to multiply numeric values. It takes two operands and produces its product as an output. When used in the context of lists `marks`, it will replicate the list a given number of times. Let's consider a given list and replicate this list 2 times and observe the output below.

```
>>>marks=[20, 40, 60]
>>>print(marks*2)
```

The above line of code will produce the output as:

```
[20, 40, 60, 20, 40, 60]
```

Concatenation Operator +

The + operator or, concatenation operator is used to concatenate two or more lists. It appends one list to another list and produces a new list as an output. Let's understand the concept of the concatenation operator using an example given below.

```
list1=["blue", "green", "magenta"]

list1=list1 + ["yellow"]

print(list1)

['blue', 'green', 'magenta', 'yellow']
```

In the given output above, we can observe that two lists are concatenated together and produce a new list.

len()

The length function `len()` is used to find out the length of a list. It returns the count of elements present in the list. The syntax of the `len()` function is as follows:

```
len(list_name)
```

Let us find out the length of the `list1` defined below. The output of the line of code should return the number of elements present in `list1`, i.e., 4.

```
>>>list1=["blue", "green", "magenta", "yellow"]
>>>print(len(list1))
4
```

min()

As the name suggests, the function `min()` returns the element from the list having the minimum value. The syntax of `min()` function when applied on a list is as follows:

```
min(list_name)
```

For example, `my_list` contains a list of integer items.

```
>>>my_list=[10, 20, 30, 40]

>>>print(min(my_list))

10
```

It has produced the output as 10, which is the minimum value in the list `my_list`.

max()

The `max()` function is designed to return the element with the highest value from a given list. To utilize this function, the syntax is as follows:

```
max(list_name)
```

Let's apply the max() function on `my_list`.

```
>>>print(max(my_list))
40
```

The function has successfully returned the maximum value of 40 from `my_list`. It is worth noting that when the elements in the list are strings, the `min()` and `max()` functions compare them based on their ASCII values. This means that the comparison is made character by character, starting from the leftmost character, until a difference is found.

sum()

The sum() function is designed to calculate the total sum of all elements within a list. It is important to note that this function cannot be applied to strings, as it only works with numerical data values. To properly utilize the sum() function, ensure that your list contains only numerical data values. The syntax for the sum() function is as follows:

```
sum(list_name)
```

For example,

```
>>>my_list=[10, 20, 30, 40]
>>>print(sum(my_list))
100
```

It has produced the output as 100 which is the sum of all the integer values present in my_list.

Indexing

Indexing is a fundamental concept in Python programming that allows you to access specific elements within a list. When applied to a list, indexing enables you to retrieve a particular element based on its position. In Python, the first element in a list has an index of 0, while the second element has an index of 1, and so on. The last element in a list has an index of n–1, where n represents the length of the list. This is known as positive indexing.

However, Python also supports negative indexing, which allows you to access elements from the end of the list. In negative indexing, the last element in a list has an index of –1, and the indexing proceeds from right to left. To illustrate the use of indexing in lists, consider the example shown in Figure 6.3. This example demonstrates how to access specific elements within a list using both positive and negative indexing.

Positive Indices	0	1	2	3
	10	**20**	**30**	**40**
Negative Indices	–4	–3	–2	–1

Figure 6.3 Demonstrating the indexing concept.

```
>>>my_list=[10, 20, 30, 40]
>>>print(my_list[-2])
30
```

It will give 30 as output. Here negative indexing is used. The element present at –2 index is 30.

Slicing

Slicing helps to retrieve a subsequence or a sublist from the existing list. Slicing works with three values: *start index, end index* and *increment value*. The start index is the index that marks the beginning of the slice. The end index, on the other hand, indicates where the slice should end. Finally, the increment or step parameter determines how many values to skip at each step while moving forward. The colon : symbol is used to separate all three parameters. The syntax for list slicing is as follows:

```
<list_name>[start:end:inc]
```

The example below shows how the indexing works.

```
>>>my_list=[10, 20, 30, 40]
>>>print(my_list[0:2])
[10,20]
```

It produces 10, 20 as an output as 10 is present at index 0 and 20 is present at index 1.

```
>>>my_list=[10, 20, 30, 40]
>>>print(my_list[0:3:2])
[10,30]
```

It produces 10, 30 as an output as there is a step count of 2. Indexing in lists is similar to that of strings, mentioned in chapter 5.

Membership Operators: `in` and `not in`

Membership operators are used to check whether an item exists in a python list or not. There are two membership operators which are `in` and `not in` keywords. These keywords are also used with `for` loop, for example, `for i in range(1,11):`

The `in` keyword returns `True` if an item exists in a list otherwise it returns `False`. Below is an example to check the existence of an element in a given list using the `in` operator.

```
>>>my_list=[10, 20, 30, 40]
>>>print(20 in my_list)
True
```

This line will produce output as `True` because 20 is indeed present in `my_list`. The `not in` keyword returns `True` if an item is not in the list, otherwise it returns `False`. Let's check if 70 is present in `my_list` or not using the `not in` keyword.

```
>>>my_list=[10, 20, 30, 40]
>>>print(70 not in my_list)
True
```

Iterating over Lists

Let's use the `in` operator in `for` loop with another example. We can iterate over lists using two ways. First method is to use `in` operator along with a `for` loop. The syntax is given below:

```
for x in list:
```

Second method is using the `range()` function with a `for` loop. The syntax will be:

```
for i in range(len(list))
```

Suppose we want to iterate through the `fruits` list using `in` and `for` loop.

```
>>>fruits = ["apple", "orange", "mango"]
>>>for x in fruits:
     print(x)
```

The output of the above code is:

```
apple
orange
mango
```

The above piece of code has printed each element of the list one by one. Let's rewrite the above code using `range()` function with `for` loop.

```
>>>fruits = ["apple", "orange", "mango"]
>>>for i in range(len(fruits)):
     print(x)
```

Output using both the ways will be the same as given above.

In addition to the operations discussed above, there are some built-in functions also that can be applied on Python lists. Table 6.2 summarizes the available functions briefly.

Table 6.2 Built-in functions on Python List

Functions	Description
`append()`	Appends elements at the end of the list
`clear()`	Removes all items from the list
`extend()`	Inserts each element of the iterable (list, set, tuple, string or dictionary) to the end of the list
`count()`	Returns the number of occurrences of a particular element in the list
`index()`	Returns the index of the element if present in the list
`remove()`	Removes the first occurrence of the given element from the list
`pop()`	It removes and returns the element present at a given index
`insert()`	Inserts the element at a given index in the list
`sort()`	This function sorts the elements of a list
`reverse()`	It reverse the ordering of all elements present in a list
`copy()`	This function creates a shallow copy of a existing list

Let's understand each function in detail using suitable examples.

6.1.2 Built-in List Functions

append()

The built-in function called `append()` is used to append elements at the end of an existing list. The syntax of `append()` function is as follows:

```
<list_name>.append(item)
```

Here, item is the element which is required to be added in the list. For example, `a` is a list consisting of two items.

```
>>>a=["Python", "C++"]
>>>a.append("Java")
>>>print(a)
['Python', 'C++', 'Java']
```

extend()

The `extend()` function is used to add items of any iterable objects or sequence type at the end of an existing list. Here, iterable objects can be anything like `lists, tuples, sets,` etc. The syntax for `extend()` function is as follows:

```
<list_name>.extend(iterable)
```

Example given below explains the concept of `extend()` function.

```
>>>list1=["Hello", "World"]
>>>list2=[1, 2, 3]
>>>list1.extend(list2)
>>>print(list1)

['Hello', 'World', 1, 2, 3]
```

Figure 6.4 illustrates the difference between `append()` and `extend()` functions.

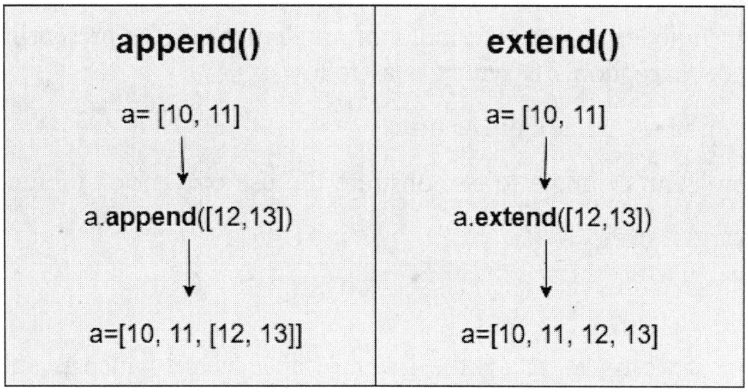

Figure 6.4 Difference between `append()` and `extend()` functions.

clear()

The `clear()` function is used to remove or clear all the elements from the list. Its syntax is as follows:

```
<list_name>.clear()
```

Let's understand how the `clear()` function is used using an example.

```
>>>my_list=[1, 2, 3, 4]
>>>print("My list before clear", my_list)

>>>my_list.clear()
>>>print("My list after clear", my_list)

My list before clear [1, 2, 3, 4]
Mylist after clear []
```

count()

It is used to count and return the number of occurrences of an element present in a list. The syntax of `count()` function is as follows:

```
<list_name>.count(element)
```

The element, whose occurrences have to be counted, is passed as argument. It takes only one argument at a time, if more than one argument is passed inside `count()` function then it raises `TypeError`. Let's understand it using an example to count the number of items present in a given list using the `count()` function.

```
>>>list1=[1, 2, 2, 3, 3, 3, 4, 4, 5]
>>>print(list1.count(3))
3
```

index()

This built-in function returns the index of an element if it is present in the list, else it raises a `ValueError` exception. Its syntax is as follows:

```
<list_name>.index(element)
```

Given below is an example to demonstrate the use of `index()` function.

```
>>>num_list=[1, 2, 3, 9, 0, 4, 6]
>>>print(num_list.index(9))
3
```

Suppose if we try to access the index of an element which is not present in the list then it will throw a `ValueError` exception. For example,

```
>>>print(num_list.index(13))
Traceback (most recent call last):
  File "C:/Users/AKANSHA/Desktop/q.py", line 2, in <module>
    print(num_list.index(13))
ValueError: 13 is not in list
```

remove()

The `remove()` function removes the first occurrence of the given element from the list. It doesn't return anything. Its syntax is as follows:

```
<list_name>.remove(object)
```

Let's understand the use of `remove()` function using an example.

```
>>>list1=[1, 2, 1, 3, 0, 5, 4, 2, 7]
>>>list1.remove(2)
>>>print(list1)

[1, 1, 3, 0, 5, 4, 2,7]
```

We can also delete items from a list using the `del` keyword.

```
>>>list1=[1,2, 1, 3, 0, 5, 4, 2, 7]
>>>del list1[3]
>>>print("List after deleting element at index 3: " ,list1)
List after deleting element at index 3: [1, 2, 1, 0, 5, 4, 2, 7]
```

We can also delete a sequence of elements from a list using `del` keyword.

```
>>>list1=[1,2, 1, 3, 0, 5, 4, 2, 7]
>>>del list1[4:6]
>>>print("List after deletion: ", list1)
List after deletion: [1, 2, 1, 3, 4, 2, 7]
```

In the first example, it will delete the item present at index 3. And in the second example it will delete elements from the start index till specified end index. We can also delete the entire list. To do so,

```
>>>del list1
```

Now, if we try to print `list1`, it will give `NameError` exception as `'list1'` is no longer defined.

```
>>>print(list1)
Traceback (most recent call last):
  File "C:/Users/AKANSHA/Desktop/q.py", line 3, in <module>
    print(list1)
NameError: name 'list1' is not defined
```

pop()

The `pop()` function removes and returns the last value from the list if no argument is passed. An index may be passed to `pop()` to remove and return the element at that index. Its syntax is:

```
<list_name>.pop(index)
```

Here, index value is optional.

Suppose we have a list `my_list` having four elements. Let's remove the element using the `pop()` function.

```
>>>my_list=[“200”, “334”, “400”, “540”]
>>>my_list.pop()
>>>print(my_list)

[‘200’, ‘334’, ‘400’]

>>>my_list.pop(1)
>>>print(my_list)

[‘200’, ‘400’, ‘540’]
```

insert()

The `insert()` function inserts a given element at a given index. It takes two parameters which are index value and element to be inserted. It follows the given syntax:

```
<list_name>.insert(index, element)
```

Let's try to insert 334 at index 1 in `my_list`.

```
>>>my_list.insert(1, 334)
>>>print(my_list)
[‘200’,‘334’, ‘400’, ‘540’]
```

Note here if the given index value is greater than the *length* of the list, in this case, the element is inserted at the end of the list.

sort()

The `sort()` function is used to sort the elements of a list in ascending or descending order. Sorting is done either on the basis of values or any user defined method. To sort the list in ascending order, syntax is:

```
<list_name>.sort()
```

Let's sort `my_list` using `sort()` function.

```
>>>my_list.sort()
>>>print(my_list)
[‘200’,‘334’, ‘400’, ‘540’]
```

To sort the list in descending order, we have to set the `reverse` parameter to `True`. Its syntax is:

```
<list_name>.sort(reverse=True)
```

For example,

```
>>>my_list.sort(reverse=True)
>>>print(my_list)
['540','400', '334', '200']
```

Now, if we want to sort the list on the basis of key values achieved by applying some functions to the objects in the list, we can pass it as a parameter inside the `sort()` function. Its syntax includes:

```
<list_name>.sort(key=function)
```

For example, we want to sort `name_list` on the basis of its length of the list elements.

```
>>>name_list=["Reeta", "Sita", "Ram", "Shyam"]
>>>name_list.sort(key=len)
>>>print(name_list)
['Ram', 'Sita', 'Reeta', 'Shyam']
```

reverse()

The `reverse()` function is an built-in function that reverses the order of all the elements of a list. Its syntax includes:

```
<list_name>.reverse()
```

For example,

```
>>>name_list.reverse()
>>>print(name_list)
['Shyam', 'Ram', 'Sita', 'Reeta']
```

copy()

The `copy()` function is a useful tool for creating a new list that is an exact replica of the original, without altering the original list in any way. This function is particularly helpful when you need to reuse the objects in the list for other purposes. To use the `copy()` function, simply call it without any parameters, and it will return a copy of the list. The syntax for using this function is as follows:

```
<list_name>.copy()
```

Let's create a copy of a given list `list1`.

```
>>>list1=[1, 0, 9, 3, 4]
>>>list2=list1.copy()
>>>print("The new list created is ", list2)
```

```
The new list created is [1, 0, 9, 3, 4]

>>>list2.append(2)
>>>print("The new list after adding one more element is ", list2)
>>>print("The older list after adding one more element is ", list1)
```

The output of the code is

```
The new list after adding one more element is [1, 0, 9, 3, 4, 2]
The older list after adding one more element is [1, 0, 9, 3, 4]
```

6.1.3 Nested Lists

A nested list is a collection of lists inside another list.

Consider the following examples:

1. `list1=[[1,2,3],[4,5,6],[7,8]]` → Here `list1` is a nested list having 3 inner lists or sublists.
2. `list2=[['yellow','green'],['orange']]` → Here `list2` is a nested list having 2 sublists.
3. `list3=['Ram', 6, 3.0, [1, 2]]` → Here `list3` contains a string, an integer, a float and another list.

Nested lists are very useful for representing any two dimensional data or tables where values are organized in rows and columns.

List Indexing for 2-Dimensional List

While accessing items of a one dimensional list, only one index value is required. But, we need to specify two indices in order to access an element from a two dimensional list. We need to write two indices in consecutive square brackets `[][]` along with the name of the list.

- First square bracket is for the row index.
- Second square bracket is for column index.

Syntax is as follows:

```
List_name[row_index][column_index]
```

Program 6.1 explains the method to access the elements from a 2D list given below.

Program 6.1: Program to access an element in a 2-Dimensional list

```
>>>#Nesting list inside another list
>>>List = [['Programming', 'Is'], ['Fun']]
>>>print("Accessing an element from a multidimensional list: ")
>>>print(List[0][0])
>>>print(List[1][0])
```

```
Accessing an element from a multidimensional list:
Programming
Fun
```

In Program 6.1 above, we accessed a 2-D list using indices. Initially, we printed the element located at `row_index` 0 and `column_index` 0, which resulted in the word `'Programming'` being printed. In the second `print` statement, we displayed the element located at `row_index` 1 and `column_index` 0 from the List. This resulted in the word `'Fun'` being printed from the given list.

This program demonstrates the use of indices to access specific elements within a 2-D list. By understanding how to properly use indices, we can manipulate and extract data from lists with ease.

6.1.4 Deep Copy and Shallow Copy

Assignment operator = when used in a program, only creates a reference to the original object. It does not create a new object. For example,

```
>>>original_list = [1, 2, 3, 4, 5]
>>>new_list = original_list
>>>new_list[2] = 10
>>>print('Original List:', original_list)
>>>print('ID of Original List:', id(original_list))

>>>print('New List:', new_list)
>>>print('ID of New List:', id(new_list))
```

The code given above creates a numeric list named as `original_list`. This list is further assigned to another variable called `new_list`. Then we tried to change the list element present at index 2 in `new_index` to 10. Furthermore, we printed the original list, `new_list` and their respective ids using `id()` function.

```
Original List: [1, 2, 10, 4, 5]
ID of Original List: 180728507592
New List: [1, 2, 10, 4, 5]
ID of New List: 180728507592
```

In the output, we have observed that changes applied to `new_list` have also been reflected in `original_list` and their id values are also the same which means these both variables are pointing to the same memory object.

Sometimes, we want to change the original list without changing it in the newly created list or vice versa. In such cases, we need to use a few methods available in Python.

1. Shallow copy
2. Deep copy

In order to use these methods, we are required to use a module named `copy`.

Shallow copy

A shallow copy is created using the `copy()` function from the `copy` module. This method produces a copy of the list that is considered to be one level deep. Unlike a deep copy, a shallow copy does not recursively copy nested objects. The syntax for creating a shallow copy is as follows:

```
copy.copy(list_name)
```

For example,

```
import copy

list1 = [10, 15, [20, 25], 30]

# using copy() to create a shallow copy
list2 = copy.copy(list1)

# displaying original elements of list1
print ("The original elements before shallow copying")
for i in range(0,len(list1)):
  print(list1[i],end=" ")

print()
# adding element to list2
list2[2][0] = 50

# checking if change is reflected in the original list
print ("The original elements after shallow copying")
for i in range(0,len( list1)):
    print (list1[i],end=" ")
```

```
The original elements before shallow copying
10  15  [20, 25] 30
The original elements after shallow copying
10 15 [50, 25] 30
```

As we can see, changes made to nested object (inner list) in `list2` are also reflected in original list `list1` which indicates that it is a shallow copy.

Deep copy

Deep copy uses a function `deepcopy()` from the `copy` module. This method generates copies of nested objects within the list, ensuring that all child objects are also duplicated. The process begins by creating a copy of the original list, and then recursively creating copies of all child objects found within.

The syntax for this method is as follows:

```
copy.deepcopy(list_name)
```

For example,

```
import copy
list1 = [10, 15, [20, 25], 30]

# using copy to deep copy
list2 = copy.deepcopy(list1)

# original elements of list1
print ("The original elements of list1 before deep copying")
for i in range(0,len(list1)):
  print(list1[i],end=" ")

print()
# adding and element to new list2
list2[2][0] = 50

# checking if change is reflected in list2
print ("The elements of list2 after deep copying")
for i in range(0,len(list2)):
    print (list2[i],end=" ")

print()

# Checking if change is NOT reflected in original list
print ("The original elements of list1 after deep copying")
for i in range(0,len(list1)):
  print (list1[i],end=" ")
```

```
The original elements of list1 before deep copying
10  15  [20, 25] 30
The elements of list2 after deep copying
10 15 [50, 25] 30
The original elements of list1 after deep copying
10 15 [20, 25] 30
```

Upon examining the output presented above, it is evident that any modifications made to the nested objects within the newly created deep copy `list2` will not have any impact on the original list `list1`. This indicates that the deep copy method has been employed, resulting in an independent copy of the list that includes all of its nested objects.

It is important to note that the distinction between shallow copy and deep copy only becomes relevant when dealing with compound objects, such as lists and class instances.

6.2 SETS

Sets are a fundamental data structure in Python that offer a powerful way to store and manipulate collections of objects. Essentially, a set is an unordered collection of unique elements that are mutable in nature. It is possible to modify a set by adding or removing elements from it. One of the key features of sets is that they do not allow *duplicate* items. This makes them ideal for tasks such as removing duplicates from a list or checking for membership in a collection. To create a set in Python, you simply use curly brackets `{}` and separate the elements with commas. If you want to create an empty set, you can use empty curly brackets.

Overall, sets are a versatile and efficient way to work with collections of data in Python. Let's understand concept of sets using examples given below:

```
>>>my_set={}
>>>print("Empty Set ", my_set)
Empty Set {}
```

To create a set with 4 elements, see the example given below.

```
>>>my_set={1, 8, 0, 9}
>>>print(my_set)
{8, 1, 0, 9}
```

We can also check the type of the above my_set variable using a `type()` function. It will return `<class set>` as an output.

To check the type of a given set,

```
>>>print(type(my_set))
<class 'set'>
```

set()

We can also use the `set()` function to convert an object, let us say a list, into a set. For example,

```
>>>colors=set(['Red', 'Blue', 'Orange'])
>>>print(colors)
{'Red', 'Blue', 'Orange'}
```

Heterogeneous set

Sets are capable of storing heterogeneous elements in it. Elements can be of any data type such as `string, int, float, boolean`. Let's create a heterogeneous set using the given example.

```
>>>my_set = {"Good", "Morning", 35, 81.2, False}
>>>print("Heterogeneous set: ", my_set)
Heterogeneous set: {False, 35, 'Good', 'Morning', 81.2}
```

Table 6.3 summarizes the operations that can be performed on a set.

Table 6.3 Operations on Sets

Operation	Description
add()	Adds a given element to a set
clear()	Removes all the elements from the set
update()	Adds the item to the set if not present already
remove()	Removes a given element from the set
pop()	Returns and removes any random element from a given set
copy()	Returns a shallow copy of a set
union()	Returns a new set that has union of all sets
intersection()	Returns a new set that has the intersection of all sets
difference()	Returns a new set that is the difference between two sets
symmetric_difference()	Returns a new set containing elements that are in any of the two given sets but not in both.
issubset()	Returns True if all elements of a set A are present in another set B
issuperset()	Returns True if all elements of a particular set are present in the original set.

6.2.1 Set Operations and Built-in Functions

add()

The add() function adds an element to a given set if that element is not already present in it. It takes only one parameter at a time. The syntax includes:

```
<set_name>.add(element)
```

Let's try to add some elements to a given set VEHICLE.

```
>>>VEHICLE={"v", "e", "h", "i", "c", "l", "e"}
>>>VEHICLE.add("s")
>>>print("The letters are ", VEHICLE)

The letters are {'e', 's', 'c', 'v', 'l', 'h', 'i'}
```

As a set is an unordered collection of elements, a new element will be added at any index.

clear()

The clear() function removes all elements from the given set. The syntax is as follows:

```
<set_name>.clear()
```

For example,

```
>>>VEHICLE={"v", "e", "h", "i", "c", "l", "e"}
>>>print("VEHICLE before clear: ", VEHICLE)
```

```
>>>VEHICLE.clear()
>>>print("VEHICLE after clear: ", VEHICLE)

VEHICLE before clear: {'c', 'v', 'i', 'h', 'l', 'e'}
VEHICLE after clear: set()
```

update()

The `update()` function adds elements from one set to another set. The syntax is:

```
<set1_name>.update(<set2_name>)
```

Here, `set1` is a set in which `set2` elements will be added. The `update()` function takes only a single parameter which can be a list, set, tuple or a dictionary. It automatically converts it into a set and adds it to a set. In the example given below, we are updating elements of `set2` with the elements of `set1`.

```
>>>list1 = [1, 2, 3]
>>>list2 = [4, 5, 6]
>>># Lists converted to sets
>>>set1 = set(list2)
>>>set2 = set(list1)

>>># Update function
>>>set1.update(set2)

>>># Print the updated set
>>>print(set1)
```

The output of the code is

```
{1, 2, 3, 4, 5, 6}
```

remove()

To remove a particular element from a set, we use `remove()` function. It takes a single argument. Its syntax is:

```
<set_name>.remove(element)
```

Let's remove the element 'e' from the set `vowels`.

```
>>>vowels={"a", "e", "i", "o", "u"}
>>>vowels.remove("e")
>>>print(vowels)

{'i', 'a', 'u', 'o'}
```

An action to remove an element which is not present in the set will raise a `KeyError` exception.

pop()

The `pop()` function removes any random element from the set. Its syntax is as follows:

```
<set_name>.pop()
```

For example,

```
>>>vowels={"a", "e", "i", "o", "u"}
>>>vowels.pop()
>>>print(vowels)

{'e', 'i', 'u', 'a'}
```

copy()

The copy() function creates a shallow copy of the existing set. It does not take any parameters. When we perform modification in the new copy of a set, no changes occur in the original set. The syntax of this function is as follows:

```
<set_name>.copy()
```

Here, set_name is the name of a set whose copy we want to generate.

Let's create a copy of a given set set1.

```
>>>set1={1, 2, 3}
>>>set2=set1.copy()
>>>print(set2)

>>>set2.add(4)
>>>print(set1)
>>>print(set2)
```

The output of the code is

```
{1, 2, 3}
{1, 2, 3}
{1, 2, 3, 4}
```

Adding a new element to set2 will not affect set1 because set2 is a copy of set1. The original set set1 remains the same as before.

union()

The insert() function is used to create a new set which is a union of all the sets. Its syntax is:

```
set1.union(set2, set3, set4,...)
```

Here, it will return a union of all the sets (set2, set3...) with set1. It will return simply set1 if no parameters are passed inside the union() function. Refer Figure 6.5.

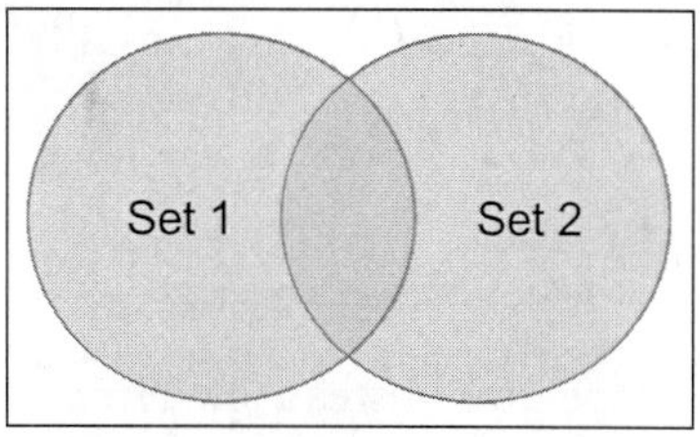

Figure 6.5 Union of two sets.

Let's try to perform a union of two sets `set1` and `set2`.

```
>>>set1 = {1, 2, 3, 4}
>>>set2 = {3, 4, 5, 8}

>>># union of two sets
>>>print("set1 U set2 : ", set1.union(set2))
```

The output of the code is shown below:

```
Set1 U set2 : {1, 2, 3, 4, 5, 8}
```

We can also use "|" operator instead of `union()` keyword to find the union of the sets.

```
>>>set1 = {1, 2, 3, 4}
>>>set2 = {3, 4, 5, 8}

>>># union of two sets
>>>print("set1 U set2 : ", set1 | set2)
```

It will produce the same result as above.

intersection()

The `intersection()` function returns a new set containing all the elements which are common in the given sets. Refer to figure 6.6. The syntax is:

```
set1.intersection(set2, set3, set4...)
```

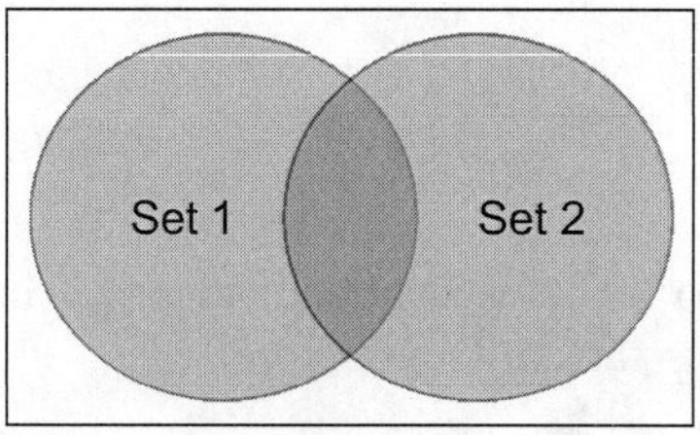

Figure 6.6 Intersection of two sets.

For example,

```
>>>set1 = {1, 2, 3, 4}
>>>set2 = {3, 4, 5, 8}

>>># intersection of two sets
>>>print("The intersection of set1 and set2 : ", set1.
intersection(set2))
```

The output of the code is

```
The intersection of set1 and set2 : {3, 4}
```

We can also use the "&" operator instead of `intersection()` keyword to find the intersection of two sets.

```
>>>set1 = {1, 2, 3, 4}
>>>set2 = {3, 4, 5, 8}

>>># intersection of two sets
>>>print("Intersection of set1 and set2 : ", set1 & set2)
```

It will produce the same output as above.

difference()

The `difference()` function returns a set which is the difference between two given sets. Refer Figure 6.7. Its syntax is:

`set1.difference(set2)` for `(set1 - set2)`

and

`set2.difference(set1)` for `(set2 - set1)`

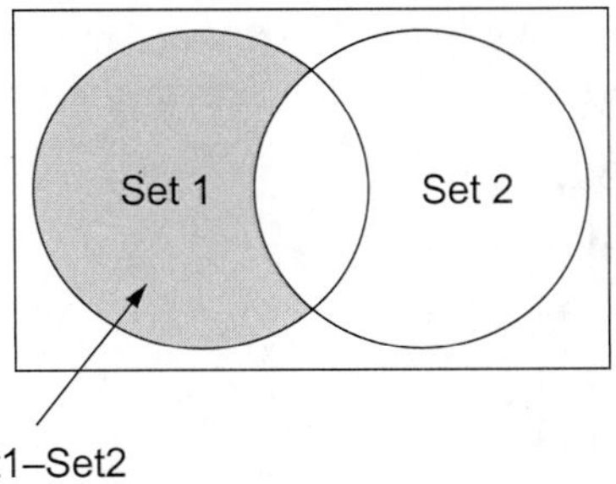

Figure 6.7 Difference between two Sets (set1–set2).

The following code finds the difference of two given sets `set1` and `set2`.

```
>>>set1 = {1, 2, 3, 4}
>>>set2 = {3, 4, 5, 8}

>>># difference of two sets
>>>print("The difference between set1 and set2 : ", set1.
difference(set2))
```

The output of the code is

```
The difference between set1 and set2 : {1, 2}
```

We can also use the "-" operator instead of `difference()` keyword to find the difference of two sets. The code will be as follows:

```
>>>set1 = {1, 2, 3, 4}
>>>set2 = {3, 4, 5, 8}

>>># difference of two sets
>>>print("The difference between set1 and set2 : ", set1 - set2)
```

symmetric_difference()

The symmetric_difference() function returns a set of all those elements which are either in set1 or set2 but not in both the sets. Refer Figure 6.8. Its syntax is as follows:

```
set1.symmetric_difference(set2)
```

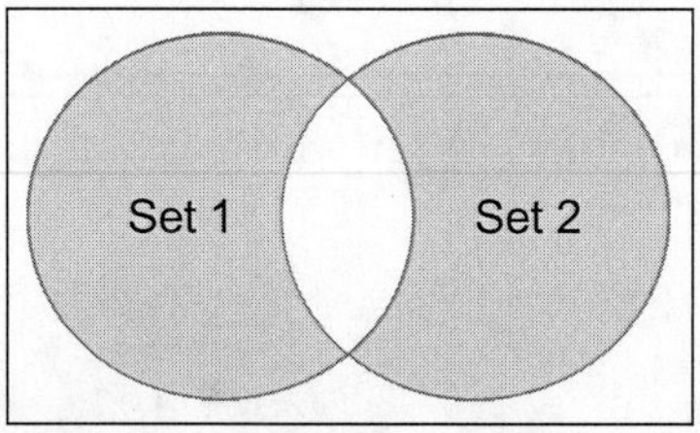

Figure 6.8 Symmetric difference of two sets.

Given list1 and list2, we first convert them into set1 and set2 respectively. Then, we perform symmetric difference of both the sets in the example given below.

```
>>>list1 = [10, 20, 30]
>>>list2 = [20, 30, 40]

>>># Convert list to sets
>>>set1 = set(list1)
>>>set2 = set(list2)
>>>print(set1.symmetric_difference(set2))
```

The output of the code is

```
{40, 10}
```

issubset()

This function returns True if all the elements of set1 are present in another set2 which is passed as an argument inside this function, otherwise it returns False. Refer to Figure 6.9. Its syntax is:

```
set1.issubset(set2)
```

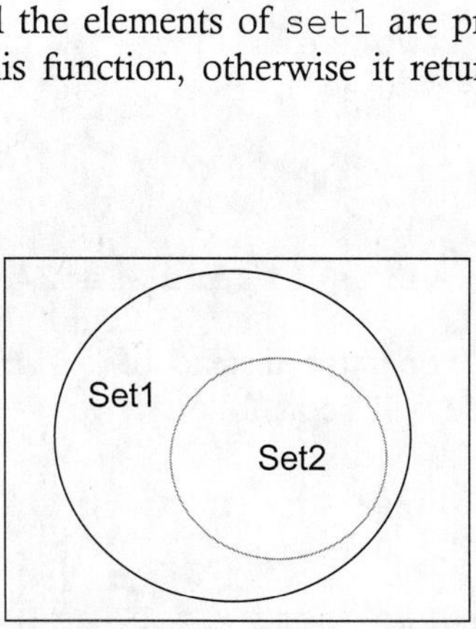

Figure 6.9 Set2 is subset of Set1.

Let's check if a set1 is a subset of set2.

```
>>>set1 = {4, 1, 0, 6}
>>>set2 = {6, 0, 4, 1, 5, 0, 3, 5}
>>>print(set1.issubset(set2))    # It will returns True
>>># set2 is not subset of set1
>>>print(set2.issubset(set1))    # It will returns False
True
False
```

issuperset()

The issuperset() function returns True only if all the elements of set1 occupies set2 which is passed as a parameter and returns False in the other case. Refer to Figure 6.10. Its syntax includes:

```
set1.issuperset(set2)
```

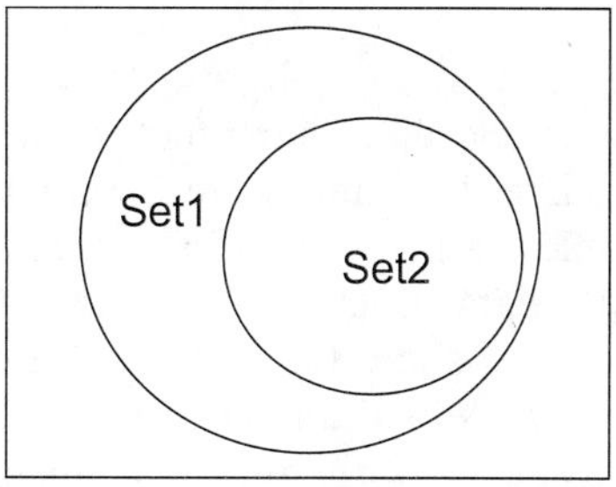

Figure 6.10 Set1 is superset of Set2.

For example,

```
>>>set1 = {4, 1, 0, 5}
>>>set2 = {6, 0, 3, 1, 5, 0, 4, 5, 9}
>>>print("set1.issuperset(set2) : ", set1.issuperset(set2))
>>># set2 is superset of set1
>>>print("set2.issuperset(set1) : ", set2.issuperset(set1))
```

The output of the code is

```
set1.issuperset(set2) : False
set2.issuperset(set1) : True
```

Program 6.2: Program to use different comparison operators along with sets

```
months_set1 = {"January", "February", "March", "April"}
months_set2 = {"January", "February"}
months_set3 = {"January", "February", "August"}
#months_set1 is the superset of months_set2 so it will print True.
print(months_set1>months_set2)
```

```
#prints false since months_set1 is not the subset of months_set2
print(months_set1<months_set2)
#prints false as months_set2 and months_set3 are not equivalent
print(months_set2 == months_set3)
```

```
True
False
Flase
```

Program 6.2 explains the use of various comparison operators like <, >, ==, >=, <= with the different sets. These comparison operators basically check whether a given set is a superset or subset or equivalent to another set or not. Depending on the comparison, the result is a boolean value i.e., `True` or `False`. Since `months_set1` is the superset of `months_set2` so the output is `True`. Further, when we tested `months_Set1<months_set2`, output is `False` since `months_set1` is not the subset of `months_set2`. Lastly, `months_set2 == months_set3` has resulted in `False` as they both are not equivalent.

6.3 TUPLES

A tuple is a collection of values enclosed in parentheses and separated by commas. Similar to lists, tuples are ordered, but unlike lists, tuples are immutable, meaning that the elements in a tuple cannot be changed. Tuples can store multiple values of different data types in a single variable, making them a versatile data structure. To create a tuple, use round brackets `()`. One unique feature of tuples is that they allow for duplicate values, meaning that the same value can appear more than once in a tuple. Additionally, tuples have an indexing property, where the first element has an index value of 0, the second element has an index value of 1, and so on. To create an empty tuple, simply use the following code:

```
>>>empty_tuple=()
>>>print("Empty Tuple ", empty_tuple)
Empty Tuple()
```

6.3.1 Tuple Operations and Built-in Functions

tuple()

The `tuple()` function is a built-in function which converts a sequence to a tuple data type.

Let's convert a string stored in `x` variable into a tuple.

```
>>>x='ILoveProgramming'
>>>print(tuple(x))
('I', 'L', 'o', 'v', 'e', 'P', 'r', 'o', 'g', 'r', 'a', 'm',
'm', 'i', 'n', 'g')
```

We can also use `range()` function to create a tuple within a given range.
For example,

```
>>>print(tuple(range(10)))
(0, 1, 2, 3, 4, 5, 6, 7, 8, 9)
```

Heterogeneous tuples

Let's create a tuple `t1` with heterogeneous elements.

```
>>>t1=(2,5,[1,7],'abc',{9,4}, (8,3))
>>>print(t1)
(2, 5, [1, 7], 'abc',{9, 4}, (8,3))
```

The above code shows the heterogeneity of a tuple as values of different data types like integer, list, string, set, etc. are stored in a single tuple.

In order to check the type of the above `t1` variable using a `type()` function.

```
>>>t1=(2,5,[1,7],'abc',{9,4}, (8,3))
>>>print(type(t1))
<class 'tuple'>
```

There is another way to create a tuple. List the items of tuples separated by commas. For example,

```
>>> t = 1,2,3,4,5
>>> print(t)
(1, 2, 3, 4, 5)
>>> print(type(t))
<class 'tuple'>
```

Singleton tuples

If a tuple contains only one element, in that case the element must be followed by a comma (,) symbol to distinguish a tuple from a parenthesized expression. This type of tuple is known as Singleton tuple.

```
>>>print(4)
4
```

The code line above shows only 4 as an integer in the output instead of tuple. To make a tuple with only 4 as an element, we must write the following code:

```
>>>print(4,)
(4,)
```

Immutability in tuples

Tuples are immutable in nature. So if we try to change an existing element in a tuple, it will throw a `TypeError` exception as the 'tuple' object does not support item assignment. For example, if we try to change an element present at index 3 in tuple `t1`, it will throw an exception.

```
>>>t1=(2,5,[1,7],'abc',{9,4}, (8,3))
>>>t1[3]=10
>>>print(t1)

Traceback (most recent call last):
  File "C:/Users/AKANSHA/Desktop/q.py", line 2, in <module>
    t1[3]=10
TypeError: 'tuple' object does not support item assignment
```

However, there might be some elements present in a tuple that are mutable in nature. Let's understand it with an example given below.

```
>>>t1=(1,2,[6,7])
>>>t1[2][1]=5
>>>print(t1)
(1, 2, [6, 5])
```

Here, as we can observe, the item is updated in the tuple. This could happen only if the element is mutable. In this example, we changed the element present in the list which is mutable in nature. That's why output resulted in no error.

Table 6.4 Operations on a Tuple

Operations	Description
Repetition Operator *	Repeats the tuple given number of times
Concatenation Operator +	Concatenates two given tuples
Function `len()`	Finds the number of elements present in a tuple
Indexing	Returns the element that is present at the specified index in a tuple
Function `count()`	Returns the frequency of occurrence of a specified element
Slicing Syntax: `start:end:inc`	Slices the sequence in a tuple
Function `max()`	Returns the maximum value in a tuple
Function `min()`	Returns the minimum value present in a tuple
Function `sum()`	Adds all the values (numeric type) in a tuple
Membership Operators: `in` and `not in`	Checks the presence of an element in tuple
Function `tuple()`	Converts an iterable sequence into a tuple

Table 6.4 illustrates some operations that can be applied on a tuple.

Repetition Operator *

The repetition operator, denoted by asterisk (*) symbol, is used to repeat a tuple for a given number of times.
For example,

```
>>>tuple1 = ('Python',)*4
>>>print(tuple1)
('Python', 'Python', 'Python', 'Python')
```

Concatenation Operator +

The concatenation operator, denoted by + symbol, is used to concatenate the elements of two given tuples. Refer to the example given below.

```
>>>tuple1=(0, 1, 2, 3)
>>>tuple2=('python', 'programming')
>>># Concatenating above two
```

```
>>>print(tuple1 + tuple2)
(0, 1, 2, 3, 'python', 'programming')
```

In Python IDLE, a tuple can not be concatenated with a string. It will throw a `TypeError` exception. Let's understand it with an example given below.

```
>>>tuple3=tuple2 + "coding"
>>>print(tuple3)
```

The code above generates the following error:

```
Traceback (most recent call last):
  File "C:/Users/AKANSHA/Desktop/q.py", line 2, in <module>
    tuple3=tuple2 + "coding"
TypeError: can only concatenate tuple (not "str") to tuple
```

`len()`

The length function `len()` retrieves the length of a given tuple. It returns an integer value which is the count of elements present in a tuple.

Let's return the length of a given tuple `tuple1`.

```
>>>tuple1=(0, 1, 2, 3)
>>>print(len(tuple1))
4
```

Indexing

Indexing can be performed on a tuple as elements in a tuple are ordered in nature. Using indexing, we can retrieve an element present at a given index value. Suppose we want to retrieve an element given at index 2 in a given tuple `tuple1`.

```
>>>tuple1=(0, 1, 2, 3)
>>>print(tuple1[2])
2
```

Also, there is an `index()` function that returns the index of the given value present in a tuple. Its syntax is as follows:

```
<tuple_name>.index(element)
```

For example, we want to find out the index value of "blue" in `color_tuple`.

```
>>>color_tuple=("red", "blue", "magenta")
>>>print(color_tuple.index("blue"))
1
```

`count()`

It returns an integer value depicting how many times an element occurs in a given tuple. Its syntax is as follows:

```
<tuple_name>.count(element)
```

Here, element is the name of the object whose frequency has to be counted. It takes only one parameter at a time. If more than one argument is passed simultaneously, it will throw an error.

Let's count the occurrence of an element 5 in a given tuple `num_tuple`.

```
>>>num_tuple=(1, 3, 2, 8, 5, 3, 4, 6, 8, 5)
>>>x=num_tuple.count(5)
>>>print(x)
2
```

Slicing

The slicing concept helps in retrieving the part of a sequence in a given tuple. It has three parameters: *start index*, *end index*, and *increment* (steps count). End and increment parameters are optional but the start parameter is required. The syntax is as follows:

```
start:end:inc
```

Suppose we want to retrieve a subset of elements from a given tuple `my_tuple`. We can write the following statements of code.

```
>>>my_tuple = (10 ,20, 30, 40)
>>>print(my_tuple[1:])
>>>print(my_tuple[::-1])
>>>print(my_tuple[2:4])
(20, 30, 40)
(40, 30, 20, 10)
(30, 40)
```

Deleting a tuple

We use the `del` keyword in order to delete all the elements of a tuple.

Let's try to delete all elements from a `num_tuple`.

```
>>>num_tuple=(1, 2, 6, 7)
>>>del num_tuple
>>>print(num_tuple)
```

This `num_tuple` is now deleted. If we try to print this tuple, it will throw an error as shown below:

```
Traceback (most recent call last):
  File "C:/Users/AKANSHA/Desktop/q.py", line 3, in <module>
    print(num_tuple)
NameError: name 'num_tuple' is not defined
```

max()

The `max()` function returns the maximum value present in a tuple.

For example,

```
>>>num_tuple=(1, 3, 2, 8, 5, 3, 4, 6, 8, 5)
>>>print(max(num_tuple))
8
```

min()

The `min()` function returns the minimum value present in a tuple.

For example,

```
>>>num_tuple=(1, 3, 2, 8, 5, 3, 4, 6, 8, 5)
>>>print(min(num_tuple))
1
```

sum()

The `sum()` function sums up all the elements present in a tuple and returns the sum.

Let's try to print the sum of all elements from a `num_tuple`.

```
>>>num_tuple=(1, 3, 2, 8, 5, 3, 4, 6, 8, 5)
>>>print(sum(num_tuple))
45
```

Membership Operators: in and not in

The membership operators `in` and `not in` check the presence or absence of an element in a tuple. The `in` operator returns `True` if an element exists in a tuple, otherwise `False`. When we use `not in` operator, it returns `True` only if an element is not present in the tuple otherwise it returns `False`.

For example, let's check the existence of an element in a tuple using `in` and `not in` operators.

```
>>>fruits_tuple=('apple', 'lichi', 'banana')
>>>print('apple' in fruits_tuple)
True
>>>print('guava' not in fruits_tuple)
True
```

Program 6.3: Program to sum all the integer elements present in a tuple

```
def addition(sample_tuple):
   #Using list() to convert tuple into a list
   list1 = list(sample_tuple)

      sum = 0      # initializing a sum variable
      for i in list1:
          sum+=i
      return sum

# initializing sample_tuple
sample_tuple = (4, 25, 2, 10, 5, 12)
print(addition(sample_tuple))
```

The output of the code is

```
58
```

In Program 6.3 above, we begin by converting the given tuple into a list using the `list()` function. This conversion is necessary to perform the summation of all elements in the tuple. However, we can simplify the code by utilizing the built-in function, `sum()`, on `list1` and returning the result instead of using a `for` loop to iterate over each element in the list. By using the `sum()` function, we can achieve the same result while reducing the number of code lines. This approach is both efficient and effective.

6.4 DICTIONARY

Python offers another built-in data structure known as a dictionary. This data structure consists of `key:value` pairs and is enclosed within curly brackets `{}`. To differentiate between the keys and values in a dictionary, we use the colon : symbol. It's worth noting that all keys and values in a dictionary can be of different types. Additionally, it's important to remember that *keys* in a dictionary are immutable, while *values* can be either mutable or immutable. It's crucial to ensure that keys in a dictionary are unique, as they serve as identifiers for values. To create and print an empty dictionary, use the following statements:

```
>>>my_dict={}
>>>print("Empty Dictionary", my_dict)

Empty Dictionary {}

>>>print(type(my_dict))
<class 'dict'>
```

6.4.1 Dictionary Operations and Built-in Functions

`dict()`

`dict()` is a built-in function that helps in creating a dictionary. Let's use this function to create a dictionary.

```
>>>my_dict = dict(student_name = "Ram", age = 23, country = "India")
>>>print(my_dict)
{'student_name': 'Ram', 'age': 23, 'country': 'India'}
```

Heterogeneous dictionary

A dictionary can store multiple types of data in the form of `key:value`.

Following examples illustrate the use of dictionaries.

```
>>>my_dict={1: 'I', 2: 'love', 3: 'Python'}
>>>print("Dictionary having only integer keys ")
>>>print(my_dict)
```

```
Dictionary having only integer keys
{1: 'I', 2: 'love', 3: 'Python'}
```

Let's create a dictionary `Dict` having different data types of `key:value` pairs.

```
>>>Dict={'Name': 'Alexa', 1: [9, 8, 7, 6]}
>>>print("Dictionary having different data types of keys ")
>>>print(Dict)

Dictionary having different data types of keys
{'Name': 'Alexa', 1: [9, 8, 7, 6]}
```

Accessing values in a dictionary

There are multiple methods to access the values within a dictionary. The initial approach involves utilizing the dictionary's name in conjunction with the corresponding key, which is enclosed in square brackets.

```
>>>my_dict={1: 'I', 2: 'love', 3: 'Python'}
>>>print(my_dict[3])

Python

>>> my_dict={1: 'I', 2: 'love', 3: 'Python'}
>>> my_dict[5]
```

In the above code, as the specified key is not present in the dictionary, a `KeyError` exception is raised by the interpreter shown below:

```
Traceback (most recent call last):
  File "<pyshell#5>", line 1, in <module>
    my_dict[5]
KeyError: 5
```

The second way to access values in a dictionary is by using a built-in function called `get()`. Its syntax is:

```
dict_name.get(key, default)
```

For example,

```
>>>a=my_dict.get(3)
>>>print(a)

Python
```

The `get()` function particularly takes two parameters. First parameter denotes the key name and the second parameter is any default value which will appear in case that key is not present in the dictionary. For example,

```
>>>stud_data={'Reema': 101, 'Jatin': 102, 'Neha': 103}
>>>print(stud_data.get('Jatin', -1))

102
```

But if the key is not present in the dictionary,

```
>>>print(stud_data.get('Radha', -1))
-1
```

In this case, the specified default value `-1` has appeared as an output. Note that if no default value is passed in `get()` function and the key that is referred is not available in the dictionary, in this case, output will be `None`.

```
>>>print(stud_data.get('Radha'))

None
```

Table 6.5 Operations on a Dictionary

Operations	Description
Function `len()`	Returns the length of the dictionary
Function `clear()`	Clears the entire dictionary
Function `get(key, default)`	Retrieves the value referred to the specified key
Function `keys()`	Returns an object displaying all the keys of a dictionary
Function `values()`	Returns a list displaying all the values present in a dictionary
Function `items()`	Returns a list comprising all the `key:value` pairs given in a dictionary
Function `max()`	Returns the maximum value of a key
Function `min()`	Returns the minimum value of a key
Function `sum()`	Sums up all the keys, assuming keys are in numeric format
Function `pop()`	Removes an element with the mentioned key
Function `popitem()`	Removes the last inserted `key:value` pair from a dictionary
Function `update()`	Updates a new `key:value` pair into an existing dictionary
Membership Operators: `in` and `not in`	Checks whether a key or value exists in a dictionary or not
Function `copy()`	Creates a copy of existing dictionary

Table 6.5 shows some basic operations that can be performed on a dictionary.

len()

The length function `len()` returns how many `key:value` pairs are present in a dictionary. Let's find out the number of `key:value` pairs present in a dictionary `calendar` given below.

```
>>>calendar={1: 'January', 2: 'February', 3: 'March', 4: 'April',
5: 'May', 6: 'June', 7: 'July', 8: 'August', 9: 'September', 10:
'October', 11: 'November', 12: 'December'}

>>>print(len(calendar))

12
```

clear()

The clear() function empties the given dictionary. It removes all the key:value pairs. For example,

```
>>>calendar.clear()

>>>print(calendar)

{}
```

keys()

The function keys() returns all the keys present in a dictionary. Its syntax is as follows:

```
<dict_name>.keys()
```

Let's try to return all the keys present in a dictionary calendar.

```
>>>calendar={1: 'January', 2: 'February', 3: 'March', 4: 'April', 5: 'May', 6: 'June', 7: 'July', 8: 'August', 9: 'September', 10: 'October', 11: 'November', 12: 'December'}

>>>print(calendar.keys())

dict_keys([1, 2, 3, 4, 5, 6, 7, 8, 9, 10, 11, 12])
```

The keys() function will always produce output of the <class 'dict_keys'> type, which is an iterable object that can be utilized with a for loop. Additionally, this outcome can be transformed into a list or tuple type.

This function generates a specific type of output, namely <class 'dict_keys'>, which is a versatile iterable object that can be easily manipulated using a for loop.

values()

The function values() gives all the values available in a dictionary. Its syntax is as follows:

```
dict_name.values()
```

For example,

```
>>>print(calendar.values())

dict_values(['January', 'February', 'March', 'April', 'May', 'June', 'July', 'August', 'September', 'October', 'November', 'December'])
```

Similar to the keys() function, the output of values() will always be of the type <class 'dict_values'>. It is an iterable object and can be used with a for loop. This result can also be converted to list or tuple type.

items()

The function items() returns all the key:value pairs in a specified dictionary. The output of this function can be understood in a way similar to keys() and values(). Each item is returned within a tuple. Its syntax is as follows:

```
dict_name.items()
```

For example,

```
>>>print(calendar.items())

dict_items([(1, 'January'), (2, 'February'), (3, 'March'), (4, 'April'),
(5, 'May'), (6, 'June'), (7, 'July'), (8, 'August'), (9, 'September'),
(10, 'October'), (11, 'November'), (12, 'December')])
```

max()

The function `max()` returns the maximum valued key among all keys present in the dictionary. For example,

```
>>>print(max(calendar))

12
```

min()

The function `min()` returns the minimum valued key among all keys present in the dictionary. For example, the `min()` function, if applied on a `calendar` dictionary, will produce the following output.

```
>>>print(min(calendar))

1
```

sum()

The `sum()` function sums up all the keys and returns the sum. Note that `sum()` can be applied only if all the keys are of numeric form. For example,

```
>>>print(sum(calendar))

78
```

So if we perform the `sum()` function on the given calendar dictionary, it returns 78 as the addition of all the keys.

pop()

The `pop()` function removes and returns the element with the specified key in a dictionary. It follows the following syntax:

```
dict_name.pop(key)
```

Let's pop a value having 2 as a key in a `calendar` dictionary.

```
>>>print(calendar.pop(2))

February
```

popitem()

The popitem() function removes and returns the last inserted key:value pair from the given dictionary. See the example given below.

```
>>>print(calendar.popitem())
(12, 'December')
```

Note here, the output is obtained in the form of a tuple.

update()

The update() function adds key:value pairs from one dictionary to another dictionary. It follows the mentioned syntax:

```
dict1.update(dict2)
```

For example,

```
>>>dict1={1: 'One', 2: 'Two', 3: 'Three'}
>>>dict2={4: 'Four', 5:'Five', 6: 'Six'}
>>>dict1.update(dict2)
>>>print(dict1)
{1: 'One', 2: 'Two', 3: 'Three', 4: 'Four', 5: 'Five', 6: 'Six'}
```

The above code has added items of dict2 to dict1.

Membership Operators: in and not in

The membership operators in and not in are used to check the existence of elements (both keys and values) in a given dictionary. The in operator by default checks the existence of a key in the dictionary and returns True if that key is present in a dictionary otherwise it returns False. But, we can also write .keys() to check the presence of it in the given keys of a dictionary.

Let's try to check the presence of both keys and values in a calendar dictionary.

```
>>>print(4 in calendar)
OR
>>>print(4 in calendar.keys())
True
```

Since 4 is present as a key in the calendar dictionary, it has returned True.

We can also check the presence of values and items using .values() and .items() functions respectively. For example,

```
>>>print('April' in calendar.values())
True
>>>print((20, 'Twenty') in calendar.items())
False
```

copy()

The `copy()` function creates a copy of the dictionary. It does not take any parameters. The syntax of `copy()` function is as follows:

```
dict_name.copy()
```

In the following example, `cal2` is a copy of the `calendar`. The changes made in `cal2` do not reflect in the `calendar`.

```
>>> calendar = {1: 'January', 2: 'February', 3: 'March', 4: 'April',
5: 'May', 6: 'June', 7: 'July', 8: 'August', 9: 'September', 10:
'October', 11: 'November', 12: 'December'}

>>> cal2 = calendar.copy()

>>> cal2[7]='XYZ'

>>> print(cal2)

{1: 'January', 2: 'February', 3: 'March', 4: 'April', 5: 'May',
6: 'June', 7: 'XYZ', 8: 'August', 9: 'September', 10: 'October',
11: 'November', 12: 'December'}

>>> print(calendar)

{1: 'January', 2: 'February', 3: 'March', 4: 'April', 5: 'May',
6: 'June', 7: 'July', 8: 'August', 9: 'September', 10: 'October',
11: 'November', 12: 'December'}
```

Program 6.4: Program to merge two different dictionaries into one

```
>>>dict1 = {'a': 10, 'b': 15}
>>>dict2 = {'c': 20, 'd': 25}
>>>merged_dict = dict1.copy()
>>>merged_dict.update(dict2)
>>>print(merged_dict)

{'a': 10, 'b': 15, 'c': 20, 'd': 25}
```

In Program 6.4 above, we have successfully merged the `key:value` pairs of two dictionaries, `dict1` and `dict2`. To begin, we created a copy of `dict1` using the `copy()` function and stored it in a new variable called `merged_dict`. From there, we utilized the `update()` function to add the elements of `dict2` to the end of `merged_dict`. This process allowed us to combine the information from both dictionaries into one cohesive unit.

6.5 COMPREHENSIONS IN PYTHON

Comprehension is a method to reconstruct the code in a short and concise manner. It provides a syntax to create new sequences including lists, sets, dictionaries using predefined sequences. It reduces the number of code lines. The core component of every comprehension method is a `for` loop. There are three types of comprehensions:

1. List comprehensions
2. Set comprehensions
3. Dictionary comprehensions

6.5.1 List Comprehension

List comprehension is a concise and efficient way to create a list in Python. This method allows you to create a new list in just one line of code, making your code more readable and easier to maintain. To use list comprehension, you simply specify a `for` loop inside square brackets. The syntax for list comprehension is as follows:

```
[<expression> for <variable_name> in <list_or_sequence> if
<condition == True>]
```

Program 6.5: Program to display the characters in a string as a list

(a) using conventional approach

```
char_list = []
for character in "Python Programming!":
   char_list.append(character)
# Display list
print(char_list)
```

```
['P', 'y', 't', 'h', 'o', 'n' ' ', 'P', 'r', 'o', 'g', 'r', 'a',
'm', 'm', 'i', 'n', 'g', '!']
```

In this method, we have simply created an empty list and started appending each character from the given string `"Python Programming!"` using a `for` loop.

(b) Using list comprehension

```
char_list = [character for character in 'Python Programming!']
#Displaying list
print("The character list using list comprehension: ", char_list)
```

```
The character list using list comprehension: ['P', 'y', 't', 'h', 'o',
'n' ' ', 'P', 'r', 'o', 'g', 'r', 'a', 'm', 'm', 'i', 'n', 'g', '!']
```

Using list comprehension in above Program 6.5, we have reduced the number of code lines by simply traversing each character from the string `'Python Programming!'`

6.5.2 Set Comprehension

This method can create a new set in a single line code. To create a set comprehension, we use curly brackets. The syntax is as follows:

```
{<expression> for <variable_name> in <list_or_sequence> if
<condition == True>}
```

Program 6.6: Print a set having only even numbers from the given input list

(a) Using conventional approach

```
my_list = [10, 20, 9, 15, 30, 4, 35, 5, 2, 6, 6, 7]
result_set = set()
# Using loop for creating result set
for i in my_list:
   if i % 2 == 0:
      result_set.add(i)
print("The resultant set using for loop: ", result_set)
```

The output of the code is

```
The resultant set using for loop: {2, 4, 6, 10, 20, 30}
```

(b) Using set comprehension

```
# Using Set comprehensions
my_list = [10, 20, 9, 15, 30, 4, 35, 5, 2, 6, 6, 7]
set_comp = {i for i in my_list if i % 2 == 0}
print("Result Set using set comprehension method :", set_comp)
```

The output of the code is

```
Result Set using set comprehension method :{2, 4, 6, 10, 20, 30}
```

In Program 6.6 above, we utilized a conventional approach by using a `for` loop to print even numbers from a given list. To determine if a number is even, we checked if it is divisible by 2 and has a remainder of 0. If it does, then it is even; otherwise, it is odd. We applied the same logic in the set comprehension method, which significantly reduced the amount of effort required.

6.5.3 Dictionary Comprehension

This method can create a new dictionary in a single line code. To create a dictionary comprehension, syntax is as follows:

```
{<key:value> for <key:value> in <sequence> if <condition == True>}
```

Program 6.7: Print a dictionary which contains only the even numbers as keys present in the given input list and calculate their square as values

(a) Using conventional approach

```
my_list = [1, 2, 3, 4, 5, 6, 7, 8, 9]

resultant_dict = {}
# Using loop for creating resultant dictionary
for i in my_list:
   if i % 2 == 0:
      resultant_dict[i] = i**2
print("The Resultant Dictionary using for loop: ", resultant_dict )
```

The output of the code is

```
The Resultant Dictionary using for loop: {2: 4, 4: 16, 6: 36, 8: 64}
```

(b) Using dictionary comprehension

```
my_list = [1, 2, 3, 4, 5, 6, 7, 8, 9]
dict_comp = {i:i ** 2 for i in my_list if i % 2 == 0}
print("The Resultant Dictionary using dictionary comprehension: ",
dict_comp)
```

The output of the code is

```
The Resultant Dictionary using dictionary comprehension: {2: 4,
4: 16, 6: 36, 8: 64}
```

In Program 6.7 above, we have computed and exhibited the squares of every even number in the provided list, `my_list`, using the exponent operator `**`. The first method employs a `for` loop and saves the outcome in `resultant_dict`. Similarly, the second method utilizes the same logic and stores the output in the `dict_comp` variable. However, this time, the solution is presented in a single line of code, demonstrating the benefits of using comprehension methods.

SUMMARY

- Objects whose internal state can be changed are called mutable objects(ex. lists) while an object who does not allow you to change its state is called an immutable object (ex. strings, tuples).
- A list is an ordered, comma separated ordered sequence of values. It is enclosed in square brackets [ ].
- Operations such as concatenation, repetition, `len`, `min`, `max`, `sum`, indexing, slicing, membership operators `(in, not in)` can be applied on a list.
- There are some built-in functions also that can be applied on Python lists such as `append`, `clear`, `extend`, `count`, `index`, `remove`, `pop`, `insert`, `sort`, `reverse`, `copy`.
- A set is a comma separated unordered collection of unique objects.
- Operations that can be performed on a set are `add`, `clear`, `update`, `remove`, `pop`, `copy`, `union`, `intersection`, `difference`, `symmetric_difference`, `issubset`, `issuperset`.
- A tuple is an ordered sequence of values enclosed in parentheses and separated by commas. It is enclosed with round brackets ().
- Operations that can be applied on a tuple are repetition, concatenation, `len`, indexing, `count`, `slicing`, `max`, `min`, `sum`, membership operators `(in, not in)`, `tuple()`.
- A dictionary is a mapping type object consisting of `key:value` pairs.
- It is enclosed within curly brackets {}.

- `len, clear, max, min, sum,` indexing, `get(key, default), keys(), values(), items(), pop, popitem, update,` membership operators `(in, not in), copy` are some operations that are applied on a dictionary.
- Comprehension is a method to reconstruct the code in a short and concise manner.

EXERCISES

6.1 Give the output that will be produced on execution of the following code segments:

```
(a) l1 = [50, 22, 'a', 'b', 23, 94]
    print(l1[3:])
(b) max(l1)
(c) type(l1[2])
(d) l2=[3,4]
    l1.extend(l2)
(e) l1.reverse()
(f) String1= " Hello first year students"
    String2= " Hello second year students"
    for i in String1:
        if i in String2:
            print(i , end=" ")
```

6.2 Consider the following two sets:

```
set_X = set(["green", "blue", "yellow", "red"])
set_Y = set (["blue", "yellow", "pink", "orange"])
```

Write the Python statements for each of the following operations:

(a) Adding an element to the set `set_X`.
(b) Compute `xUy` as a union of `set_X` and `set_Y`.
(c) Compute `x minus y` as the set difference between `set_X` and `set_Y`.
(d) Remove "blue" from `set_X`.

6.3 Consider the tuple t1 defined below:

```
t1 = (12, 5, 2, 4, 17, 44, 7, 6, 9, 10)
```

Write a Python statement to:

(a) Print first half of the values of `t1` in one line and the other half in another line.
(b) Produce a list comprising all the even numbers in the tuple `t1`.
(c) Check whether the element 44 is present in the `t1` or not, if yes, print the message "Element is there in the tuple".
(d) Display the last element from the tuple.
(e) Calculate the sum of all the elements.
(f) Print the given tuple in reverse order.

6.4 Find the output of the following code:

(a)
```
def fname(n):
    for i in range(n):
        if i==3:
            return 0
        else:
            print('i=', i)
print('output=', fname(5))
```

(b)
```
names={'DELHI':5,'BOMBAY':6,'GOA':3}
print(list(names.keys()))
print(names.get('RANCHI', 'NONE'))
```

(c) Find the content of S after the execution of the following statements?

```
S1='EXECUTION'
S=S1[0::3] * 3
```

6.5 Using both loop and list comprehension methods, calculate the cube of the first five natural numbers. Consider the sample input and output given below:

```
Input Sample: n = 4
Output Sample: 100
```

$1^3 + 2^3 + 3^3 + 4^3 = 100$

6.6 Write a program to interchange the first and last elements in a list. Take a list as input from the user.

6.7 State any three differences between lists and tuples. Also, show their usage using an example.

6.8 Perform the following operations on the given list:

```
L = [3, 8, 1, 6, 2, 10, 3, 5]
```

(a) `L.insert(3, 20)`
(b) `L.index(12)`
(c) `L.append(7)`
(d) `L.count(3)`
(e) `L.pop()`
(f) `L.min()`

6.9 Write a function to find the common elements from the two lists. Take lists as user input.

6.10 State any two advantages of comprehensions method over conventional approach using suitable examples.

7

Introduction to Classes and Objects

When learning any programming language, it is often iterated that coding helps solve real-life problems, i.e., create the automated version of a manual solution to the problem.

A point to ponder here would be that to model real-life applications or situations, the information needed is also in a certain structure and format. This is where **object-oriented programming** comes into picture.

The object-oriented paradigm of programming focuses on modeling the data and functionalities associated with real world entities, by means of *classes* and *objects*. The aim is to *encapsulate* the information and methodology that defines a real world entity, and create a template. This template is called a *class*. In order to represent a particular instance of this entity, an *object* of the corresponding class is created.

In this chapter, we aim to cover the usage of classes and objects in Python. In addition to this, we study the key concepts of object-oriented programming, namely encapsulation, inheritance and polymorphism.

7.1 INTRODUCTION

7.1.1 Object-oriented Programming Concepts (OOPs)

Being object oriented is a very striking feature in any programming language. Object-oriented Programming Concepts, commonly known as OOPs, allow to model real-life entities and the functionalities associated with them. For this purpose, *classes and objects* are put at work. In this type of programming paradigm, the data being used is considered as an object which has certain features and functionalities associated with it. For example, consider implementing an application that needs to work with cars. Hence, the object here would be a car and its features could be color, manufacturer, model and price as shown in Figure 7.1.

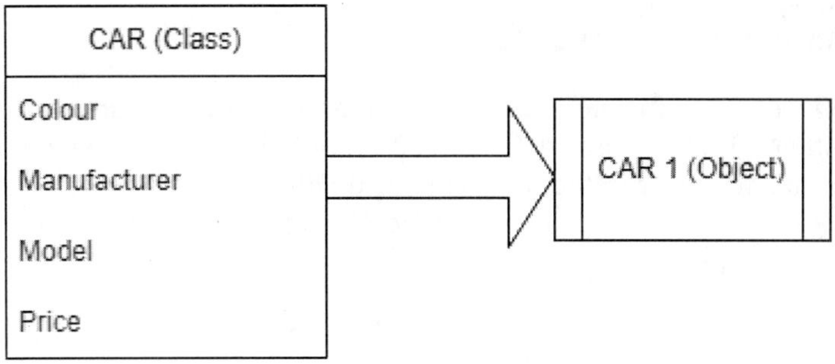

Figure 7.1 Class and Object.

7.1.2 Need for Classes

When considering the example stated above, one might question the benefit of using classes to store real-life data. It can conveniently be said that a lot of problems can be solved by programming without using OOPs concepts. So what is the need?

Let us understand this by extending our example of cars. If we need to save data of one car, we may use a dictionary.

```
car1 = {'color' : 'gray', 'manufacturer' : 'Hyundai', 'model' : 'M56', 'price' : 500000}
```

The programmer may then define functions that will work on this type of data. Now let us try to understand some shortfalls of this approach.

- For a few more cars, the programmer may bear the overhead of typing this data repeatedly. But what if there are hundreds of cars whose data has to be stored?
- Further, there are chances of potential non-uniformity in this case. For a `car1`, the programmer might have spelt the key as "`model`" and maybe for `car5`, it was typed as "`Model`". Assume that a function defined in this application has a statement `print(car['model'])`. This statement will give an error when executed for `car5` and it will be very difficult to debug this.
- The reader may argue that the code was checked several times and that the scope of occurrence of such typing errors was negligible. Even if that was the case, assume that at a later point of time, the application also wants to store the mileage for each of the cars in its database. The programmer will now have to modify each dictionary created and add another key value pair. There may be chances of typing error or a possibility of leaving out any car.

It is admitted here that these issues may be resolved to some extent by creating a data structure which is a list of dictionaries and by using loops on it. However, it will be a complex and redundant approach storing different values each time for the same keys.

A better way to store such information would be to somehow create a blank template or blueprint and then just create more copies of it adding different values for each object. This is exactly what is achieved by classes and objects. The concept is elucidated in more detail in the following section.

7.2 CLASSES AND OBJECTS

A class is defined as a template or a blueprint that defines the structure of a real world entity. Classes are often known as user defined data types, i.e., they will have certain data members and functions, all coming together as one named entity. The name of a class follows the same rules as variable naming. It is a good practice to capitalize the first letter of the class name. The syntax of a class is:

```
class <class_name>:
    #class body
```

Let us create an empty class and study some basic features.

```
class Empty:
        '''This is an empty class.
        It contains some documentation
        which may be accessed using __doc__'''
print(Empty.__doc__)
```

This class named `Empty`, contains nothing but what is identified as a multi-line comment. Recall the documentation done in functions. It is a string enclosed in triple quotes, added in the beginning of the function body. Similarly a class can also be documented by adding some information about its purpose. Outside the class, there is a `print()` statement that accesses and displays the documentation of this class. The documentation string of the class is accessed by writing class name followed by a *dot* and `__doc__` as

```
Empty.__doc__
```

It is a good practice to add docstring to classes.

7.2.1 Attributes

The class body follows indentation rules and comprises some data members, also known as *attributes*. They correspond to the attributes or characteristics of the real-life object. For example, if we are trying to store information about Pet animals, we will create a class called `Pet`. The attributes in this class could be the following:

- `pet_type` : a string type variable that holds the type of pet
- `pet_name` : a string variable that stores the name of pet
- `color` : a string variable which stores the color of the pet.

and several others such as name, habitat, etc. Note that it is up to the programmer how many and which characteristics of the entity will be represented by attributes in the class. Moreover, these variables need not be of the same data type. They may be assigned some default values in this template, known as class. Let us create the `Pet` class having the aforesaid attributes.

```
class Pet:
    pet_type = "cat"
    pet_name = "liz"
    color = "white"
```

7.2.2 Methods

In addition to attributes, any entity also has some associated functionality. For instance, a pet could be named, adopted, missing, etc. For each of these, a class contains some functions or class *methods*. The syntax to define these functions is the same as studied earlier in Chapter 4, except that these functions will be defined inside the scope of a class. Methods in a class can be used to perform any task associated with the entity.

Let us make some additions to class Pet.

```
class Pet:

    def __init__(self):
        self.pet_type="dog"
        self.pet_name="cru"
        self.color="brown"

    def display(self):
        print("The pet is a", self.pet_type, "called",
        self.pet_name, ". \nIt is", self.color, "in color.")

    def change_type(self, t):
        self.pet_type = t

    def change_name(self, n):
        self.pet_name = n

    def change_color(self, c):
        self.color = c
```

After this code is executed, the interpreter knows that a template named Pet exists and that it has certain attributes and functions. It has been established that a class is an entity that binds data and methods together. This is an OOP concept known as *encapsulation*.

7.2.3 Instantiation and Objects

As mentioned earlier, a class is a user defined data type and when variables of this data type are created, they are called *objects* of that class. Objects are also known as instances, and hence the process of creating objects is called *instantiation*.

Consider an analogy to understand this concept. A college has put up a form on its website to gather data of student achievements. Now this form may have some fields namely, student name, course, year, etc. It may also have features such as reset, preview and submit. Up till here, it is similar to just defining a class. But how is it used? Say, the form on the website gets used when a student fills it out, and possibly many more students fill in the same form. Similarly, a class is used when it is **instantiated**. In order to do that, we create objects of that class. Let us now use the Pet class by creating some objects.

Program 7.1: Create a class to store details of a Pet. Add required attributes and methods. Create some objects of this class

```
class Pet:
    def __init__(self):
        self.pet_type="dog"
        self.pet_name="cru"
        self.color="brown"
    def display(self):
        print("The pet is a", self.pet_type, "called",
        self.pet_name, ". \nIt is", self.color, "in color.")
    def change_type(self, t):
        self.pet_type = t
    def change_name(self, n):
        self.pet_name = n
    def change_color(self, c):
        self.color = c
#creating first object of Pet class
pet1 = Pet()
print("Type of first object : ", type(pet1))
print("Details of first pet :")
pet1.display()
print()
#creating second object
pet2 = Pet()
pet2.change_type("cat")
pet2.change_name("norris")
print("Details of second pet object :")
pet2.display()
```

When Program 7.1 is executed, the output first displays details of the first pet and then the second pet. The output is shown below.

```
Type of first object : <class '__main__.Pet'>
Details of first pet :
The pet is a dog called cru.
It is brown in colour.

Details of second pet object :
The pet is a cat called norris.
It is brown in colour.
```

Now let us understand how this is working. We know that after a class is defined, a template definition by the name `Pet` is stored. In the definition of this class, the data members – `pet_name`, `pet_type` and `color`, have already been assigned a value. So whenever we create an object of this class, it will have these values only for the data members.

Next, an object named `pet1` was created by the statement `pet1 = Pet()`. The part `Pet()` is a call to a special method called the *initializer* or *constructor* (`__init__()`) of the class, which creates an object of type `Pet`, returns its memory location, and it is stored in the object called `pet1`. This is evident when the type of this object is displayed in the next line. Figure 7.2 depicts that `pet1` is an object of type `Pet` stored in the memory. It stores certain values for the class attributes.

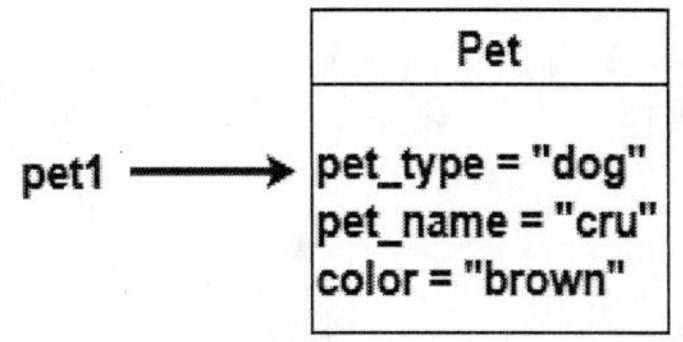

Figure 7.2 pet1 as an object of class Pet.

7.2.4 Accessing Data and Methods

There are some more statements in the class `Pet` whose working will be discussed in this section. In the statement `pet1.display()` the "." is called the *dot operator*. It is used to access the functions or variables associated with the class object. So, here when `display()` method is called, it is called with respect to object `pet1`. Not only methods, the dot operator can also be used to access the data members associated with the object. For example, when the statement `print(pet1.pet_name)` is executed, the output will be `cru` as shown in Figure 7.3. *Everything defined inside a class can be accessed from anywhere in the program, only by using an object of that class, if the method or attribute is not hidden.*

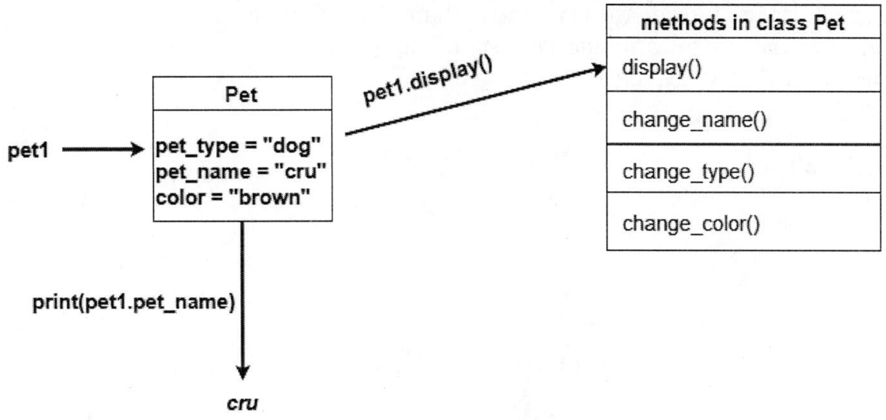

Figure 7.3 Accessing attribute *pet_name* and method *display()* using object, *pet1* dot operator.

Now what if we need to store data for a different pet? The statement `pet2 = Pet()` creates another object named `pet2`. At this stage, `pet2` holds the same data as stored in the object `pet1`. The statements:

```
pet2.change_type("cat")
pet2.change_name("norris")
```

change these values of `pet_type` to `"cat"` and `pet_name` to `"norris"`, by calling the respective methods as shown in Figure 7.4. The change in the object is reflected by the output.

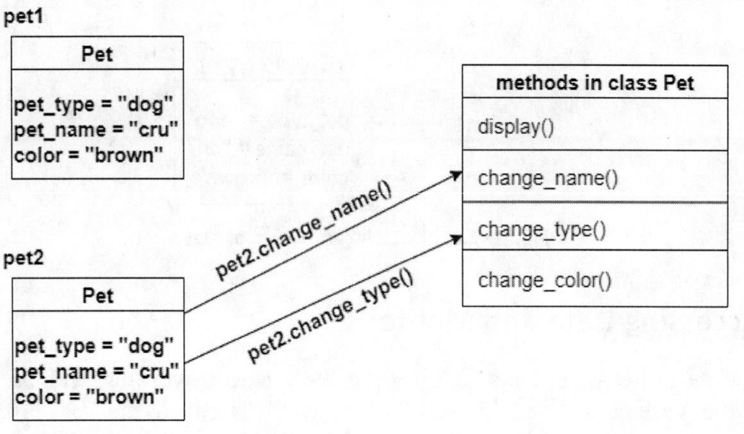

Figure 7.4 New object *pet2*, accessing methods using it.

7.2.5 self

A point to be observed in the above example is the parameter named `self` in the methods of `class Pet`. This variable holds a reference to the calling object. And that is why all values of the attributes used inside the class method are those represented by the calling object. Inside the class methods, if an attribute corresponding to the calling object needs to be used, it is preceded by `self`, as depicted in the Figure 7.5.

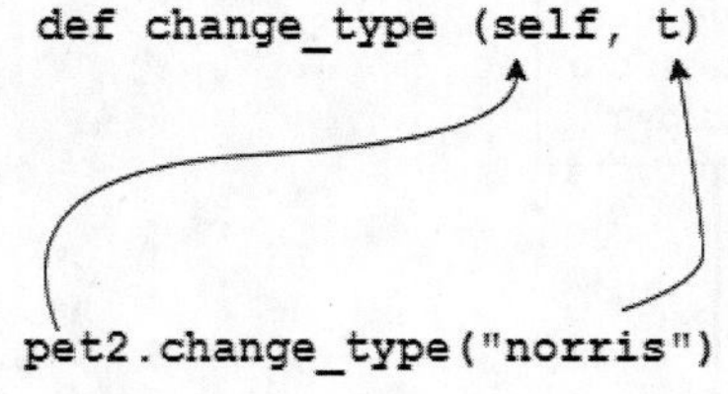

Figure 7.5 Object reference as *self* parameter.

It must also be noted that `self` is not a keyword, hence, the programmer may give any other name to this parameter holding the reference to the calling object. However, this should always be the first parameter in the class method. If this parameter is not specified, an error will occur as shown in Program 7.2.

Program 7.2 Program to demonstrate the use of self parameter

```
class A:

    def __init__(self, num):
        self.num = num

    def increment(x):
        self.num = self.num+x

ob = A(57)
ob.increment(23)
```

The output of Program 7.2 is shown below:

```
Traceback (most recent call last):
File "C:/Users/Hp/Desktop/Samples/Chapter8/self.py", line 11, in <module>
  ob.increment(23)
TypeError: increment() takes 1 positional argument but 2 were given
```

The error says that the signature of `increment()` method mentions only 1 parameter, but at the time of call, 2 arguments were given. Note that, one argument is the number *23* and the second argument is the reference of the object `ob`. Although we never pass it explicitly as an argument, yet internally it is passed to the method.

7.3 SPECIAL FEATURES OF A CLASS

7.3.1 Constructor (_init_)

The `Pet` class defined earlier is syntactically correct. It fulfills the desired purpose. However, it might be said that the functioning of the class is not practical enough. If the user wished to store information about a hamster named Abc, having color black, it does not make much sense to first let the object be a dog named Cru, having color brown and then updating the features. The values that the variables associated with an object will hold, should be decided when the object is created, or constructed. For this purpose, we use a special method called a *constructor*.

A constructor is a special type of method that is called automatically when an object of a class is created. It may or may not have parameters. However, it will definitely have the *self* parameter. A constructor does not have a return type. Unlike other programming languages, in Python, the name of the constructor is the same for every user-defined class, irrespective of the class name. A constructor in Python is named as `__init__` (the word init, preceded and succeeded by double underscores). As the name suggests, when this method is executed, it initializes all attributes. The variables can be initialized to any default value. Let us see a simple example.

Program 7.3: Program to demonstrate a constructor

```
class Fraction:

    def __init__(self):
        self.numer = 0
        self.denom = 1

    def display(self):
        print("The fraction is =", self.numer, "/", self.denom)

f1 = Fraction()
f1.display()
```

Consider class Fraction, which has two variables, `numer` and `denom`. Suppose we want to set default values of `numer` to 0 and `denom` to 1. The corresponding statements for this are mentioned in the `__init__()` method. The above code will display the fraction as **0/1**. One may add other methods to this class to set some user defined values for numerator and denominator. Another way of setting the numerator and denominator to some user defined values is depicted in Program 7.4.

Program 7.4: Program to demonstrate constructor with arguments

```
class Fraction:

    def __init__(self, numer, denom):
        self.numer = numer
        self.denom = denom

    def display(self):
        print("Fraction is =", self.numer, "/", self.denom)

n = int(input("Enter numerator :"))
d = int(input("Enter denominator :"))
f2 = Fraction(n,d)
f2.display()
```

In this approach, we add two additional arguments to the `__init__()` method. The values for numerator and denominator are taken as user input and are passed to the constructor when the object is instantiated. The output of Program 7.4 is shown below.

```
Enter numerator :6
Enter denominator :28
Fraction is = 6 / 28
```

At this point, the reader is encouraged to modify this constructor to accommodate the situation where a fraction is to be created without any user defined values, i.e., the fraction is to be initialized with some default values of numerator and denominator.

7.3.2 Destructor (__del__)

Up till now, it has been established that a constructor is called when an object of a class is created. The purpose of a constructor is to appropriately initialize the attributes with either default or user defined values. This object occupies some memory. Once an object has been used, or when the program is ending, the object is deleted and that is when a *destructor* is called.

A *destructor* is a special method that is called when the object is to be destroyed and the memory occupied by it is freed. Destructors in Python have a special name : `__del__` (the word del preceded and succeeded by double underscores). A destructor is either called automatically when the scope of an object has ended; or when an object is explicitly deleted using the `del` keyword. Let us understand this using Program 7.5.

Program 7.5: Program to demonstrate a destructor

```
class Demo:

  def __init__(self):
    print("Inside constructor, object created")

  def __del__(self):
    print("Inside destructor, object destroyed")

def create_objects():
  print("Inside function..")
  d2 = Demo()
  print("Leaving function..")

print()
print("Object 1")
d1 = Demo()
del d1

print()
print("Object 2")
create_objects()
```

The output of Program 7.5 is shown below.

```
Object 1
Inside constructor, object created
Inside destructor, object destroyed

Object 2
Inside function..
Inside constructor, object created
Leaving function..
Inside destructor, object destroyed
```

Observe here that one object, `d1` was created globally, outside of any scope. The statement `del d1` is used to explicitly delete the object `d1`, even though its scope has not ended yet because its scope is the entire program. The second object, `d2` is created inside a method. So, when the method ends, the object `d2` automatically gets destroyed. The output corresponding to both these scenarios is depicted above. Try removing the statement `del d1`; observe and understand the new output.

7.3.3 __str__ Method

In a previous example, we created a method named `display()` explicitly, to print the fraction. Later, when the fraction is to be printed, that method is called with the class object. Python classes provide a more sophisticated way of displaying the data stored in an object. It is the `__str__` method. It is defined inside the class with the following syntax:

```
def __str__(self):
    #return <details about the object, that need to be displayed>
```

When using it in a program it is invoked in 2 possible ways:

```
1. print(str(<class_object_name>))
2. print(<class_object_name>.__str__())
```

Let us modify the `Fraction` class slightly to include this feature.

Program 7.6: Program to demonstrate the use of __str__ method

```
class Fraction:

    def __init__(self, numer, denom):
        self.numer = numer
        self.denom = denom

    def __str__(self):
        return "The fraction is = " + str(self.numer) + "/" + str(self.denom)

print("Fraction :")
f2 = Fraction(4, 9)
print(str(f2))
```

The output of Program 7.6 is shown below:

```
Fraction :
The fraction is = 4/9
```

Program 7.7: Modify the Fraction class to include the following functionalities:

- Convert a fraction to mixed fraction if needed
- To perform the addition of 2 fractions.

```
class Fraction:
    '''
    This class works with fractions. It has 3 attributes - numerator,
    denominator and the whole number. It has a constructor, an
    __str__method, a method to convert fraction to mixed form and
    another  method to add 2 fractions.
    '''
    def __init__(self, num, den):
        '''
        parameters - class instance, numerator, denominator purpose
        - Initializes the attributes, and checks if the fraction is
        to be converted to mixed form
        '''
        assert den>0, "Denominator should be non zero"

        self.num = num
        self.den = den
        self.wh = 0
        if self.num>self.den:
            self.mixed()

    def __str__(self):
        '''
        Returns a string displaying the fraction
        '''
        if self.wh!=0:
            return "The mixed fraction is {} ({}/{})".format(self.wh,
            self.num, self.den)
        else:
            return "The fraction is {}/{}".format(self.num, self.den)

    def mixed(self):
        '''
        converts fraction to its mixed form
        '''
        self.wh = self.num//self.den
        temp = self.num%self.den
        self.num = temp

    def addition(self, f2):
        '''
        parameters - class instance, fraction object
        purpose - adds the two fractions
        return value - a new fraction object
        '''
```

```
        denom = self.den * f2.den
        numer = self.num*f2.den + f2.num*self.den
        result = Fraction(numer, denom)
        return result
f1 = Fraction(3, 4)
print("F1 : ", f1)

f2 = Fraction(14, 8)
print("F2 : ", f2)

r = f1.addition(f2)
print("F1 + F2 = ", r)
```

The output of Program 7.7 is shown below.

```
F1 : The fraction is 3/4
F2 : The mixed fraction is 1 (6/8)
F1 + F2 = The mixed fraction is 1 (16/32)
```

7.4 DATA HIDING

Data Hiding is the process of making certain attributes and methods in the class as "private" or "hidden". It is used to prevent any unintended or malicious access to the data. On the basis of whatever has been learnt till now, any attribute or method in the class may be accessed using an object instance of that class. In order to avoid any accidental modification to the attribute values, that particular data member may be made *hidden.*

- The hidden members of a class can only be accessed from within the class methods.
- *Hidden class members cannot be accessed using an object from outside the class.*
- To make a data member hidden, its name should be preceded with a pair of underscores. (Ex. `self.__age=5`)
- To make a method hidden, its name should be preceded with a pair of underscores. (Ex. `def __showdata(self)`)

Let us see an example depicting hiding of data.

Program 7.8: Program to depict hidden data

```
class HidingDemo:

    def __init__(self, a, b):
        self.__a = a
        self.b = b

    def set_a(self, value):
        self.__a=value

    def get_a(self):
        return self.__a
```

```
obj1 = HidingDemo(15, 45)
print("Value of b = ", obj1.b)
obj1.b += 20
print("New value of b = ", obj1.b)

#print(obj1.a)

print("Value of a = ", obj1.get_a())
obj1.set_a(38)
print("New value of a = ", obj1.get_a())
```

Note that the class `HidingDemo` has 2 data members, `a` and `b`. While `a` is hidden and represented as `self.__a`, `b` is not. When an object is created, `a` gets the value 15 and `b` is assigned 45. The next statement tries to access `b` from outside the class using the dot operator and the object, and the statement executes successfully. In the following statement, the value of `b` is appropriately incremented, and then again displayed.

If the commented statement is executed, the following error occurs. Since the attribute `a` is hidden inside the class, an attempt to access it outside leads to this error.

```
Value of b = 45
New value of b = 65
Traceback (most recent call last):
  File "c:/Users/Hp/Desktop/Samples/Chapter8/data_hiding.py", line 19,
in <module>
    print(obj1.a)
AttributeError: 'HidingDemo' object has no attribute 'a'
```

The subsequent set of statements attempt to access and modify the values of attribute `a` by calling the methods defined for the same purpose. These `get` and `set` methods are commonly called - *getter - setter* or *accessor - mutator*. The output of Program 7.8 is as follows:

```
Value of b = 45
New value of b = 65
Value of a = 15
New value of a = 38
```

Note that methods inside the class may also be hidden. However, this should be done carefully keeping in mind that if hidden, they cannot be accessed from outside the class.

Program 7.9: Create class Student having attributes as name, age, roll number and marks in 3 subjects. Add a method *compute()* that computes and returns the average marks and the highest marks scored by the student and make this method hidden. Add an `__str__` method to display the details, thi method should invoke *compute()*. Also add a constructor. Of all the data in this class, only the roll number of students should be accessible outside, rest should be hidden.

```
class Student:
   def __init__(self, roll, n, a, marks):
      self.rollno = roll
      self.__name = n
      self.__age = a
      self.__marks = marks

   def __str__(self):
      r = self.__compute()
      av = r[0]
      hi = r[1]
      return "Student Name\t:{}\nRoll Number\t:{}\nAge\
      t\t:{}\nMarks\t\t:{}\nAverage\t\t:{}\nHighest\t\t:{}".
      format(self.__name, self.rollno, self.__age, self.__marks,
      av, hi)

   def __compute(self):
      return round(sum(self.__marks)/3,2), max(self.__marks)

rollno = int(input("Enter student's roll number : "))
sname = input("Enter name of student : ")
age = int(input("Enter age of student : "))
m = []
print("Enter marks in 3 subjects : ")
for i in range(3):
   t = float(input())
   m.append(t)
s1 = Student(rollno, sname, age, m)
print(s1)
```

The output of Program 7.9 is shown below.

```
Enter student's roll number : 42
Enter name of student : shaheen
Enter age of student : 16
Enter marks in 3 subjects :
88.75
91.5
89.5
Student Name  : shaheen
Roll Number   : 42
Age           : 16
Marks         : [88.75, 91.5, 89.5]
Average       : 89.92
Highest       : 91.5
```

7.5 STATIC ATTRIBUTES AND METHODS

7.5.1 Static Attributes

We have studied till now about the data and methods in a class, how to use them and hide them. In all the examples covered till now, we have seen that each instance of a class holds its own copy of the data, which means, changing the value of an attribute for one object will not impact the value of that attribute for the other object(s). However, there exists a concept in classes where some data is shared among all class objects, i.e., if any changes are made globally to that data, they will be visible in each object. The attributes defined in a class which are shared by all instances of the class are known as *static attributes* or *class variables.* Figure 7.6 depicts the above concepts.

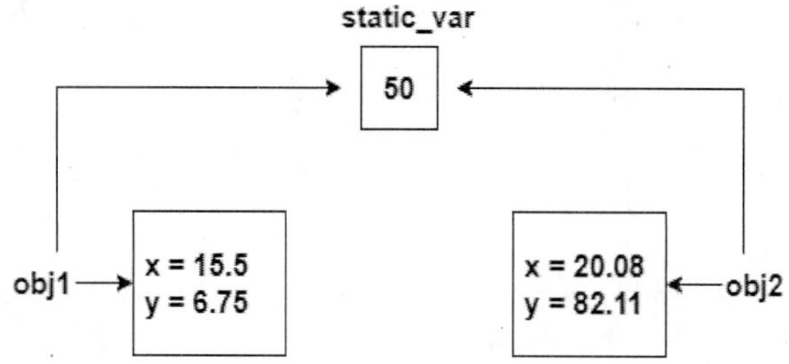

Figure 7.6 Class variable shared among all objects of the same class.

Unlike other programming languages such as C++ or Java, Python does not require the keyword *static* to precede the attribute name in the class definition. In order to make a variable static, it is defined inside the class, but outside any method, even outside a constructor as shown in the code below:

```
class StaticDemo:
    static_var = 0
    def __init__(self, x, y):
        self.x = x
        self.y = y
```

Note that here, the attribute `static_var` is a static variable or class variable and is not restricted to any particular object. Instead, it is associated with the class. On the other hand, the attributes `x` and `y` are instance variables as they are used only by the reference of an object/instance.

In order to use a static variable, its name must be preceded with the class name and the dot operator. Program 7.10 briefly explains the usage of a static variable.

Program 7.10 Program to demonstrate the use of static variable

```
class StaticDemo:
    static_var = 0

    def __init__(self, x, y):
        self.x = x
        self.y = y
```

```
    def __str__(self):
        return "x = " + str(self.x) + "\ny = " + str(self.y)

obj1 = StaticDemo(4.5, 19.25)
print("Object 1", obj1, sep="\n")

obj2 = StaticDemo(35, 103.4)
print("Object 2", obj2, sep="\n")

print("Static variable = ", StaticDemo.static_var)

#modifying static variable
StaticDemo.static_var += 50
print("After modification...")
print("Static variable = ", StaticDemo.static_var)

#accessing static variable using object
print("Static variable using 1st object = ", obj1.static_var)
print("Static variable using 2nd object = ", obj2.static_var)
```

In this class named `StaticDemo`, there is 1 static variable, 2 instance variables and 2 methods - `__init__()` and `__str__()`. Two objects of this class are created, both having different attribute values. Observe that whether inside a method or outside the class, the instance variables are accessed only using an object. Next, we access the static variable outside the class by prepending the name of the class and dot operator (`StaticDemo.static_var`). Using the same syntax, we increment `static_var` by 50 and display its value.

The following 2 statements attempt to access `static_var` using the objects and both yield the same value. Although this is syntactically correct, in practice one should not access static variables using object instances as they are bound to the class and not with a particular object. The output of Program 7.10 is shown below:

```
Object 1
x = 4.5
y = 19.25
Object 2
x = 35
y = 103.4
Static variable = 0
After modification...
Static variable = 50
Static variable using 1st object = 50
Static variable using 2nd object = 50
```

7.5.2 Static Methods

On similar lines, the methods defined inside a class also work on specific instances. This is ascertained by the fact that the first parameter in the parameter list of methods is a variable referencing the calling object or instance. Hence, the methods we have seen till now are known as *instance methods.* The methods that are associated with the class, but not to any objects are known as *static methods.* They serve a purpose associated with the class (the entity) however, they are not performing any instance specific tasks.

Since these methods are not restricted to be working with an object, they do not have the self parameter, i.e., the object reference usually passed to other class methods is not passed to a static method. In order to make a method static the `@staticmethod` function decorator is added right above the function definition. It guides the interpreter to make the following method static. The syntax is as follows:

```
@staticmethod
def getS():
    returns
```

Similar to static attributes, accessing a static method does not require using an object. Since it is bound to the class, it is accessed using the class name only. Say, the above method belongs to the class `StaticDemo`, then it is called like `StaticDemo.getS()`. Observe the absence of self parameter here. Note that a class may have any number of static attributes and methods as per the application. Let us see an example using both—a static method and a static attribute. Here, we attempt to count the number of objects created of this class. To store the count, we create a static variable and a static method that returns this count.

Program 7.11: Program to demonstrate the use of static variable and static method

```
class StaticDemo:

    countInst = 0
    def __init__(self, n, a):
        StaticDemo.countInst += 1
        self.name = n
        self.age = a

    @staticmethod
    def getCount():
        return StaticDemo.countInst

ob1 = StaticDemo("Abc", 16)
print("Number of objects ... ", StaticDemo.getCount())

ob2 = StaticDemo("Def", 19)
print("Number of objects ... ", StaticDemo.getCount())
```

When an object of a class is created, the first method that gets invoked is `__init__()`. Hence, the count is incremented in that method. So, whenever an instance is created, this static count is incremented by 1. A simple static method is created, which returns the `countInst` variable when invoked. The output of Program 7.11 is shown below:

```
Number of objects . . . 1
Number of objects . . . 2
```

It must be emphasized here that static attributes and static methods are bound to the class and not any specific object. Hence, it is not only a good practice, but it is also more logical *to access or modify a static attribute within a static method only*. Another implementation that one may focus on is that the static variable may also be hidden. Let us see a working example.

Program 7.12: Create class Person having attributes—ID, name, sex, ptype, age. The attribute ptype can have values—'E' (employee), 'S' (Student) and 'O' (Other). Create some objects of this class and maintain a count of each ptype. Add appropriate methods to display details of each person, to display the count of each type and an appropriate constructor.

```
class Person:
   __employee=0
   __student=0
   __others=0

   def __init__(self, pid, n, s, ptype, age):
      assert ptype in "ESO", "Invalid ptype!"
      self.pid = pid
      self.name = n
      self.sex = s
      self.ptype = ptype
      if ptype=="E":
         Person.__employee+=1
         elif ptype=="S":
            Person.__student+=1
         else:
            Person.__others+=1
         self.age = age

   def __str__(self):
      if ptype=="E":
         temp = "employee"
      elif ptype=="S":
         temp = "student"
      else:
         temp = "others"
         return "PID - "+str(self.pid)+"Name - "+self.name+"Sex - "
           +self.sex+"Age - "+str(self.age)+"Ptype - "+temp

   @staticmethod
   def getCounts():
      return Person.__employee, Person.__student, Person.__others

p1 = Person(101, "Alicia", "F", "E", 32)
p2 = Person(102, "Mark", "M", "E", 29)
```

```
p3 = Person(103, "Ray", "F", "E", 36)
p4 = Person(104, "Smith", "M", "S", 15)
p5 = Person(105, "Stevie", "F", "S", 14)
p6 = Person(106, "Alex", "M", "O", 39)

print("Count of Persons : ")
res = Person.getCounts()
print("Employees : ", res[0])
print("Students : ", res[1])
print("Others : ", res[2])
```

The output of Program 7.12 is shown below.

```
Count of Persons :
Employees : 3
Students : 2
Others : 1
```

We would like to highlight at this point that if *n* objects of the same class need to be created, it can be done using a list. The programmer can create a list of objects by taking input for each object. Refer to the following code snippet.

```
n = int(input("Enter number of objects to be created : "))
people = []
for i in range(n):
  print("Enter data for object", i+1, ":")
  Pid = int(input("Enter pid : "))
  Pname = input("Enter name of the person :")
  g = input("Enter gender :")
  a = int(input("Enter age : "))
  people.append(Person(Pid, Pname, g, a))
```

Similarly, data stored like this can be printed by iterating over the list of objects :

```
for i in range(n):
  print(people[i])
```

7.6 REUSING A CLASS

In the beginning of this chapter, it was stated that classes aid reusability. There are many ways to reuse a class that has already been created. One way is to create and use objects in the same program where the class was created. Another way would be to create a class in a separate file and save it as *filename.py*, and then import this to another program and then use it.

Let us create a file named *People.py* and add the code for class `Student` created earlier in *People.py*. Note that just the class definition is to be added in this file.

Now this class can be used in another program, as shown below.

```
from People import Student
s1 = Student(1, "Aarti", 15, [92, 91.5, 90])
print(s1)
```

Note that more class definitions can be added to a single file and can be imported as needed. Another way to use a class is to create its object inside another class as shown in the following program.

Program 7.13: Program to create an object of a class inside another class

```
from People import Student
class CollegeStudent:
    def __init__(self, stu, college_name):
        self.student = stu
        self.cname = college_name

    def display(self):
        print(self.student)
        print("College name : ", self.cname)

cs1 = CollegeStudent(Student(20, "Naman", 16, [80, 85, 89]), "St. Peter's")
cs1.display()
```

Note that we imported the pre-existing class `Student`, which stores the student's roll number, name, age and marks. In addition to this, if the application demands to store the college name as well, then instead of modifying the entire student class, the attribute college name can be stored in a new class. Having an object of a class as a data member within another class, is known as *composition*. In order to create its object, the `Student` class was first imported, and then all the methods and attributes accessible using a `Student` object can be accessed from here. Thus, in the `display()` method of class `CollegeStudent`, the statement `print(self.student)` invokes the `__str__()` method of `Student` class. The output of Program 7.13 is:

```
Student Name   : Naman
Roll Number    : 20
Age            : 16
Marks          : [80, 85, 89]
Average        : 84.67
Highest        : 89
College name   : St. Peter's
```

SUMMARY

- A class is a blueprint or template which creates a user defined data type. It contains some data, known as attributes and functions, known as methods.
- Classes are a way to implement real world entities. The use of classes and some of its properties is known as Object-oriented Programming.
- Objects of a class are its instances. They are variables of the type of the class.
- Every object has its own copy of the attributes of class.
- The data and methods of a class are accessed using the object and dot operator.
- Every method defined inside a class must have the first parameter as a reference to the calling object. This parameter is generally known as *self*, however, it can have any other valid variable name.
- `__init__()` method is known as the constructor. This method is invoked automatically when an object is created. It is used to initialize all data members of the class associated with the object.
- `__del__()` is the destructor method. It is invoked when an object is either explicitly deleted, or if its scope ends.
- The `__str__()` method returns a string describing the calling object.
- Data and methods in a class may be hidden from outside access, i.e., it is possible to restrict an object to access some data and methods. This is done by prepending the data variable or method name by __ (double underscore).
- A static attribute or class variable is a variable defined within the class, but outside the init method. All objects of the class share the same copy of the static variable.
- A static method is bound not to specific objects, but with the class. They do not do a task specific to any object. However, their purpose is linked to the entity represented by the class.
- Both, static method and static attribute are accessed by prepending the name of the class and a dot operator.
- A class can be defined and kept in a separate file and used in another program by importing it.
- One class may have the object of another class as its data member. This is known as *composition.*

EXERCISES

7.1 Define constructor and its properties. Can a class have multiple constructors? Why?

7.2 Differentiate between instance variables and class variables.

7.3 What is the first parameter in a class method?

7.4 How are static attributes and methods accessed?

7.5 Create a `class Polygon`. Add attributes to store the `name of the polygon`, `number of sides` and `the length of all sides`. Add methods to return the shortest side, to compute the perimeter of the polygon. Assign the name of the variable based on the number of sides. Display the name of the polygon and sides in the overridden `__str__` method.

7.6 Modify the `class Fraction` to perform functions like subtraction, multiplication and division. Also add a method to convert the fraction to its lowest form.

7.7 Modify the `class Student` to also store the grade of each student. If average marks are > 90, assign 'A+' grade, else if marks are in the range 75 to 80 then 'A' grade and so on. The grade should be hidden and accessible only from within a function. The method to compute grades should also be hidden and must not be accessible by an outside object.

7.8 Create a `class Interest`. It should have attributes to hold `PersonID`, `PersonName`, `Principal` and `Time`. Also store the type of interest - 'c' for compound and 's' for simple interest. It should be entered by the user. The rate of interest is 2.5% and 3% per annum for simple and compound interest respectively. Add methods to compute simple or compound interest based on the user's choice. Also calculate the amount payable by the end of the time period. Ensure that all attributes are hidden from outside access. Use getter and setter methods to access data.

7.9 Spot the error(s) or find the output of the following code snippets.

(a)

```
class Demo:

    def __init__(self, n, a):
        __pname = n
        __age = a

    def display(self):
        print(self.__pname, "\t", self.__age)

d = Demo("abc", 5)
d.display()
print(d.pname)
```

(b)

```
class S:
    __c = 0

    def __init__(self):
        self.x = 1.8
        self.y = 0.6
        S.__c += 1

    @staticmethod
    def getC():
        return S.__c

o1 = S()
print(S.getC())
o2 = S()
print(S.getC())
```

(c)

```
class Temp:

  s = "hello"

  def __init__(obj):
    obj.x = 50
    obj.y = "xyz"

  def __str__(obj):
    return "x = "+str(obj.x)+"\ty = "+obj.y

t1 = Temp()
print(str(t1))
print(Temp.s)
print(t1.s)

t2 = Temp()
t1.s = "world"

print(t1.s)
print(t2.s)
print(Temp.s)
```

(d)

```
class Try:

  def __init__(self, objname):
    self.obj = objname
    print("Hi", self.obj, sep=" : ")

  def __del__(self):
    print("Bye-Bye", self.obj, sep=" : ")

def func():
  t = Try("t")

t1 = Try("t1")
func()
del t1
```

8

More About Classes

In the previous chapter, we learnt about the basic structure of a class. It embodies some data and methods corresponding to a real world entity. It was also mentioned that classes implement Object-oriented Programming in Python. The Object-oriented Programming paradigm considers data as an object. A class is a blueprint containing the features and methods of that object. Object-oriented Programming concepts (OOPs) are a set of concepts associated with programming. In this chapter we aim to cover these concepts, their details and their use with classes.

8.1 ABSTRACTION AND ENCAPSULATION

The word *abstract* means something that exists but cannot be seen. In the context of classes, abstraction means hiding of unnecessary details from the user. In order to provide a better separation among the user and the program, classes provide abstraction by hiding the implementation details from the user. It is just the constructors, methods, etc. which can be accessed using the class object and hence, a user can perform the desired task.

Although the details are hidden, yet the user is able to perform any desired task. This happens because the class object is a variable whose data type is the corresponding class. Using the associated methods, any application can make use of class functionalities. Hence, classes are also known as *Abstract Data Types* (*ADT*). This property helps to implement different data structures used in some trivial computer algorithms.

In a class, data of various types and methods associated with a real world object come together as a single data type. The property of combining data and methods under one named entity is known as *encapsulation*. Encapsulation is closely knit with abstraction in the sense that only when data and methods are encapsulated, their implementation details, i.e., how they are interacting and interfacing, are hidden from the end user.

8.2 INHERITANCE

The ability of a class to be able to derive the attributes and functions of an existing class is known as *inheritance*. The class which derives these functionalities is called the *child* or *derived* class and the class from which this class inherits the properties is called *parent* or *base* class.

The concept of inheritance is very useful in OOPs. One of the major advantages of using classes is the reusability of code, as the same class can be used to store data for similar objects, and can even be imported to various other programs. Inheritance aids reusability by allowing *child* class to reuse information and attributes of parent class.

8.2.1 Parent–Child Class Relationship

As mentioned earlier, inheritance involves a relationship between two classes, wherein one class inherits or receives the attributes and methods of another class. The class which inherits from another class is called the *child* class or *derived* class or *subclass*. The class from which the child class inherits, is called the *parent* class or *base* class or *superclass*. The syntax of implementing inheritance is as follows:

```
class Parent:
  #data and methods of Parent class

class Child(Parent):
  #this Child class has inherited from
  #the class named Parent
  #It might have some data and methods of its own
```

Consider the `Person` class example discussed in the previous chapter. There we created an attribute—`person_type` which denoted if the `Person` is an employee or student. However, the concept of inheritance makes the implementation of this example easy and clear. It is understandable that `Employee` and `Student` are both special cases of `Person` class, in the sense that they use the existing attributes of class `Person` - `name`, `age`, etc. and could also have their own attributes such as `Salary` for `Employee` and `Marks` for `Student`. The child class is also known as a *specialization* of the parent class for this reason and the parent class is known as the *generalization*. Figure 8.1 depicts the Parent class and Child class relationship.

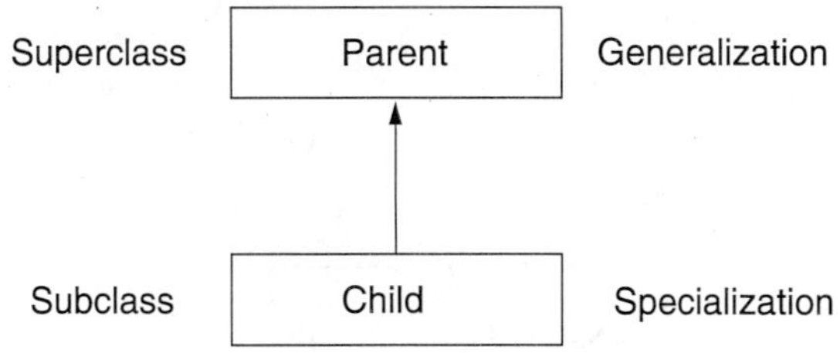

Figure 8.1 Parent-child class relationship.

In order to understand the working of inheritance, consider Program 8.1.

Program 8.1: Program to demonstrate inheritance

```
class A:
    def __init__(self, x):
        self.ax = x
        print("In class A constructor..")

    def __str__(self):
        return "ax = "+str(self.ax)


class B(A):
    def __init__(self,x,y):
        self.by = y
        print("In class B constructor..")

    def __str__(self):
        return "by = "+str(self.by)

    def show(self):
        print("In class B")
        #print("ax = ", self.ax)
        print("by = ", self.by)

obja = A(45)
print(obja)

objb = B(77.75)
print(objb)
objb.show()
```

The output of Program 8.1 is shown below:

```
In Class A Constructor..
ax = 45
In Class B Constructor..
by = 77.75
In Class B
by = 77.75
```

However, once we remove the comment from the statement `print("ax = ", self.ax)`, the following error pops up.

```
In class A constructor ..
ax = 45
In class B constructor ..
by = 77.75
In class B
Traceback (most recent call last):
  File "c:/Users/Hp/Desktop/Samples/ch8_exl.py", line 32, in <module>
    objb.show()
  File "c:/Users/Hp/Desktop/Samples/ch8_exl.py", line 24, in show
    print("ax = ", self.ax)
AttributeError: 'B' object has no attribute 'ax'
```

This is because, in the scope of object `objb`, the attribute `ax` was never initialized. So even though the syntax has made class B a subclass of class A, the purpose of inheritance is still unfulfilled. Section 8.2.2 covers the solution to this.

8.2.2 Subclassing and `super()`

In the example above, the *child* class has extended or inherited the *parent* class and all its accessible data and methods. However, we did not use any *parent* class attribute inside the *child* class yet. Logically, it makes sense that when we create a *child* class object, we also initialize the attributes it has inherited from the *parent*. The following Program 8.2 is a modified version of Program 8.1 which shows how attributes of the *parent* class will be initialized using an object of *child* class.

Program 8.2: Program to demonstrate initializing the attributes of the parent class

```
class A:

    def __init__(self, x):
        self.ax = x
        print("In class A constructor..")

    def __str__(self):
        return "ax = "+str(self.ax)

class B(A):

    def __init__(self, x, y):
        self.by = y
        print("In class B constructor..")
        super().__init__(x)

    def __str__(self):
        return "by = "+str(self.by)

    def show(self):
        print("In class B")
        print("ax = ", self.ax)
        print("by = ", self.by)
```

```
obja = A(45)
print(obja)
print("End parent object")
print("\nCreating child object...")
objb = B(77.75)
print(objb)
objb.show()
```

The statement `super().__init__()` inside the constructor of the *child* class invokes the constructor of the *parent* class. If the constructor is parameterised, the arguments needed by the parent class constructor are passed in this statement - `super().__init__(x)`. *Note that while using this syntax, the self parameter isn't passed.* The same task can also be done by the statement `<ParentClassName>.__init__(<arguments>)`. This process of invoking parent class constructor from the child class is known as *subclassing*. Figure 8.2 demonstrates subclassing.

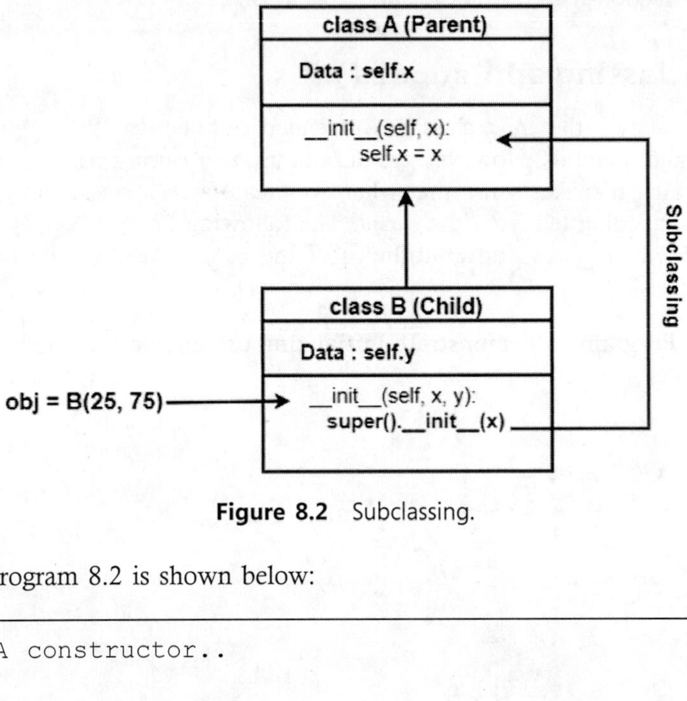

Figure 8.2 Subclassing.

The output of Program 8.2 is shown below:

```
In class A constructor..
ax = 45
End parent object

Creating child object...
In class B constructor..
In class A constructor..
by = 77.75
In class B
ax = 14.25
by = 77.75
```

Observe that objects of class A (parent) will be created in the same way as they would have been without A being the parent class. However, the signature of the constructor for child class B, has now changed. It now needs a value for x as well, which will be passed to the parent class constructor. Also note that now when a reference is made to attribute ax using an object of child class B, there is no error and it gets displayed. Some more cases of scope and access rules are covered in the subsequent section.

8.2.3 Scope and Access Rules for Single Inheritance

The form of inheritance where a one child class extends one parent class, is known as *single inheritance.* There exist other forms of inheritance as well and in each, there are different rules of scope and access. One of the main purposes of object-oriented programming is to implement real world entities and the relationships among them. Hence, one must be careful about the data and methods associated with the entities while modeling relationships between them.

One rule of access is that the hidden attributes and methods of the parent class are not accessible by the child class object as well. Let us see an example.

Program 8.3: Program to demonstrate accessing hidden attributes

```
class Parent:

    def __init__(self, x, y):
        self.__x = x
        self.y = y

    def __str__(self):
        return "x="+str(self.__x)+"\ny="+str(self.y)

class Child(Parent):

    def __init__(self, x, y, z):
        self.z = z
        super().__init__(x,y)

    def __str__(self):
        return "x="+str(self.__x)+"\ny="+str(self.y)+"\nz="+str(self.z)

c = Child(20, 40, 60)
print(c)
```

Here, the parent class has a hidden attribute, x. The child class constructor sends a value of 20 to x. However, it is not possible to access variable x using the child class object. Thus, the execution of this code results in an error as shown below:

```
Traceback (most recent call last):
  File "c:/Users/Hp/Desktop/Samples/ch8_ex2.py", line 21, in <module>
    print(c)
File "c:/Users/Hp/Desktop/Samples/ch8_ex2.py", line 18, in _str_
    return "x="+str(self._x)+"\ny="+str(self.y)+"\nz="+str(self.z)
AttributeError: 'Child' object has no attribute '_Child_x'
```

The only way by which a hidden attribute of the parent class can be accessed in a child class is by using the *getter-setter* methods. If the parent class has appropriate, non-hidden *get* and *set* methods corresponding to every hidden attribute, then the child class can access the hidden values using these methods. It is illustrated in the next example.

Program 8.4: Program to demonstrate hidden attributes using get and set methods

```
class Parent:

    def __init__(self, x, y):
        self.__x = x
        self.y = y

    def __str__(self):
        return "x="+str(self.__x)+"\ny="+str(self.y)

    def getx(self):
        return self.__x

    def setx(self, a):
        self.__x = a

class Child(Parent):

    def __init__(self, x, y, z):
        self.z = z
        super().__init__(x,y)

    def __str__(self):
        return "x="+str(self.getx())+"\ny="+str(self.y)+"\nz="+str(self.z)

c = Child(20, 40, 60)
print(c)
c.setx(100)
print("\nAfter modifying value of x :")
print(c)
```

We have modified the previous code to add methods `getx()` and `setx()` in the Parent class. Now instead of accessing variable x as `self.__x`, the child class gets its value by `self.getx()`. An object of the child class may also modify the value of x by using the `setx()` method. The output of Program 8.4 is as follows.

```
x=20
y=40
z=60

After modifyinq value of x :
x=100
y=40
z=60
```

8.2.4 Method Overriding

Method overriding is a very common phenomenon in inheritance. If there is a method in the child class which has the same signature as the method in the parent class, but the child class method is doing some different or additional work, the child class method is said to *override* the parent class method. This process is known as *method overriding*. As a result of method overriding, when an object of child class invokes such a method, the child class copy of that method is invoked, not the parent class copy. The Program 8.5 illustrates this.

Program 8.5: Program to demonstrate method overriding

```
class Parent:

    def __init__(self, x, y):
        self.__x = x
        self.y = y

    def __str__(self):
        return "x="+str(self.__x)+"\ny="+str(self.y)

    def getx(self):
        return self.__x

    def setx(self, a):
        self.__x = a

    def hello(self):
        print("In parent class...")

    def bye(self):
        print("Parent class Bye method...")


class Child(Parent):

    def __init__(self, x, y, z):
        self.z = z
        super().__init__(x,y)

    def __str__(self):
        return "z="+str(self.z)

    def hello(self):
        print("In child class...")

c = Child(20, 40, 60)
print(c)   #invokes __str__ from child class
c.hello() #invokes hello() from child class
c.bye()    #invokes bye() from parent class
```

The output of Program 8.5 is shown below.

```
z = 60
In child class ...
Parent class Bye method ...
```

Note that the child class overrides two methods of the parent class - the `__str__()` and `hello()` methods. Observe the following points with reference to the above example when an object of child class is created:

- When the statement `print(c)` executes, it invokes the `__str__()` method from Child class, not the parent one.
- Similar process happens when the `hello()` method is invoked.
- However, observe that the `bye()` method exists only in the parent class. Hence, when the statement `c.bye()` executes, it calls the `bye()` method from the parent class. This method is not overridden.

Let us try to understand another fact associated with method overriding. Suppose a method, say `hello()` exists in the parent class and it takes an integer as an argument. Its child class defines method `hello()` with no argument. What happens if `hello()` is invoked with an instance of the child class?

Program 8.6: Program to demonstrate method overriding with variable arguments

```
class Parent:

    def __init__(self, x, y):
        self.__x = x
        self.y = y

    def hello(self, number):
        print("In parent class...")
        print("Number = ", number)

class Child(Parent):

    def __init__(self, x, y, z):
        self.z = z
        super().__init__(x,y)

    def hello(self):
        print("In child class...")

c = Child(20, 40, 60)
c.hello()
c.hello(56)
```

The output of Program 8.6 is shown below:

```
In child class ...
Traceback (most recent call last):
  File "C:\Users\Hp\Desktop\Samples\ch8_ex2.py", line 38, in <module>
    c.hello(56)
TypeError: hello() takes 1 positional argument but 2 were given
```

Execution of the above code is terminated due to an error. The statement `c.hello()` yields the expected output. However, when `hello(56)` is called using the child class object, it results in an error. This happens because the child class has no knowledge of any method named `hello()` that takes an argument. It has overridden that method with a new copy of `hello()` that it defined. Notice that similar is the case with the `__init__()` method in both parent and child class. The constructor of the parent class takes 2 arguments. However, constructor of the child class takes 3 arguments. Hence, when an object of child class is created, it requires 3 arguments only. Try creating an object of the child class having 2 arguments, and observe that the error is similar to the one depicted above.

If this is how inheritance works, is there no way to access the parent class method's copy? There definitely is a way. Notice that in the example shown above, the child class constructor accepts arguments for itself, and for the parent class data as well. Next, it invokes the parent class constructor using the `super()` command. The `super()` command gives an option to invoke some method of the superclass or the parent class.

8.2.5 Types of Inheritance

What we have studied till now is known as *single inheritance.* It is the most basic type of inheritance where a child class inherits from exactly one class. However, Python provides different types of inheritance as well. In this section, we aim to cover some of them.

Multiple Inheritance

When the child class can inherit from more than one class as in Figure 8.3, it is known as *multiple inheritance.* In such a case, the accessible data and methods from all the base classes will be inherited by the child class. The syntax to implement multiple inheritance is:

```
class Child (Parent1, Parent2 ,..., ParentN):
    #class body
```

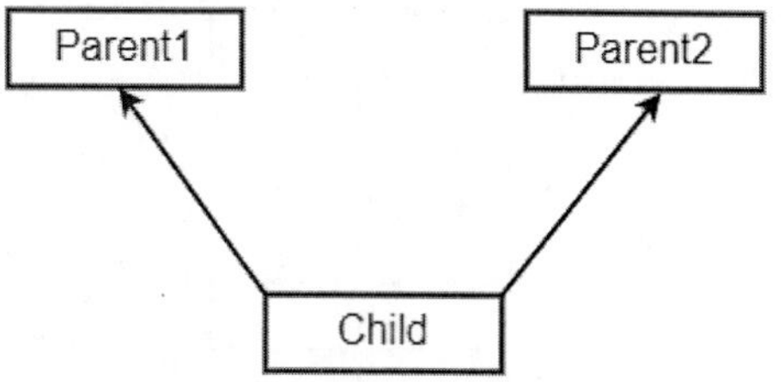

Figure 8.3 Multiple Inheritance.

Program 8.7 Program to demonstrate multiple inheritance

```
class P1:

    def __init__(self):
        print("In class P1")

class P2:

    def __init__(self):
        print("In class P2")

class Child(P1, P2):

    def __init__(self):
        super().__init__()
        print("In class Child")

obj = Child()
```

The output of Program 8.7 is shown below:

```
In class P1
In class Child
```

Here the child class inherits from classes `P1` and `P2`. Take note that the order in which a child inherits multiple classes matters. For instance, `P1` is mentioned first here. So, when a call to the superclass' constructor is made, the constructor of `P1` is invoked. Try mentioning `P2` first and note the change in output.

Multilevel Inheritance

This type of inheritance visualizes the relationship of grandparent, parent and child. In multilevel inheritance, a class is derived from a superclass, which itself is derived from some other class. This relationship is depicted in Figure 8.4.

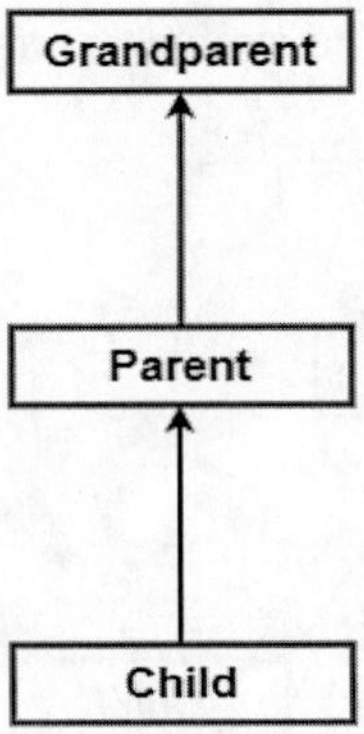

Figure 8.4 Multilevel Inheritance.

The syntax to implement multilevel inheritance is not very different. There is now a chain of parent-child classes.

Program 8.8: Program to demonstrate multilevel inheritance

```
class Grandparent:

  def __init__(self):
    print("This is class Grandparent")

class Parent(Grandparent):

  def __init__(self):
    super().__init__()
    print("This is class Parent")

class Child(Parent):

  def __init__(self):
    super().__init__()
    print("This is class Child")

c = Child()
```

When an object of the child class is created, its constructor is called. Now the constructor in the child class is invoking the constructor of its superclass, which is parent. The parent class constructor is using the `super()` construct to invoke the constructor of its parent class, i.e., grandparent. The `__init__()` method of grandparent prints its statement. Then control goes back to the second statement in the constructor of parent, and the text gets printed. Next, the control goes back to the `__init__()` method of the child class. This flow of execution in Program 8.8 results in the output shown below.

```
This is class Grandparent
This is class Parent
This is class Child
```

Hierarchical Inheritance

When multiple child classes are derived from the same parent class, it is known as *hierarchical* inheritance. Consider the following example to understand the working.

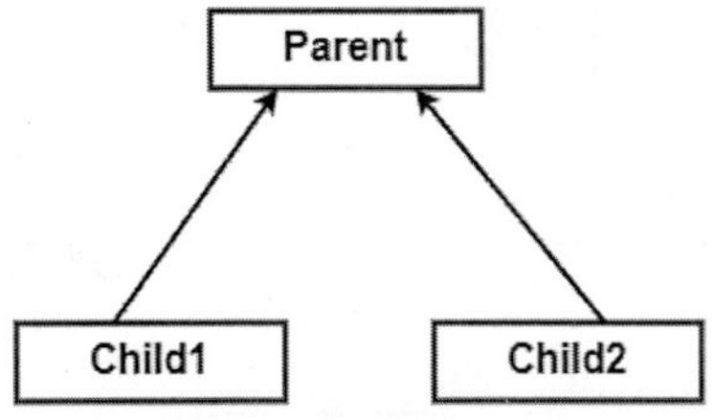

Figure 8.5 Hierarchical inheritance.

Program 8.9: Program to demonstrate hierarchical inheritance

```
class Parent:

    def __init__(self):
        print("\n\nParent Class")

class A(Parent):

    def __init__(self):
        super().__init__()
        print("Child class A")

class B(Parent):

    def __init__(self):
        super().__init__()
        print("Child class B")

ca = A()
cb = B()
```

There is a class Parent in Program 8.9. Class A and class B, both inherit from Parent and hence depict the hierarchical structure of inheritance. The output is shown next.

```
Parent Class
Child class A

Parent Class
Child class B
```

Hybrid Inheritance

A flow of inheritance that combines all—single, multiple, multilevel and hierarchical inheritance, is said to be following *hybrid* inheritance. It combines features of all types of inheritance as shown in Figure 8.6 and hence, gives more flexibility.

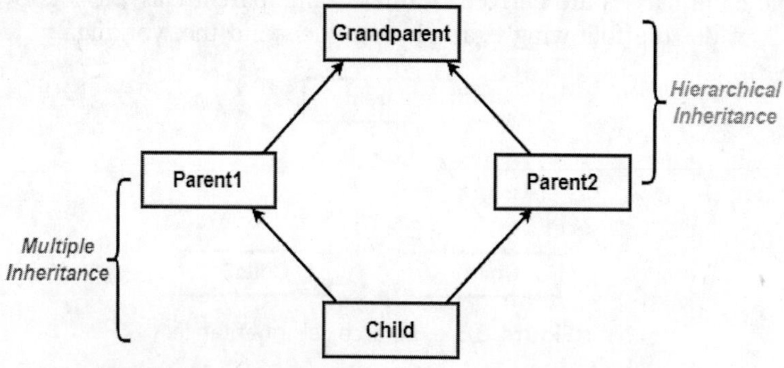

Figure 8.6 A possible structure for Hybrid Inheritance.

8.3 POLYMORPHISM

The word *poly* stands for *many* and the word *morph* stands for *forms*. So literally, the word polymorphism means *taking many forms*. In programming, polymorphism is often used in the context of methods. When functions having the same name but different parameters as per their signature are known as polymorphic functions. It means that when a call to the method is made, the decision as to which method of that name is called depends upon the arguments passed.

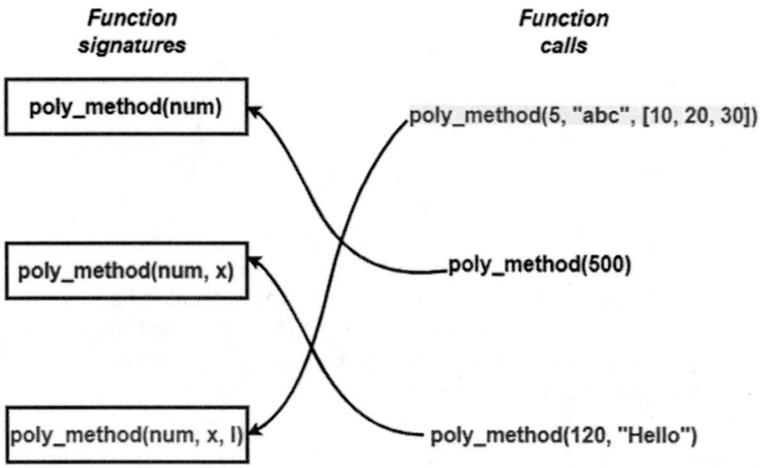

Figure 8.7 Polymorphism depicted via different function signatures and corresponding calls.

8.3.1 Polymorphism in Built-in Functions

While several other programming languages allow creating different functions having the same name but different parameters, Python does not allow the same. Python implements polymorphism using default parameters. It is interesting to note at this point that up till now, we have used polymorphism without explicitly realizing it. Many built-in Python functions implement polymorphism.

Consider the following sequence of Python commands that call the `range()` function.

```
>>> print(list(range(10)))
[0, 1, 2, 3, 4, 5, 6, 7, 8, 9]
>>> print(list(range(4,10)))
[4, 5, 6, 7, 8, 9]
>>> print(list(range(2, 20, 2)))
[2, 4, 6, 8, 10, 12, 14, 16, 18]
```

We know that the `range()` function can take 3 possible arguments—*start, stop* and *step*. If not given, *start* has a default value of 0 and *step* has a default value of 1. So when `range()` is called with just one parameter, it is considered as the *stop* value. If 2 arguments are provided, then `range()` considers the first one as *start* and second as *step*. In order to provide a customized step size, we must provide all the three parameters—*start, stop* and *step*. Only then the appropriate output is obtained. Observe here that the same function name is being used to call `range()` function to do different tasks. This is how polymorphism is implemented in Python.

While the `range()` function uses number of arguments as the basis to distinguish between types of calls, the `len()` function uses the type of argument to distinguish among calls and how it will work. The following commands depict this.

```
>>> len("this is a string")
16
>>> len([12, 15, 88])
3
>>> len(25)
Traceback (most recent call last):
  File "<pyshell#2>", line 1, in <module>
    len(25)
TypeError: object of type 'int' has no len()
```

The first command calls `len()` on a string while the second calls it with a list. The way of counting elements is different for a string and a list. Observe that it gives an error when we try to invoke `len()` with an integer. This happens because `len()` works only with sequence data types and based on its definition and implementation, `len()` function knows how to handle different data types. On similar lines, we can also define a method with default parameters to implement polymorphism.

8.3.2 Polymorphism in Classes

Python does not allow multiple definitions of a method having the same name present in a single class. So one way of doing it, if necessary, is to use default arguments as depicted in Section 8.3.1. Polymorphism is demonstrated in Program 8.10 below:

Program 8.10: Program to demonstrate polymorphism in classes

```
class PolyDemo:

    def __init__(self, name=" ", age=10, state="New Delhi"):
        self.name = name
        self.age = age
        self.state = state

    def incr_age(self, inc=2):
        self.age += inc

    def __str__(self):
        return "\nName : "+self.name+"\tAge :" + str(self.age)+
        "\tState :" + self.state

per1 = PolyDemo("Karan")
print("\nFirst object :")
print(per1)
```

```
per2 = PolyDemo("Rutuja", 29)
print("\nSecond object :")
print(per2)

per3 = PolyDemo()
print("\nThird object :")
print(per3)

print("*****"*10)
per1.incr_age(5)
print("\nFirst object after age increment of 5:")
print(per1)

per3.incr_age()
print("\nThird object after default age increment:")
print(per3)
```

This class has two methods that are implementing polymorphism. First is the constructor, `__init__()` method. All of its parameters are default, which means that an object of this class can be created without any arguments, as is the third object. It is also possible to create objects by giving one or two parameters as done by the first and second object respectively. The second method implementing polymorphism is the `incr_age()` method. The value by which `age` is to be incremented is set to 2 and it will be used if this method is invoked without an argument as object `per3` does. This method can also be invoked with a single argument, as `per1` does, which will be considered as an increment to the `age`. The output of Program 8.10 is shown below:

```
First object :
Name : Karan    Age : 10     State : New Delhi
Second object :
Name : Rutuja   Age : 29     State : New Delhi
Third object :
Name :          Age : 10     State : New Delhi
**************************************************
First object after age increment of 5:
Name : Karan    Age : 15     State : New Delhi
Third object after default age increment:
Name :          Age : 12     State : New Delhi
```

This just demonstrates the case of a single class. But we have studied that classes can have a relation via inheritance. And polymorphism works there too. At this point, the reader must understand that every class that is defined is a subclass to the *object* class in Python. One can check the relationship between various classes and objects using some built-in functions. Some of them are listed below:

- `isinstance(objname, classname)`–returns `True` if the object is an instance of the class, else `False`

```
>>> isinstance(6, object)
True
>>> isinstance("Hello", object)
True
>>> isinstance(25, str)
False
>>> isinstance(int, object)
True
```

- `issubclass(classA, classB)`–returns `True` if `classA` is a subclass of `classB`

```
>>> issubclass(list, object)
True
>>> issubclass(list, str)
False
>>> issubclass(int, object)
True
```

This essentially means, that whenever any class is created it is the child class of the predefined `object` class. This `object` class has certain methods defined in it, including the `__str__()` method. Therefore, even if we do not provide the `__str__()` method in our class, then the `__str__()` method of the parent class, i.e., `object` class is invoked when needed. For example:

```
class Account:

   def __init__(self, ano, n, t):
      self.acno = ano
      self.name = n
      self.atype = t

a1 = Account(123456, "ABC", "savings")
print(str(a1))
```

The output of the above code is given below:

```
<__main__.Account object at 0x000002011E9B2E08>
```

Although the class `Account` does not have an `__str__()` method yet, when we try to print its object, we do get an output that is provided by the `object` class. If an `__str__()` method is defined in the `Account` class, it will override the one provided in the `object` class.

8.3.3 Dynamic Binding and Method Order Resolution

It was seen in the previous section that if the child class does not have a particular method, but the Parent class has it, then the copy of parent class method is invoked. Let us see another example for this.

Program 8.11: Program to demonstrate dynamic binding

```
class Person:

    def __init__(self, name, age):
        self.name = name
        self.age = age

    def __str__(self):
        return "\nName : "+self.name+"\nAge : "+str(self.age)

class Student(Person):

    def __init__(self, sname, sage, inst):
        super().__init__(sname, sage)
        self.inst_name = inst

class Employee(Person):

    def __init__(self, ename, eage, org):
        super().__init__(ename, eage)
        self.org_name = org

    def __str__(self):
        return "\nEmployee's name is "+self.name+". Their age is
        "+str(self.age)+", currently working for "+self.org_name

p1 = Person("Sakshi", 23)
s1 = Student("Akash", 15, "DU")
e1 = Employee("Jayesh", 34, "ABC Inc.")

print(p1)
print(s1)
print(e1)
```

The output of Program 8.11 is shown below.

```
Name : Sakshi
Age : 23

Name : Akash
Age : 15

Employee's name is Jayesh. Their age is 34, currently working for ABC Inc.
```

The first object, `p1`, is an object of `Person` class so `print(p1)` invokes `__str__()` from `Person` class. The third object, `e1` is an object of `Employee` class which is a subclass of `Person` class. The statement `print(e1)` looks for `__str__()` method in the `Employee` class and invokes that. The second object, `s1`, is an object of the `Student` class that inherits `Person` class. The statement `print(s1)` attempts to look for the `__str__()` method in the `Student` class, but that class does not override the `__str__()` method. So, the corresponding method is looked for in the parent class `Person` and the `__str__()` method in `Person` is invoked with an object of `Student` class.

In this situation, the decision of which method corresponding to a particular object will be invoked, is delayed till the statement is executed. This is known as *dynamic binding*. Not only with user defined classes, but also with other built-in objects such as `str`, `list`, etc., dynamic binding is witnessed in the sense that the same variable name can be associated with different data types at later stages of the program. How which operators or functions will act on these objects is decided at runtime, owing to dynamic binding.

In case of classes, the process to find and decide which method is to be invoked corresponding to an object, is known as *Method Order Resolution*. There is an order in which the interpreter looks for the matching method to execute. Suppose that `x` is an object of class `c`, which is a subclass of class `p1`, which is further a subclass of `p2`. When `x` invokes a method, its copy is first searched in `c`, then in `p1` if it is not defined in `c` and in `p2` if it is defined neither in `c` nor in `p1`. This is known as method order resolution. The explanation here corresponds to multilevel inheritance. Method order resolution is different for different types of inheritance as depicted in Figure 8.8.

Figure 8.8(a) shows multilevel inheritance. Assume a statement `c.method()` where `c` is an object of the `Child` class. First, the method is searched for in `Child`, then in `Parent` and then in `Grandparent`. The search stops as soon as the method is found in any of these classes. Figure 8.8(b) shows hierarchical inheritance. The order of method resolution here is direct, as both `Child1` and `Child2` are separate from each other and have the same parent. So whenever

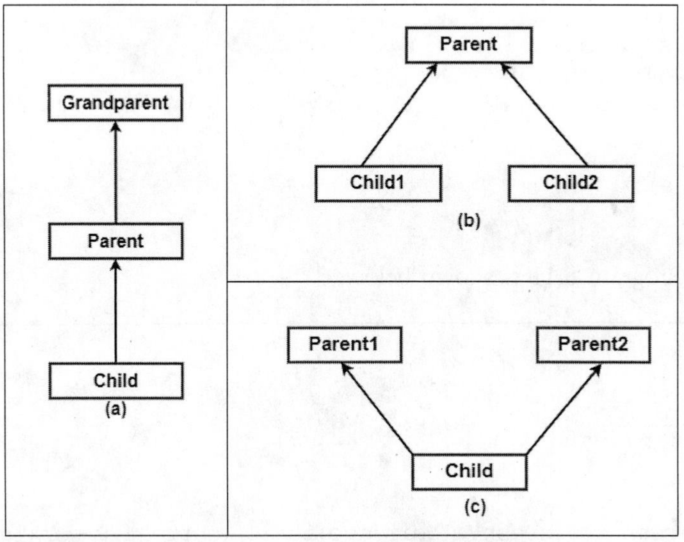

Figure 8.8 Method order resolution in different types of inheritance.

an object of `Child1` is created, and it invokes a method, it is first looked for in `Child1` and then in `Parent`; similarly for `Child2`. Figure 8.8(c) depicts multiple inheritance. Consider a statement `c.method()` where `c` is an object of `Child` class. If the `Child` class was created by writing : `class Child(Parent1, Parent2)`, then the order of resolution is—Child → Parent1 → Parent2. Had the class definition been class `Child(Parent2, Parent1)`, the order of resolution would have been Child → Parent2 → Parent1.

SUMMARY

- The pillars of Object-oriented Programming are: Abstraction, Encapsulation, Inheritance and Polymorphism.
- Abstraction means hiding unnecessary implementation details from the user in order to achieve a better separation.
- Combining methods and data as a single entity inside a class is known as Encapsulation.
- Inheritance allows two classes to establish a Parent-Child like relationship where the child class inherits some data and methods from the parent class.
- Only the non-hidden features of the parent class are inherited by the child class.
- The child class is also known as subclass or specialization whereas the parent class is known as the superclass or generalization.
- A method in the child class can invoke the same method of the parent class by using the `super()` statement.
- Invoking the superclass' constructor from the subclass' constructor is known as subclassing.
- When the child class implements a method having the same name as a method in the parent class, it is said to override the parent class method.
- Inheritance is of several types, including—multiple, multilevel, hierarchical and hybrid.
- Polymorphism is the property that allows a method to be used in different ways based on either the number of arguments or on the basis of the calling object.
- In Python, the same function cannot exist with the same name but different signatures. Hence, polymorphism is implemented using default parameters.
- The decision of which method corresponding to an object is to be invoked, is delayed until runtime. This is known as dynamic binding.
- The order in which the appropriate or matching method is looked for in the classes involved in inheritance, is known as method order resolution.

EXERCISES

8.1 Explain the usage of `super()`.

8.2 Define ADT.

8.3 Multilevel inheritance attempts to implement the grandparent relationship. Which inheritance implements sibling relationship? Explain.

8.4 Find the error in the following programs, and suggest appropriate solutions.

(a)

```
class X:
    def __init__(self, val):
        self.vx = val
class Y(X):
    def __init__(self, val):
        self.vy = val
ob = Y("hello")
print(Y.vy)
print(Y.vx)
```

(b)

```
class Parent:
    def __init__(self, x, y):
        self.__x=x
        self.__y=y

class Child(Parent):
    def __init__(self, x, y, z):
        super().__init__(x,y)
        self.z = z

    def __str__(self):
        return "\nx="+self.x+ "\ny="+ self.y + "\nz=" +self.z
ch_ob = Child(52, 105,100)
```

8.5 Consider the following program. Determine its output and identify the type of inheritance.

```
class A:
    def __init__(self):
        print("A")
class B:
    def __init__(self):
        print("B")
class C(B,A):
    def __init__(self):
        super().__init__()
        print("C")
class D(C):
    def __init__(self):
        super().__init__()
        print("D")
```

```
class E(C):
  def __init__(self):
    super().__init__()
    print("E")
o1 = A()
o2 = C()
o3 = E()
```

8.6 What is the output of the following program:

```
class First:
  def __init__(self, v):
    self.msg = v

  def __str__(self):
    return self.msg
class Second(First):
  def __init__(self, v1, v2):
    super().__init__(v1)
    self.msg2 = v2

  def __str__(self):
    return self.msg+ "   *****  " + self.msg2
f = First("Hello")
print(f)
s = Second("Hello", "World")
print(s)
```

8.7 Would the following program generate an error or give an output? Explain.

```
class Parent:
  def __init__(self, x= "Parent object"):
    self.p = x

  def __str__(self):
    return "Parent class str method" + self.p
class Child(Parent):
  def __init__(self, x, y):
    super().__init__("Child object calling Parent constructor")
    self.c = y

o1 = Parent()
print(o1)
o2 = Parent("New Parent object")
print(o2)
o3 = Child("Parent via Child", "Child")
print(o3)
```

8.8 Consider the following relationship among 5 classes:

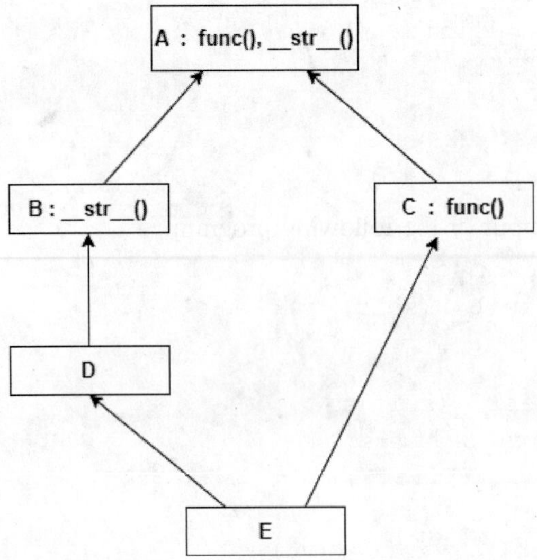

(i) Identify the various types of inheritance relationships involved.

(ii) Assume that `eobj` is an object of `class E`, `cobj` is an object of `class C` and `dobj` is an instance of `class D`. Using Method order resolution, determine which method will be invoked by the following calls: (For `eobj`, consider both possible definitions of `class E`, i.e., `class E(D,C)` and `class E(C,D)` and determine outputs of (a) and (b) for each case)

(a) `eobj.func()`
(b) `print(eobj)`
(c) `print(dobj)`
(d) `print(cobj)`

(iii) Write a program to implement this structure.

8.9 Write a program to implement a `class TwoD` that has 2 hidden data members `x` and `y` which represent the coordinates in plane. Add appropriate constructor, and methods to compute the distance of a point from the origin, length of a line, the difference between lengths of 2 lines, method to check if 2 points lie on a line.

Use this class to create a new `class ThreeD` which has one data member, `z`. Override the methods to compute distance of a 3D point from origin and to check if 2 points lie on the same plane.

8.10 Create a `class Student` having hidden data members—`university enrolment number, name, aadhar card number and course`. Add methods to show the details of the student. Create 2 classes using the `class Student` –`ExStudent` and `CurrentStudent`.

The `class ExStudent` should have data members—`degree certificate number and passing year`. Create a method to print all details of the student given the degree certificate number as an argument.

The `class CurrentStudent` should have data members—`roll number`, `semester` and `attendance in current semester`. Create a method to print all details of the student given the roll number as an argument.

9

Files and Exceptions

Files are collections of data which are stored permanently. Files are used where the data is huge and the same data might be used in different applications. These files reside on secondary storage devices and are also referred to as named locations on the disks to store related data. Files can be used subsequently in future as the data in them is stored permanently.

Files support read and write operations. Before any operation can be performed on files, they have to be opened in the correct mode. After processing, the files should be closed.

9.1 FILE CONCEPTS

Python supports three types of files: text files, CSV files and binary files. Text files usually contain sequences of character data. The characters in a text file are encoded using ASCII and Unicode encoding schemes. Binary files store the data in the form of bytes. The binary files are capable of storing text, image, audio and video data. A text file can be opened using any text editor like Notepad on Windows and vi on UNIX. Since, the binary files represent different types of data like text, image, audio and video, they can be opened in different applications depending upon the type of data.

A file can be accessed by giving its *path*, which indicates its *location* on the disk. The path can be written as absolute or relative. The absolute path name always starts with the drive letter, for e.g. *c:\python\sampledata.txt*. The absolute path indicates the complete path starting from the root directory followed by the sub-directory structure. Hence, the absolute path is machine dependent. However, the relative path is always written with respect to the current working directory, for, e.g., if the current directory is *c:\python* then *sampledata.txt* is the relative path with respect to the current working directory.

9.2 FILE HANDLING

9.2.1 Opening a File

Before any operations can be performed on a file, it has to be *opened* in a correct mode. Python has the `open()` function for opening the files.

```
filehandle = open(filename, mode)
```

The `open()` function returns a file object also called a *file handle*, this is referred for performing further operations on the file. In order to open a file, the *filename* and *mode* have to be specified. The mode specifies whether we want to open the file for *read*, *write* or *append* operations.

```
f1=open("student.txt","r")  # opens the file for reading only
f2=open("student.txt","w")  # opens the file for writing only
```

The various file modes available in Python are given in the Table 9.1:

Table 9.1 File Opening Modes

Mode	Description
"r"	Opens a file for reading.
"w"	Opens a file for writing. If the file does not exist, it will be created and if the file already exists, its contents will be replaced.
"a"	Opens a file for appending the data at the end of the file.
"t"	Opens a file in text mode.
"rb"	Opens a file for reading binary data.
"wb"	Opens a file for writing binary data.
"+"	Opens a file for updating (reading and writing)

```
f3=open("C:\python\marks.txt","a")
```

In the above Python statement, the absolute path name of the file `marks.txt` has been specified and the file will be opened in append mode. The append mode adds the new data at the end of the file.

9.2.2 Closing a File

After all the operations on the file are complete, it should be closed. Closing the file ensures that resources used by the file are returned to the system and no file operation can be performed on it. The file is closed in Python by invoking the `close()` function as shown below:

```
f.close()
```

Once the file is closed, read or write operations cannot be performed and doing so results in an I/O error as shown below:

```
Traceback (most recent call last):
 File "C:/Users/HP/AppData/Local/Programs/Python/Python37/file1.py",
    line 17, in <module>
f.read()
ValueError: I/O operation on closed file.
```

9.2.3 Writing Data into a File

Before data can be written on a file, it has to be opened in “w” (write) or “a” (append) mode. If the file to be opened does not exist, it is created and if the file already exists, the contents are overwritten unless it is opened in the “a” (append) mode. The function for writing data in a file is the `write()` function. The Program 9.1 shows the use of `write()` function to create a file.

Program 9.1: Program to create a file using write() function

```
f.open("citynames.txt", "w")
f.write("Delhi\n")
f.write("Mumbai\n")
f.write("Chennai\n")
f.write("Jaipur\n")
f.close()
```

Program 9.1 first opens the file `citynames.txt` in the “w” (write) mode. If the file does not exist, it is automatically created and if the file is already present, the `write()` function will overwrite all the contents of this file. The next four lines use the `write()` function to write names of 4 cities. The names of the cities are written on a separate line since the newline character `\n` is used at the end of each string. Lastly, the file is closed. The file `citynames.txt` created by the above program can be located in the current working directory and the contents of the file are shown below:

```
Delhi
Mumbai
Chennai
Jaipur
```

In the Program 9.1, we have used single line strings to be written in a file. It is also possible to write a multi-line string in a file as shown below:

```
f.write('''This is a multi-line string. We are demonstrating in
python, how a multi-line string can be written in a file. The string
to be written should be enclosed in triple quotes.''')
```

Python has a `writelines()` function which enables writing multiple lines together in one command. The lines to be written are to be passed as a list argument in the `writelines()` function as in Program 9.2.

Program 9.2: Program to create file with multiple lines using writelines() function

```
f=open("mfile.txt","w")
lines=["This is the first line\n","This is the second line\n",
  "This is the third and the last line\n"]
f.writelines(lines)
f.close()

f=open("mfile.txt","r")
print(f.read())
f.close()
```

The output of the code above is as follows:

```
This is the first line
This is the second line
This is the third and the last line
```

The `write()` function can also be used when some contents have to be appended at the end of an existing file. After we have created the `citynames.txt` file in Program 9.1, the `write()` function can be used to add data to the end of the file as shown in the code snippet below:

```
f.open("citynames.txt", "a")
f.write("Hyderabad\n")
f.write("Kolkatta\n")
f.close()
```

The above code opens the file `citynames.txt` in the "a" (append) mode, which means that the data will be written at the end of the file, so even if the file already exists, the `write()` function does not result in overwriting the previous contents of the file. The contents of the file `citynames.txt` created by above code is as given below:

```
Delhi
Mumbai
Chennai
Jaipur
Hyderabad
Kolkatta
```

9.2.4 Reading Data from a File

In order to read the contents of a file, the file has to be opened in the "r" (read) mode, after which the `read()` function is used to read the file. For example,

```
f = open("citynames.txt", "r")
print(f.read())
```

The above code opens the file `"citynames.txt"` which has been created in section 9.2.3, in the read mode, thereafter the `read()` function has been used.

```
Delhi
Mumbai
Chennai
Jaipur
Hyderabad
Kolkatta
```

The `read()` function retrieves the contents of the entire file. If the file that is to be opened in read mode does not exist, it generates an error. It is important to specify the correct *path* of the file to be read. If the file doesn't exist, it results in `FileNotFoundError` exception as shown below because the file with the name `citynames1.txt` doesn't exist.

```
Traceback (most recent call last):
  File "C:/Users/HP/AppData/Local/Programs/Python/Python37/file1.py",
  line 13, in <module>
    f=open("citynames1.txt","r")
FileNotFoundError: [Errno 2] No such file or directory: 'citynames1.txt'
```

Python has other read functions to read the data in different sizes. Sometimes, we need to read the data in smaller chunks and sometimes line-by-line. The `read(size)` function is used to read the `size` number of bytes from the file. The Program 9.3 demonstrates how the `read(size)` is used to read 7 bytes from the file.

Program 9.3: Program to read the file in chunks of bytes

```
f=open("fulltext.txt","w")
f.write("This book is a complete guide on Python for beginners")
f.close()
f=open("fulltext.txt","r")
print(f.read(7))
```

The output of the code is shown below:

```
This bo
```

It can be seen that the first 7 characters "This bo" of the file have been read.

Python also provides the `readline()` function to read individual lines from a file. This function reads the file from the current position till the newline character, which marks the end of the line.

Program 9.4: Program to demonstrate the use of readline() function

```
f=open("citynames.txt","r")
no_of_lines=2
for i in range(no_of_lines):
  print(f.readline())
f.close()
```

The Program 9.4 will read 2 lines from the file. The `readline()` function is being called from inside a loop, to read the lines from the file as specified in the variable `no_of_lines`. The output of the above code is shown below:

```
Delhi
Mumbai
```

Lastly, there is a `readlines()` function that returns all lines from the current position in a file in the form of a list. In Program 9.5, we have extended the previous code where the first two lines from the file are being read by the `readline()` function and then the `readlines()` function is called, which reads the remaining lines from the file after the third line.

Program 9.5: Program to demonstrate the use of readlines() function

```
f=open("citynames.txt","r")
no_of_lines=2
for i in range(no_of_lines):
    print(f.readline())
print(f.readlines())
f.close()
```

The output of Program 9.5 shows the first two lines as output of the `readline()` function executed twice in the loop. The rest of the lines in the file are read together with the `readlines()` function, which generates a list of the remaining lines

```
['Chennai\n', 'Jaipur\n', 'Hyderabad\n', 'Kolkatta\n']
```

```
Delhi

Mumbai

['Chennai\n', 'Jaipur\n', 'Hyderabad\n', 'Kolkatta\n']
```

All the read functions in Python return null string or empty values when the end of file (EOF) is reached.

9.2.5 Seek and tell Functions

Initially, when the file is opened the file pointer is positioned at the beginning signified as position 0. The `tell()` function is used to know the current position of the file pointer in a file.

Program 9.6: Program to demonstrate the tell() function

```
f=open("citynames.txt","r")
print("Initial Position : ",f.tell())
print(f.read(6))
print("After reading 6 character: ",f.tell())
```

In Program 9.6, when the file is opened for reading the file pointer is positioned at the beginning, i.e., position 0. After reading the 6 characters "Delhi\n", the file pointer is positioned at 7. Here, "\n" is treated as 2 different characters and not as a single character, hence the position of the file pointer is 7 and not 6. The output is shown below:

```
Initial Position : 0
Delhi

After reading 6 character : 7
```

The `seek()` function in Python changes the position of the file pointer to a specific offset with respect to a reference point. The syntax of the function is:

```
seek(offset, reference point)
```

The offset is the distance from the reference point. The reference point is by default 0, which means absolute file positioning, 1 is meant for seek relative to the current position and and 2 is for seek relative to the end of the file.

Program 9.7: Program to demonstrate the use of seek() function

```
f=open("citynames.txt","r")
print("Initial Position : ",f.tell())
print(f.read(6))
print("After reading 6 character: ",f.tell())
f.seek(0)
print("After repositioning :", f.tell())
```

In Program 9.7, the f.seek(0) function positions the file pointer to the absolute 0 position. The output is shown below:

```
Initial Position : 0
Delhi

After reading 6 character : 7
After repositioning : 0
```

9.2.6 Using Multiple Files in a Program

We can use multiple files in a program. It is important that the files are opened in the correct mode. If we have three files `a.txt`, `b.txt` and `c.txt` and the data from these files is to be combined in a fourth file `d.txt`, we have to open the files `a.txt`, `b.txt` and `c.txt` in the *read* mode and `d.txt` in the *write* mode.

Program 9.8: Program to demonstrate the use of multiple files in a program

```
f1=open("a.txt","r")
f2=open("b.txt","r")
f3=open("c.txt","r")
f4=open("d.txt","w")

result1=f1.read()
result2=f2.read()
result3=f3.read()

f4.write(result1)
f4.write(result2)
f4.write(result3)

f1.close()
f2.close()
f3.close()
f4.close()
```

In Program 9.8, file `a.txt`, `b.txt` and `c.txt` are opened in the read mode, the content is read in `result1`, `result2` and `result3` and then written to `d.txt`, which was opened in the write mode.

The Program 9.9 below demonstrates how to count vowels in a given text file `file.text` and store the count of each vowel in a dictionary.

Program 9.9: Program to count the vowels in a file and store the result in the dictionary

```
dict={}
def freq_vo():
   f=open("file.txt","r")    # opens the file in the read mode
   countv=0
   set1=set("aeiouAEIOU")
   g=f.read()
   lower_g=g.lower()
   for ch in lower_g:
      if(ch in set1):
         countv+=1
         x=g.count(ch)  # gets the count of each vowel in the file
         dict[ch]=x  # writes the vowel & its count in the dictionary
   print("No. of vowels=",countv)
   print("Dictionary =",dict)
   f.close()
#main program
freq_vo()          # calls the function to count vowels in the file
```

The output of Program 9.9 is given below:

```
No. of vowels= 477
Dictionary = {'u': 43, 'a': 112, 'i': 118, 'e': 115, 'o': 82}
```

9.3 USING CSV FILES

The *comma separated value* (.csv) files are most commonly used to store real life data from real world applications and use it for various processing. The `csv` files are normally created using spreadsheet software like MS Excel, etc. The `csv` file can be created by typing the data in a spreadsheet software as shown in Figure 9.1 and saving it with the extension `.csv`.

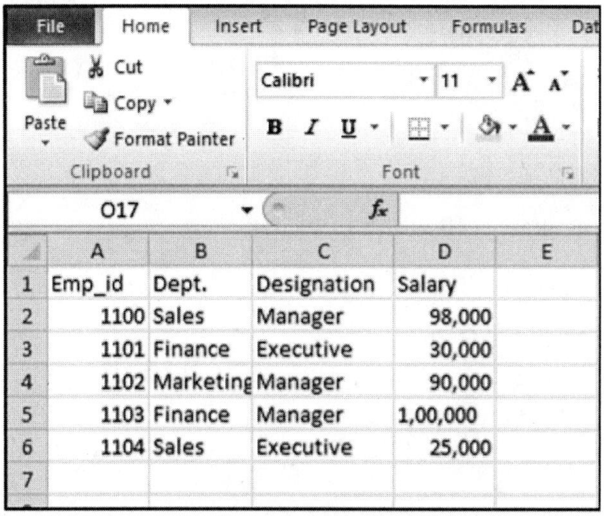

	A	B	C	D	E
1	Emp_id	Dept.	Designation	Salary	
2	1100	Sales	Manager	98,000	
3	1101	Finance	Executive	30,000	
4	1102	Marketing	Manager	90,000	
5	1103	Finance	Manager	1,00,000	
6	1104	Sales	Executive	25,000	
7					

Figure 9.1 Salary_Data.csv

The csv file shown in Figure 9.1 is "Salary_Data.csv". The data in this `csv` file is separated by commas. When we open the file in the notepad, the output appears as shown in Figure 9.2.

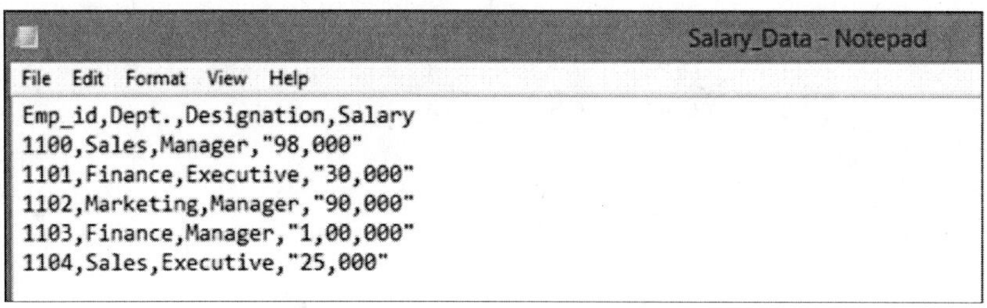

Figure 9.2 Salary_Data.csv in notepad.

It has headings for each column in the first row. All the subsequent rows have data separated by commas. Python supports the `csv` files and provides separate functions for its processing.

9.3.1 Reading a csv File

Python has a `csv` package which contains methods for handling `csv` files. We have to first import the `csv` package, open the file in an appropriate mode and then perform operations on the file. The Program 9.10 shows how the `csv` file "student.csv" is opened for reading and each row in the file is printed. The `csv` package is first imported using the `import` statement. The `open()` function is used for opening the file as we have been doing above for other files. The `reader()` function is used for reading the `csv` file. It returns an iterable object containing all rows in the file and each row is printed using a `for` loop. After printing all the rows, the file is closed.

Program 9.10: Program to demonstrate reading a csv file

```
import csv
file = open("student.csv","r")
reader=csv.reader(file)
for row in reader:
   print(row)
file.close()
```

The output of Program 9.10 is shown below:

```
['Roll_No', 'Name', 'Marks']
['101', 'Arjit', '90']
['102', 'Chetan', '98']
['103', 'Shubh', '88']
['104', 'Ritwik', '89']
['105', 'Aayansh', '92']
['106', 'Siddarth', '79']
```

Python has a `readlines()` method for reading all the rows of the `csv` file and storing them as a list.

Program 9.11: Program to demonstrate use of readlines() function in csv file

```
import csv
with open('Salary_Data.csv') as file:
   content = file.readlines()
header = content[:1]
rows = content[1:]
print(header)
print(rows)
file.close()
```

In the Program 9.11, the `readlines()` method reads all the lines from the file `'Salary_Data.csv'` and stores them in the list `content.` The first element from the list, which is the header row, is assigned to the variable `header` and all subsequent rows are assigned to the variable `rows`. The output is shown below:

```
['Emp_id,Dept.,Designation,Salary\n']
['1100,Sales,Manager,"98,000"\n', '1101,Finance,
Executive,"30,000"\n', '1102,Marketing,Manager,
"90,000"\n', '1103,Finance,Manager,"1,00,000"\n',
'1104,Sales,Executive,"25,000"\n']
```

9.3.2 Writing to a csv File

Python provides a `writer()` method for creating a writer object for a `csv` file. After creating the `writer` object, the `writerow()` and `writerows()` method can be used for writing a single or multiple rows in a `csv` file. The Program 9.12 opens the `'Marks_Data.csv'` file in the `write` mode. The `writerow()` method is used to write the header row and the `writerows()` method is used for writing all subsequent rows in the file.

Program 9.12: Program to demonstrate writing in the csv file

```
import csv
header = ['Name', 'Marks1', 'Marks2','Marks3']
data = [['Arpit', 82, 90, 94], ['Archit', 64, 75, 87], ['Jack', 85, 98, 67]]
filename = 'Marks_Data.csv'
file = open(filename, 'w', newline="")
csvwriter = csv.writer(file)
csvwriter.writerow(header)
csvwriter.writerows(data)
file.close()
```

The Program 9.12 creates the `csv` file `'Marks_Data.csv'` file as shown below:

9.4 ERRORS AND EXCEPTIONS

Errors can be defined as problems in the program which result in the abrupt termination of the program or incorrect output. There are mainly two types of errors in a program:

1. Syntax Errors
2. Logical Errors or Exceptions

When the Python program is not written in accordance with the rules laid out by the language, it results in a syntax error. The syntax errors are detected by the Python interpreter and prevent the execution of the statement till the error is corrected. Hence, syntax errors are also called compile time errors. Syntax error might occur if the variable name has some special characters, colon is missing after logical expression in *if* statement or *else*, print statement is written without parenthesis. These errors occur when syntax rules of the Python language are not followed. Few instances of syntax errors are given below:

```
>>> num+1 = 2
SyntaxError: can't assign to operator
>>> for i in range (2,12,2)
SyntaxError: invalid syntax
```

Sometimes, the program is written according to the syntax rules of the language, even then the program returns some error which cannot be detected by the interpreter before the execution of the program. Such errors are called exceptions and occur during the program execution. An exception occurs when we try to divide by zero, try to access elements in a list beyond the specified range, when we try to use a non-existent file, etc.

Python represents these exceptions as Python objects. Whenever an exception occurs, a `Traceback` object is called, which displays the name of the error, its description, the sequence of statements which led to the exception and the line number where the error occurred.

```
Traceback (most recent call last):
  File "C:/Users/HP/AppData/Local/Programs/Python/Python37/filel.py",
  line 13, in <module>
    f=open("citynames1.txt","r")
FileNotFoundError: [Errno 2] No such file or directory: 'citynames1.txt'
```

Figure 9.3 Example of Exception.

In Figure 9.3, the name of the exception is `FileNotFoundError,` which occurs at line 13 in the statement `f=open("citynames1.txt","r")` because the file `citynames1.txt` does not exist.

Some of the most commonly occurring exceptions are explained below:

1. **ZeroDivisionError**

   This exception occurs every time we try to perform division by zero, for example:

```
>>> 2/0
Traceback (most recent call last):
  File "<pyshell#3>", line 1, in <module>
    2/0
ZeroDivisionError: division by zero
```

   In the above example, the divisor in the expression `2/0` is zero, which has resulted in the `ZeroDivisionError` exception.

2. **NameError**

   This exception occurs when we try to use a variable, which has not been defined, for example:

```
>>> a + (32 - 40)
Traceback (most recent call last):
  File "<pyshell#4>", line 1, in <module>
    a + (32 - 40)
NameError: name 'a' is not defined
```

In the above example, the expression `a + (32 - 40)` is using a variable `'a'` whose value is undefined. This results in the `NameError` exception.

3. **TypeError**
   This exception occurs when we are using inappropriate data types in an expression or function.

```
>>> 'a' + 45
Traceback (most recent call last):
  File "<pyshell#9>", line 1, in <module>
    'a' + 45
TypeError: can only concatenate str (not "int") to str
```

In the above example, `'a' + 45` the string `'a'` is an inappropriate data type used with the addition operator.

4. **ValueError**
   This exception occurs whenever an invalid value is given to a function/expression even though the data type of the value is correct. In the example below, `-1` has been given as an argument to the `sqrt` function, which results in the `ValueError`. Even though the datatype of the argument to the `sqrt` function is integer, the negative value is inappropriate.

```
>>> import math
>>> print(math.sqrt(-1))
Traceback (most recent call last):
  File "<pyshell#13>", line 1, in <module>
    print(math.sqrt(-1))
ValueError: math domain error
```

5. **IndexError**
   This exception occurs whenever an index, which does not exist in a sequence, is accessed.

```
>>> a=[1,2,3,4,5]
>>> print(a[7])
Traceback (most recent call last):
  File "<pyshell#1>", line 1, in <module>
    print(a[7])
IndexError: list index out of range
```

In the above example, a list is defined as `a=[1,2,3,4,5]`, since `a[7]` is being accessed through the print statement, it returns the `IndexError` exception. The valid index range is from 0 to 4, accessing any index outside this range results in the exception.

The table 9.2 gives the list of other exceptions.

Table 9.2 Exceptions

Exception	Description
ArithmeticError	When an error occurs in evaluating numeric expression.
EOFError	When the end of file (EOF) condition is reached.
FloatingPointError	When an error occurs in floating-point calculation.
ImportError	When a module to be imported does not exist.
IndentationError	When incorrect indentation is specified.
MemoryError	When the program runs out of memory.
SystemError	When a system error occurs

9.5 EXCEPTION HANDLING

When a program encounters some errors, exceptions are raised. When these exceptions occur, the program cannot proceed and will crash. The interpreter displays an error message and the program comes to an unexpected halt.

9.5.1 `try` statement

Exceptions can be handled in Python using the `try` statement. The statements which can generate exceptions are written inside the `try` statement and the code for handling the exception is written inside the `except` clause.

The syntax of try and except statement is given below:

```
try:
    code which can generate errors.
except:
    code for handling the exception.
except:
     code for handling the exception.
.
.
.
.
else:
   code for handling exceptions other than the ones listed above.
finally:
     code to be executed after exception handling.
```

The code which is likely to generate the exception is written inside the `try` statement and the code for handling the exception is written inside the `except` clause. If the exception does not occur, the normal flow of the program continues and the `except` clause is not executed. For example:

Program 9.13: Program to demonstrate the use of try..except statement

```
num=int(input("Enter a number : "))
try:
    result=1/num
    print(result)
except:
    print("Error has occurred")
    print("Try again")
```

The output of the above Program 9.13 is given below:

```
Enter a number : 34
0.029411764705882353
```

```
Enter a number : 0
Error has occurred
Try again
```

When number 34 is entered, its reciprocal is calculated successfully and the result is printed. But, when zero is given as input, the expression will generate *division by zero* error and the program will halt abruptly. Since the `except` clause is given, this error will be handled by it and it prints the error message and the program does not crash.

9.5.2 Handling multiple exceptions

If only one `except` clause is given, then all the exceptions will be handled in the same way. This is not a good programming practice. It is possible to specify separate exception handling code for different exceptions using multiple `except` blocks.

```
try:
    #code which can generate errors.
except TypeError:
    #code for handling only the TypeError exception.
except ValueError:
    #code for handling only the ValueError exception.
except IndexError:
    # code for handling only the IndexError exception.
```

As shown above, separate exception handling code is written for separate exceptions.

When `TypeError` occurs, the code below `except TypeError` will be executed, similarly different code blocks have been defined for `ValueError` and `IndexError` exceptions.

9.5.3 `try` with `else` clause

When the code written in the `try` block does not generate an error, it might be required to execute certain code. For such situations, the code can be written inside the `else` block as shown in Program 9.14.

Program 9.14: Program to demonstrate the use of else block

```
num = int(input("Enter a number: "))
try:
    assert num % 2 == 0
except:
    print("Not an even number!")
else:
    result = 1/num
    print(result)
```

When an odd number is entered, the `assert` statement returns `false` and hence an exception is generated. The code in the `except` block is executed. But when the input is an even number, the `assert` statement returns `true` and hence the code in the `else` block is executed. The output of the Program 9.14 is shown below.

```
Enter a number : 5
Not an even number:
```

```
Enter a number : 6
0.16666666666666666
```

9.5.4 `try` with `finally` clause

If we wish to execute some code irrespective of whether an exception has occurred or not, the code should be written in the `finally` block. It is an optional block and is generally used for releasing the resources at the end of the program. For example:

```
try:
    f = open("test.txt", "r")
finally:
    f.close()
```

The code above shows that the code written in the `finally` block, i.e., `f.close()`, will be executed whether or not the `try block` generates an `exception.` The `finally` block has a file closing statement, which should be executed before the program terminates.

Further, an exception can be raised explicitly by using the `raise` clause followed by the name of the exception and a string enclosed in parenthesis to be displayed when the exception occurs.

Program 9.15: Program demonstrate the use of raise statement

```
num = int(input("Enter a positive integer: "))
try:
    if num <= 0:
        raise ValueError
except ValueError:
        print("Negative")
finally:
        print("The program is over")
```

In Program 9.15, when a positive number is entered, no exception is raised and only the code in the `finally` block is executed. When a negative number is entered, the exception `ValueError` is raised explicitly, so the code in the `except` block is executed followed by the `finally` block. Both the outputs of Program 9.15 are shown below:

```
Enter a positive integer: 7
The program is over
```

```
Enter a positive integer: -6
Negative
The program is over
```

9.6 USER-DEFINED EXCEPTIONS

Programming in real-life applications, we need to put several restrictions on the data to be used by the program, for example age cannot be negative, year cannot be negative, salary lies between a particular range and so on. In Python, the programmer can create customized exceptions to enforce constraints on the values of the variables. Such exceptions are called user-defined exceptions.

User defined exceptions are implemented using `assert` statements to raise an exception explicitly or by defining custom classes for these exceptions.

9.6.1 `raise` Statement

We have seen in the earlier sections how inbuilt exceptions are automatically raised by the program using `try..except` block, however we can also raise the exceptions explicitly by using the `raise` statement inside the `try..except` block. Consider the code given below:

```
age=int(input("Enter age : "))
yearOfBirth= 2022-age
```

```
print("Year of Birth is:")
print(yearOfBirth)
```

The above code will calculate the year of birth from the age of a person. The `age` variable should be a positive integer. If a negative number is entered as `age`, the program will not report any error or raise any exception, but will give a logically incorrect result as shown below:

```
Enter age : -45
Year of Birth is:
2067
```

As can be seen from the output above, when −45 is entered as the `age`, the program does not raise any exception. We can use the `raise` statement within the `try..except` block to put a constraint that age should be positive.

Program 9.16: Program to demonstrate the use of raise statement

```
try:
    age= -40
    print("Age : ",age)
    if age<0:
        raise ValueError
    yearOfBirth= 2022-age
    print("Year of Birth is:")
    print(yearOfBirth)
except ValueError:
    print("Age cannot be negative")
```

In the Program 9.16, if the `age` variable has a negative value, the exception `ValueError` is raised explicitly using the `raise` statement and the control moves to the `except` block and prints "`Age cannot be negative`". The output is shown below:

```
Age : -40
Age cannot be negative
```

9.6.2 Exception for `assert` Statement

As we have studied in chapter 4, the `assert` statement can be used to implement constraints on the values of the variables. A condition can be specified with the `assert` statement and if the condition is not met, the `AssertionError` will automatically be raised.

We have used the `assert` statement in the program below to enforce that the `age` is positive, if a negative number is entered for `age`, the `AssertionError` will automatically be raised.

Program 9.17: Program to demonstrate the use of assert statement

```
age= -40
print("Age : ",age)
assert age>0
yearOfBirth= 2022-age
print("Year of Birth is:")
print(yearOfBirth)
```

The output of Program 9.17 below shows that when a negative number is entered for age, an `AssertionError` exception is raised since the exception is not handled.

```
Age: -40
Traceback (most recent call last):
  File "C:/Users/HP/AppData/Local/Programs/Python/Python37/expl.py",
  line 3, in <module>
    assert age>0
AssertionError
```

We can handle this `AssertionError` exception by writing the code in `try..except` block as in Program 9.18.

Program 9.18: Program to demonstrate handling `AssertionError` exception

```
try:
    age= -40
    print("Age : ",age)
    assert age>0
    yearOfBirth= 2022-age
    print("Year of Birth is:")
    print(yearOfBirth)
except AssertionError:
    print("Age cannot be negative")
```

The output of Program 9.18 is shown below, when the age is entered as –40, an `AssertionError` exception occurs, which is handled by the except clause and it prints `"Age cannot be negative"`.

```
Age : -40
Age cannot be negative
```

9.6.3 Defining User Defined Exceptions

The user defined exception can be handled by creating a custom class. This custom class will have the desired exception name and will be derived from the `Exception` class. For example if an exception with the name `User_defined_Exception` is to be handled, a class with the name `User_defined_Exception` has to be created, which will be extended from the super class `Exception`. To generate the exception, the `raise` statement can be used and the `User_defined_Exception` exception is handled in the `except` block.

For example, if we wish to create a user defined exception `ZeroAge` when zero is entered as age, the following custom class is created.

Program 9.19: Program to create a user-defined exception

```
class ZeroAge_Exception(Exception):
  pass
try:
    age =0
    print ("Age : ",age)
    if (age == 0):
        raise(ZeroAge_Exception("User defined exception"))
    print("Age is ", age)
except ZeroAge_Exception:
    print("ZeroAge Exception : Age cannot be Zero")
```

In Program 9.19, when age is zero, the `try` block in the program throws the `ZeroAge` exception using `raise` keyword. The exception is then handled by the `except` block. If we give the correct value for age as input, it will print the age. The output of the code above is given below:

```
Age : 0
ZeroAge Exception : Age cannot be Zero
```

9.7 DEBUGGING

Debugging is the process of finding errors or bugs in the code. The process of debugging involves testing the program on various inputs and stepping through the code line by line to verify the logic of the program. Python has the `pdb` module which supports debugging. This module is based on the class pdb which uses `bdb` (basic debugger functions) and `cmd` (support for line-oriented command interpreters) modules.

The `pdb` module supports interactive debugging by allowing setting of breakpoints, stepping through the code, viewing stack traces, etc. The debugger can be used in two ways:

9.7.1 Debugging within the Program

Import the `pdb` module and then use the `pdb.set_trace()` commands. Here a breakpoint is created on a line below where `set_trace()` has been placed. In the Program 9.20, a breakpoint is created after line 5.

Program 9.20: Program to demonstrate the use of Pdb

```
import pdb
x=int(input("Enter number: "))
fact=1
pdb.set_trace()            #breakpoint
for i in range(1,x+1,1):
      fact=fact*i

print("Factorial = ",fact)
```

When the program 9.20 is executed, the pdb command appears at the breakpoint as shown below:

```
Enter number: 4
> c:\users\hp\appdata\local\programs\python\python37\factpdb.py(6)
<module>()
-> for i in range(1,x+1,1):
(Pdb) |
```

Now, the pdb commands can be used to navigate through the code. Some of the commands are given in Table 9.3.

Table 9.3 Commonly used pdb Commands

Command	Description
n(ext)	Continue execution until next line in the current function (It executes the called functions also)
s(tep)	Executes the next line only either in a called function or the next line in the current function
w(here)	Print the stack trace
enable	Enable the specified breakpoint
h(elp)	Print the list of all pdb commands

9.7.2 Debugging from the Command Line

In order to run the Python debugger from the command line, run the following command:

```
python -m pdb fact.py
```

The program can be debugged using the pdb commands given in Table 9.3, the step-by-step execution of the program to calculate factorial of a number is given in the output below:

Command Prompt - python -m pdb fact.py

```
C:\Users\HP\AppData\Local\Programs\Python\Python37>python -m pdb fact.py
> c:\users\hp\appdata\local\programs\python\python37\fact.py(3)<module>()
-> x=int(input("Enter number: "))
(Pdb) n
Enter number: 3
> c:\users\hp\appdata\local\programs\python\python37\fact.py(4)<module>()
-> fact=1
(Pdb) n
> c:\users\hp\appdata\local\programs\python\python37\fact.py(6)<module>()
-> for i in range(1,x+1,1):
(Pdb) n
> c:\users\hp\appdata\local\programs\python\python37\fact.py(7)<module>()
-> fact=fact*i
(Pdb) n
> c:\users\hp\appdata\local\programs\python\python37\fact.py(6)<module>()
-> for i in range(1,x+1,1):
(Pdb) n
> c:\users\hp\appdata\local\programs\python\python37\fact.py(7)<module>()
-> fact=fact*i
(Pdb) n
> c:\users\hp\appdata\local\programs\python\python37\fact.py(6)<module>()
-> for i in range(1,x+1,1):
(Pdb) n
> c:\users\hp\appdata\local\programs\python\python37\fact.py(7)<module>()
-> fact=fact*i
(Pdb) n
> c:\users\hp\appdata\local\programs\python\python37\fact.py(6)<module>()
-> for i in range(1,x+1,1):
(Pdb) n
> c:\users\hp\appdata\local\programs\python\python37\fact.py(9)<module>()
-> print("Factorial = ",fact)
(Pdb) n
Factorial =  6
--Return--
> c:\users\hp\appdata\local\programs\python\python37\fact.py(9)<module>()->None
-> print("Factorial = ",fact)
(Pdb)
```

SUMMARY

- File is a collection of data.
- The `open()` method is used to open a file. The first argument of the method is the name of the file and the second argument is the mode in which the file is to be opened. The file can be opened in “r” (read), “w” (open) and “a” (append) mode.
- The `close()` method is used for closing a file.
- The `read()` and `write()` methods are used for reading from and writing into a file respectively.
- The `readline()` function reads the file from the current position till the newline character. The `readlines()` function returns all the lines of the file in the form of a list.

- The `seek()` function changes the position of the file pointer to a specific offset with respect to a reference point. By default the reference point is 0.
- The `tell()` function is used to know the current position of the file pointer in a file.
- The `writelines()` function which enables writing multiple lines together in one command. The lines to be written are to be passed as a list argument in the `writelines()`.
- Exceptions are errors which occur during the program execution.
- Some of the commonly occurring exceptions:

Exception	Description
`NameError`	When a name specified is not found.
`TypeError`	When an inappropriate data type is used in an expression or function.
`ValueError`	When an invalid value is given to a function/expression even though the data type of the value is correct.
`ZeroDivisionError`	When we try to perform division by zero.
`IndexError`	When an index which does not exist in a sequence is accessed.
`ArithmeticError`	When an error occurs in evaluating numeric expression.
`EOFError`	When the end of file (EOF) condition is reached.
`FloatingPointError`	When an error occurs in floating-point calculation.
`ImportError`	When a module to be imported does not exist.
`IndentationError`	When incorrect indentation is specified.
`MemoryError`	When the program runs out of memory.
`SystemError`	When a system error occurs.

- `try...except` statement is used for handling exceptions. `Try` block has the statement which can potentially generate exceptions and `except` block has the statements for handling exceptions, `else` block has code to be executed when the exception does not occur and `finally` block has statements which will be executed irrespective of whether the exception occurs or not.

EXERCISES

9.1 Briefly explain the various modes in which a file can be opened.

9.2 Consider two files "input.txt" and "output.txt". Write a Python program to read the string data linewise from the file "input.txt" and write only that data to the file "output.txt" whose length is an even number.

9.3 Write a Python program to count the number of characters, words and lines in a file.

9.4 Write a Python program that replaces text in a given input file. The program should prompt the user to enter the name of the input file, the string to be replaced and the new string. The revised text should be written in the a new output file.

9.5 Write Python statements for the following:

(a) To open file "names.txt" in read, write and append mode.
(b) To read 20 characters from a file.
(c) To read a line from a file.
(d) To read all lines from a file.
(e) To read complete data from a file.
(f) To write multiple lines to a file from a list.
(g) To change the offset of the file to 10.
(h) To get the current offset of a file.

9.6 Explain the various types of errors.

9.7 How are exceptions different from errors?

9.8 What are the advantages of exception handling?

9.9 What is the output of the following code:

```
def func1():
    a=12
    b=a/0
   try:
        func1()
        except ZeroDivisorError:
               print("error: division by error")
        except IndexError:
               print("error: access error")
```

9.10 For the given code:

```
try:
  statement1
  statement2
  statement3
except Exception1:
      statement4
except Exception2:
      statement5
finally:
           statement6
statement7
```

(a) Which statements will be executed when `Exception1` occurs?
(b) Which statements will be executed when no exception occurs?

10

Sorting and Searching Techniques

10.1 SORTING TECHNIQUES

Sorting means organization of the data. There are some sorting algorithms used to arrange the elements present in a given list in some order. Sorting of elements could be done in any fashion such as ascending and descending order. The output achieved after performing sorting techniques over a sequence of elements is a reordered set of input elements. Sorting algorithms play a vital role when it comes to reducing the complexity of a given problem definition. Different sorting algorithms could be classified based on certain aspects which include number of comparisons, number of swaps or inversions, amount of memory usage, using recursive or non-recursive methods, stability and adaptability of a sorting algorithm.

In this section, we will study about different sorting techniques used to sort the data. The three most commonly used sorting algorithms are *Selection Sort, Insertion Sort* and *Bubble Sort.*

10.1.1 Selection Sort

It is one of the simplest sorting algorithms. In this technique, we consider two sub-lists: *sorted* and *unsorted.* The algorithm works by finding the smallest element in the unsorted sub-list and swapping it with the first element in the unsorted sub-list. In this way, the smallest element in the unsorted sub list moves to the correct position in the unsorted sub-list. Hence, in every iteration one element moves from the unsorted part to the sorted part. The list gets sorted in n−1 iterations. The step-by-step description of the selection sort is given below:

1. Initially, the complete list is considered unsorted and sorted list is empty
2. Repeat for n – 1 times
   (a) Find the smallest element of the unsorted part
   (b) Swap it with the first element of the unsorted part

Let us understand the selection sort algorithm using an example. Suppose, we have a list of five elements 11, 29, 23, 8, 35. Initially, we consider the complete list as unsorted.

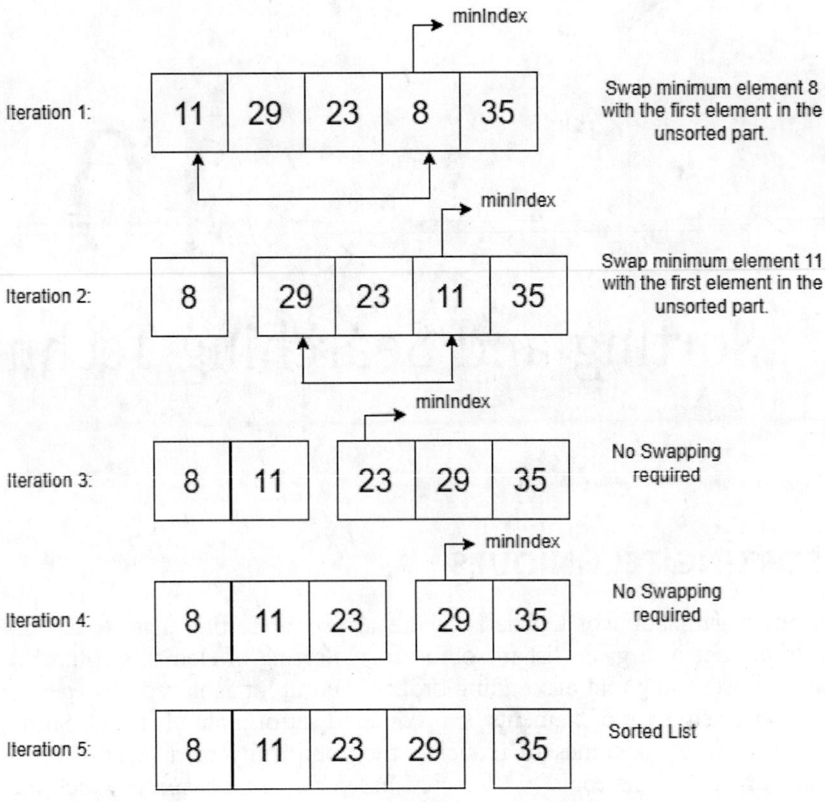

Figure 10.1 Working example using Selection sort.

In the first iteration, we traverse the entire list and find the smallest element which is 8 at index `minIndex`. We swap it with the first element in the unsorted part which is 11 as shown in Figure 10.1. After the first iteration, 8 is placed at the correct position and now constitutes the sorted part. In the second iteration, we find the next smallest element present in the remaining set of elements and exchange it with the second element positioned in the list. In this manner, we keep on traversing all the elements until we place each and every element in its correct position. Basically, if there exists `n` elements in the list then in total it requires `n-1` passes to sort them. Program 10.1 demonstrates the selection sort.

Program 10.1: Program to sort a list using selection sort

```
def selectionSort(mylist):
    for i in range(0, len(mylist) - 1):
        minIndex = i
        for j in range(i+1, len(mylist)):
            if mylist[j] < mylist[minIndex]:
                minIndex = j
        mylist[minIndex], mylist[i] = mylist[i], mylist[minIndex]
```

```
mylist = eval(input("Enter a list of elements you want to sort: "))
print("Sorted list is ")
selectionSort(mylist)
print(mylist)
```

The output of Program 10.1 on two different inputs is shown below:

```
Enter a list of elements you want to sort: [10,15,20,23,55]
Sorted list is
[10, 15, 20, 23, 55]


Enter a list of elements you want to sort: ['Kiwi','Banana',
'Apple','Pineapple','Mango']
Sorted list is
['Apple', 'Banana', 'Kiwi', 'Mango', 'Pineapple']
```

This sorting technique is very easy to implement but not considered as efficient as other sorting techniques. It is considered as in-place sorting technique because it requires no extra memory space to perform sorting. Selection sort works well when the list of entries is small in size and cost associated with every swap is not a big deal.

10.1.2 Insertion Sort

Insertion sort is a simple comparison sorting technique. In the insertion sort algorithm, we divide the list into two sub-lists. The left part of the list is considered as *sorted* and the right part of the list is an *unsorted* list having elements which need to be positioned in correct order. In every pass, we try to decrease the length of the unsorted sub-list by inserting one element from the unsorted list at its correct position in the sorted sub-list. The algorithm initially assumes that the *first* element of the list is sorted already. Every element in the unsorted sub list is compared with the elements of the sorted sub list, starting from the rightmost element and inserted at the correct position.

This algorithm is easy to implement and works pretty well for small input values. Similar to selection sort, insertion sort is also an in-place algorithm that does not require any extra storage space to sort the data values. Insertion sort also works appropriately for an already partially sorted list, which highlights another feature of adaptability. Considering that the list is to be sorted in ascending order, the step-by-step explanation is given below:

1. Initially, sorted sub-list consists of the first element and unsorted sub-list has the rest
2. Repeat for n – 1 times
   (a) Pick the first element in the unsorted sub-list, say *ele*
   (b) If *ele* is less than elements in the sorted sub-list then
      (i) Shift the elements in the sorted part to the right by one position
   (c) Insert *ele* at the current index in the sorted part

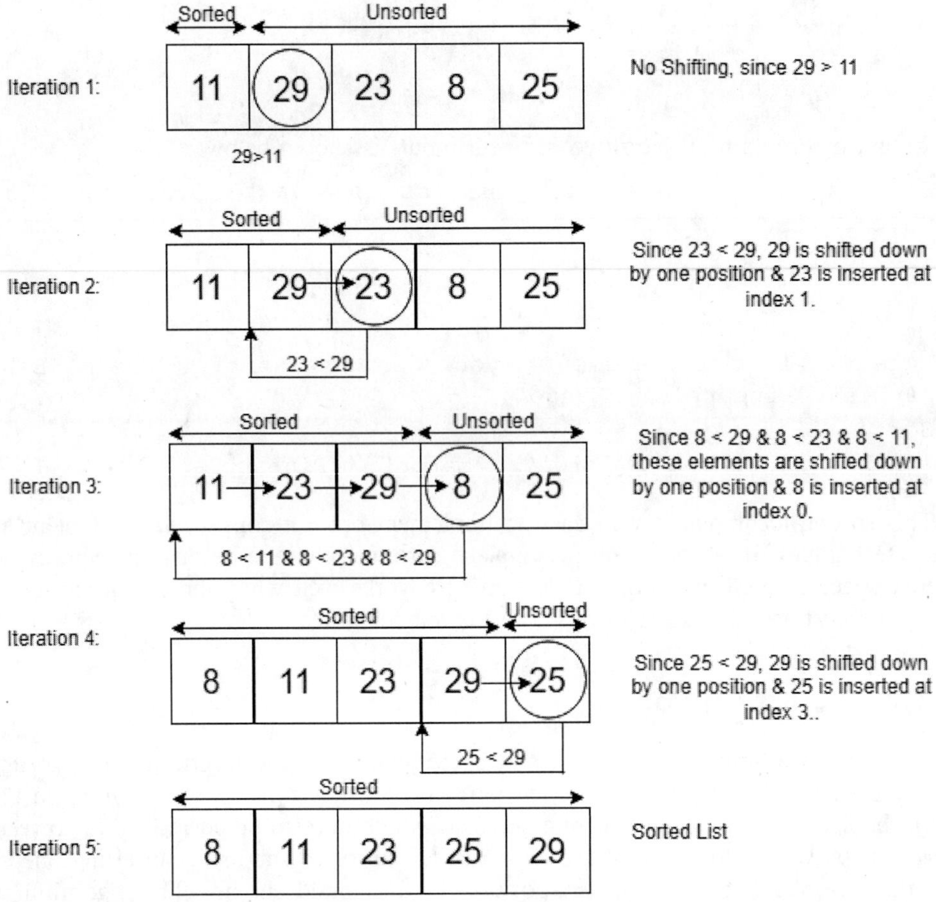

Figure 10.2 Working example of Insertion sort.

Let us understand the working of insertion sort with the help of an example given in Figure 10.2. Consider a list of five integer elements: 11, 29, 23, 8, 25. Initially, 11 is considered to be in the sorted sub-list and rest elements in the unsorted sub list. We pick one element in every iteration from the unsorted part and find its correct position in the sorted part and insert it. In every iteration, the size of sorted sub-list increases by 1 element and size of unsorted sub-list reduces by 1 element. In the first iteration, we pick 29 and compare it with all the elements in the sorted sub list starting from the right hand side. Since, 29 is greater than 11, the comparison stops here and it is not inserted anywhere in between but at the end only. Now, 11 and 29 are in the sorted sub list. In the second iteration, we pick 23 and start comparing it with the elements in the sorted part starting from right, i.e., 23 is compared with 29, since 23 < 29, we shift 29 one place to the right, making place for 23. We then compare 23 with 8, since 23 is greater than 8, we do not compare further. Now, 23 is inserted at index 1. Program 10.2 demonstrates the insertion sort.

Program 10.2: Program to sort the list of elements using Insertion Sort

```
def insertionSort(mylist):
    for i in range(1, len(mylist)):
        temp = mylist[i]
        j = i-1
        while j >=0 and temp < mylist[j]:
            mylist[j+1] = mylist[j]
            j -= 1
        mylist[j+1] = temp

mylist = eval(input("Enter a list of elements you want to sort: "))
print("Sorted list is ")
insertionSort(mylist)
print(mylist)
```

The output of Program 10.2 for two sample inputs is given below:

```
Enter a list of elements you want to sort: [11,29,23,8,35]
Sorted list is
[8, 11, 23, 29, 35]


Enter a list of elements you want to sort: ['Jaipur','Ahmedabad',
'Delhi','Nagpur','Meghalaya','Chennai']
Sorted list is
['Ahmedabad', 'Chennai', 'Delhi', 'Jaipur', 'Meghalaya', 'Nagpur']
```

10.1.3 Bubble Sort

Bubble sort is considered as the easiest sorting algorithm among all the sorting techniques. It works on the logic of repeatedly swapping the adjacent elements until we get the entire list sorted. It compares every adjacent pair and swaps their positions if they are not in the correct order. It keeps on repeating this process until the entire data is sorted. The step-by-step explanation is given below:

1. Repeat for n–1 times
   (a) Compare the adjacent pair of elements.
   (b) If they are not in the correct order then swap them.

Let's understand the working of bubble sort using an example. Consider a list consisting of 15, 13, 18, 16 and 12. In the first iteration, we will start comparing elements pairwise. Initially, the adjacent pair values will be compared. If the values are in the incorrect position, they will be swapped.

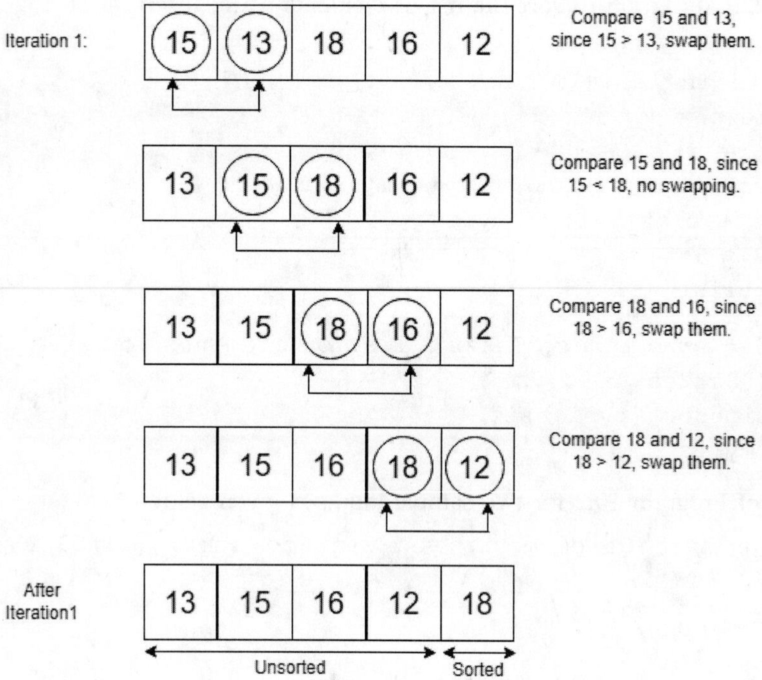

Figure 10.3 First iteration of bubble sort.

At the end of the first iteration, the largest value, i.e., 18 is correctly placed at the end of the list as shown in Figure 10.3. Now, again we will traverse the entire list in the same manner but this time the length of the list will be reduced by one i.e., len(mylist) –1 as one element is already placed at its correct location at the end of the list. The same process is performed until we achieve a new sorted list. The second iteration is shown in Figure 10.4.

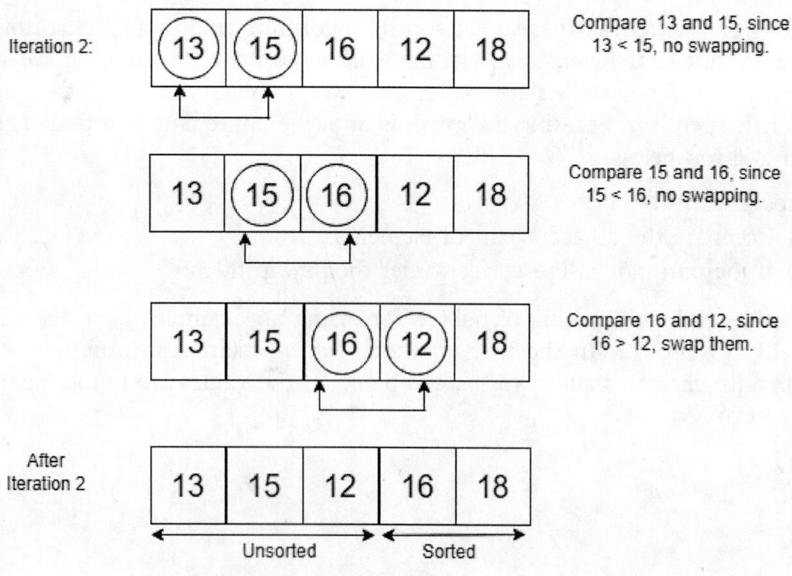

Figure 10.4 Second iteration of bubble sort.

After the second iteration 16 moves down and now the sorted part consists of 16 and 18. Third iteration is shown in Figure 10.5.

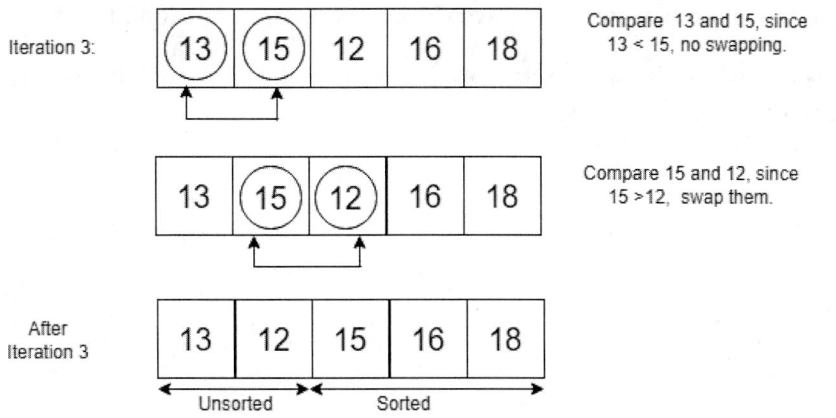

Figure 10.5 Third iteration of bubble sort.

After the third iteration the sorted part consists of 15, 16 and 18. The fourth iteration is shown in Figure 10.6.

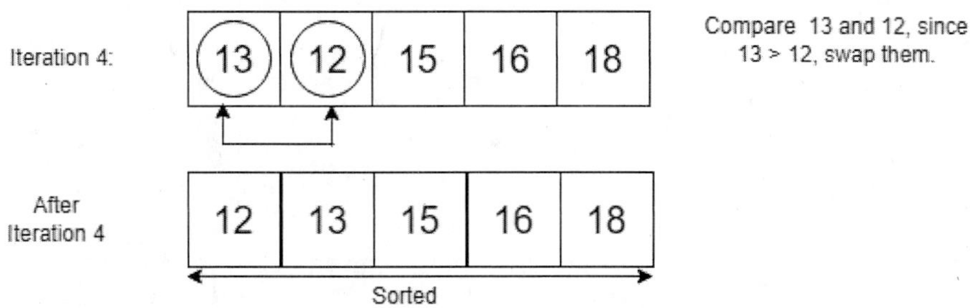

Figure 10.6 Fourth iteration of bubble sort.

After the fourth iteration, the complete list is sorted. Program 10.3 demonstrates the bubble sort.

Program 10.3: Program to sort the list of elements using Bubble Sort

```
def bubbleSort(mylist):
    n = len(mylist) - 1
    for i in range(0, n):
        for j in range(n, i, -1):
            if mylist[j] < mylist[j-1]:
                mylist[j], mylist[j-1] = mylist[j-1], mylist[j]

mylist = eval(input("Enter a list of elements you want to sort: "))
print("Sorted list is ")
bubbleSort(mylist)
print(mylist)
```

The code in Program 10.3 will not run efficiently if the list is fully sorted because it will still make all the comparisons, despite having all the elements positioned at their correct places. We can reduce the number of swaps and avoid the unnecessary evaluation in this existing version of bubble sort by modifying it a little as in Program 10.4. We can use a temporary boolean variable, let's say called as `swapped`, which is currently set as `False`. If any swapping occurs, it is changed to `True`, otherwise, it remains `False`. At the end of iteration, if the value of a temporary variable happens to be `False`, this means no swapping occurs. This implies that all the elements are already sorted and hence there is no need to go to the next iteration.

Program 10.4: Improved program to sort the list of elements using Bubble Sort

```
def bubbleSort(mylist):
    n = len(mylist) - 1
    for i in range(0, n):
        swapped = False
        for j in range(n, i, -1):
            if mylist[j] < mylist[j-1]:
                swapped = True
                mylist[j], mylist[j-1] = mylist[j-1], mylist[j]
        if swapped == False:
            break

mylist = eval(input("Enter a list of elements you want to sort: "))
print("Sorted list is ")
bubbleSort(mylist)
print(mylist)
```

The output of Program 10.4 for two sample inputs is given below:

```
Enter a list of elements you want to sort: [15,13,18,16,12]
Sorted list is
[12, 13, 15, 16, 18]

Enter a list of elements you want to sort: ['Ritu','Lavina','Ri
tisha','Anju','Manisha','Priya']
Sorted list is
['Anju', 'Lavina', 'Manisha', 'Priya', 'Ritisha', 'Ritu']
```

The bubble sort heavily relies on swapping, hence it is not considered to be an efficient algorithm for big datasets. But, the simplicity of the algorithm makes it popular for many applications.

10.2 SEARCHING TECHNIQUES

Searching techniques involve looking for an element in a sequence-type data structure. The idea is to traverse the sequence data and show results whether the item that was being looked for has been found or not. Some implementations may also return the position where the element was found. Two most commonly used searching techniques are *Linear search* and *Binary search.*

10.2.1 Linear Search

This is the most basic type of searching algorithm. As its name suggests, linear search works by linearly looking through the list of elements and checking if the list element matches the item. Once the match is found, the algorithm stops. Program 10.5 shows the implementation of linear search. In case the element is not found, the function returns `False`, else it returns `True`. The time taken by linear search to find an element is directly proportional to the size of the list.

Program 10.5: Program to search an element using Linear Search

```
def linear(elements, item):
    for x in elements:
        if x==item:
            return True
    return False

elements = [45, 199, 256, 31, 19, 26]
search_ele=int(input("Enter the element to be searched : "))
r1= linear(elements, search_ele)

if r1==True:
    print(search_ele, " - Element found!")
else:
    print(search_ele, " - Element not found")
```

The output of Program 10.5 for two different elements is as given below:

```
Enter the element to be searched : 31
31  - Element found!

Enter the element to be searched : 100
100  - Element not found
```

It may be noted here, that there may be different ways to implement this algorithm. One can also return the index of the element, if found. However, the structure of the loop remains the same. The reader is encouraged to try similar versions of the technique.

10.2.2 Binary Search

Binary search is a more efficient technique as compared to linear search. It requires that the list of elements be sorted in either ascending or descending order. For simplicity here, we consider a list arranged in ascending order.

Binary search is called so, because it splits the list into half and works only on one half. It compares the element at the middle position, *mid* with the element to be searched, *item*. If they match, then the element is found. If the *item* is less than the element stored at *mid*, the left half of the array is searched; else if the item is greater than the element at *mid*, then the right half of the element is searched. This technique follows the following steps:

1. Initialize variables begin = 0, end = n–1 (where n is the number of elements in the list)
2. While begin < end
   a. Set variable mid = (begin+end)/2
   b. Compare element at mid with item (*item* : element to be looked for)
   c. If item < element at mid
      Traverse the left half of the list, set variable end = mid–1
   Else if item > element at mid
      Traverse the right half of the list, set variable begin = mid+1
   Else if item == element at mid
      The element is found and algorithm returns `True`.
3. If begin>=end, the element is not in the list and algorithm returns `False`.

Program 10.6: Binary Search

```
def binarysearch(elements, item):

    begin = 0
    end = len(elements)-1
    while begin<end:
        mid = (begin+end)//2
        print("Mid is ",mid)
        if elements[mid] == item:
            return mid
        elif item<elements[mid]:
            print("Search the left part")
            end = mid-1
        elif item>elements[mid]:
            print("Search the right part")
            begin = mid+1
    return -1

elements = [19, 26, 31, 45, 199, 256]
search_ele=int(input("Enter the element to be searched : "))

r = binarysearch(elements, search_ele)

if r== -1:
    print("Element not found")
else:
    print("Element found at index ", r)
```

Figure 10.7 demonstrates the stepwise working of binary search when the element to be searched is 199. In the first iteration, `mid` = (0+5)//2 is 2, so 199 is compared to elements[2], i.e., 31, since 199 > 31, the search would continue in the right half from `mid+1` to `end` and the left half is discarded. In the second half, `mid`= (3+5)//2 is 4, so 199 is compared to elements[4], i.e., 199, the search ends here since the element is found.

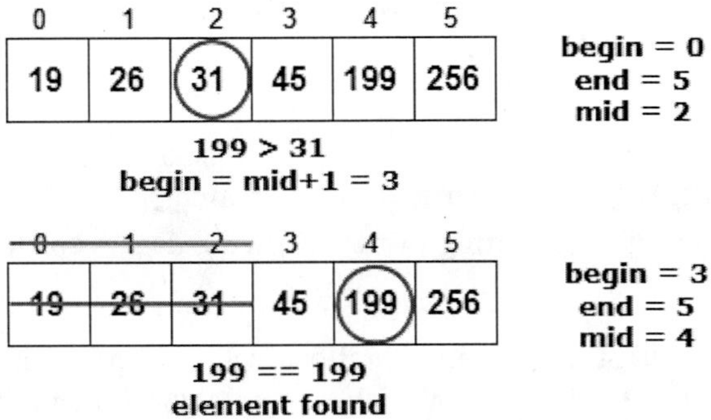

Figure 10.7 Demonstration of binary search.

The output of Program 10.6 on two different elements to be searched is shown here:

```
Enter the element to be searched : 199
Mid is  2
Search the right part
Mid is  4
Element found at index  4

Enter the element to be searched : 100
Mid is  2
Search the right part
Mid is  4
Search the left part
Element not found
```

SUMMARY

- Sorting means organization of the data.
- There are some sorting algorithms used to arrange the elements present in a given list in some order.
- The three most commonly used sorting algorithms are Selection Sort, Insertion Sort and Bubble Sort.
- Selection sort relies on finding the smallest element in the unsorted part and swapping with the first element in the unsorted part.
- Insertion sort finds the correct position of each element by comparing it with the elements in the sorted part and inserting it.

- Bubble sort compares the adjacent pair of elements and swapping them if they are not in the correct order.
- Linear search is the simplest search algorithm in which the element to be searched is compared with every element serially.
- Binary search requires the list to be in the sorted order. It works on half the list based on the value of the element to be searched with respect to the middle element.

EXERCISES

10.1 Differentiate between the linear and binary search.

10.2 Explain the step by step sorting of the following data with the help of selection sort:

`20, 10, 40, 70, 50, 100, 80`

10.3 Consider a sorted list, how many iterations will be required if we apply selection sort, insertion sort and bubble sort. Which sorting algorithm will you prefer to use for a sorted list and why?

10.4 For the given list `12, 16, 18, 22, 28, 32, 40` which algorithm can be used for searching.

10.5 In the question 10.4, apply binary search to find the element `32`, explain the values taken by begin, mid and end in every iteration.

10.6 Given the step by step explanation to sort a given list using insertion sort:

`"Quick" , "radix" , "merge", "selection", "bubble", "insertion"`

10.7 Sort the list given in question 10.6 using bubble sort, giving step by step details.

11

Python Modules

Python is a programming language which is considered as a beginner's language because it is very easy to learn and code with. Python is considered as a powerful language as it has many built-in functions, modules, libraries and packages that makes it effortless to write the programs in it. In this chapter, we will discuss in detail about two of the many modules available in the Python language.

A module in Python is a set of functions designed for a particular application. Related functions are clubbed together in a file to create a module. The file containing code for a module has an extension *.py*. Modules aid in the reusability and easy organization of pieces of code. These modules can be imported and used within other programs to obtain desired output. Regardless of the number of times a module is imported in a program, it will always be loaded only once.

11.1 NUMPY MODULE

The `NumPy` module provides functions to work with arrays. `NumPy` stands for Numeric (or Numerical) Python. It consists of multidimensional array objects and assembly of different tools that helps in working with arrays. `NumPy` provides the capability to perform major mathematical computations and logical operations efficiently. There are also functionalities for working with linear algebra, generating random numbers, matrices, and fourier transformation. `NumPy` arrays are quite powerful and efficient as compared to Python lists when it comes to working.

Basically, arrays are a type of data structure that store multiple values. `NumPy` is considered as one of the most popular modules among researchers, statisticians and data scientists to carry out heavy mathematical computations. When it comes to the code execution time, `NumPy` arrays are much faster than traditional Python lists because of its locality of reference feature. Locality of reference in computer science is the way of storing `NumPy` arrays in a continuous fashion inside the memory, unlike lists. That's why accessing and manipulating these arrays are much easier. Practically, an array is the same as a list in Python but fundamentally, there is a huge difference in their respective programming. Let us discuss more about it in detail.

11.1.1 Installation of NumPy

The `NumPy` module does not come pre-installed with the Python distribution. To install `NumPy` on a system, we use the popular Python package installer, `pip`. The command is:

```
pip install numpy
```

Once `NumPy` is installed, we need to import it in our program at the very beginning using the keyword `'import'`. Below is the command,

```
import numpy as np
```

Once it is imported, we can use it in our code. Here `np` is the alias (or nickname) used to refer to it throughout the program conveniently. We use the `as` keyword to create an alias. For example, let's create a `NumPy` array consisting numbers containing values ranging from 1 to 10 using `array()` function of the `NumPy` module:

```
>>>import numpy as np
>>>arr = np.array([1, 2, 3, 4, 5, 6, 7, 8, 9, 10])
>>>print(arr)
```

The output of the code is

```
[1, 2, 3, 4, 5, 6, 7, 8, 9, 10]
```

We can also check the version of `NumPy` using the following command:

```
import numpy as np
print(np.__version__)
```

The version is:

```
1.21.6
```

Here `__version__` is an attribute which stores the version string.

We can verify whether an array is a `NumPy` array or not using `type()` function.

```
>>>print(type(arr))
```

The output is

```
<class 'numpy.ndarray'>
```

The output `<class 'numpy.ndarray'>` confirms that it is indeed a `NumPy` array. Here, `ndarray` is the class of `NumPy` arrays. It stands for N-dimensional array.

11.1.2 Creating Arrays using NumPy

To create an `ndarray` object, a list, tuple or any other array-like object is passed as an argument to the `array()` function. It will eventually be converted to `ndarray`. For example, Let's pass a tuple inside `array()` function to create a `NumPy` array:

```
import numpy as np
arr = np.array((1, 2, 3, 4))
print(arr)
```

The output of the above example is

```
[1 2 3 4]
```

Remember that you only need to import a NumPy module once in a program, that too, in the very beginning of it.

NumPy dimensions are called *axes*. The number of axes present in a NumPy array are called *rank*. NumPy allows to create and work with multidimensional arrays as well.. Let's see an example of each type.

In a 1-D array, we have elements only in one dimension. The output here will be a simple 1-D list. In case of 2-D or multidimensional arrays, output will be like a nested list. For example,

```
>>>import numpy as np
>>>arr = np.array([1, 2, 3])
>>>print(arr)
```

The output of the above code is

```
[1 2 3]
```

For creating a 2-D NumPy array, we have 1-D arrays as its elements. They often represent matrices. For example,

```
>>>import numpy as np
>>>arr = np.array([[1, 2, 3], [4, 5, 6]])
>>>print(arr)
```

The output of the above code is

```
[[1 2 3]
  [4 5 6]]
```

Similarly, 3-D arrays are created using 2-D arrays, also called *matrices*. For example,

```
import numpy as np
arr = np.array([[[1, 2, 3], [4, 5, 6]], [[1, 2, 3], [4, 5, 6]]])
print(arr)
```

The output of the code is shown below:

```
[[[1 2 3]
  [4 5 6]]

 [[1 2 3]
  [4 5 6]]]
```

11.1.3 `ndim` Keyword

The dimensions of a NumPy array can be checked using the ndim attribute that returns an integer whose value is equal to the number of dimensions of the array. Let's understand it using some examples.

```
import numpy as np
a = np.array(13)
b = np.array([1, 2, 3, 4])
c = np.array([[1, 2, 3], [4, 5, 6]])
```

```
print(a.ndim)
print(b.ndim)
print(c.ndim)
```

The output of the code is

```
0
1
2
```

We can also create any higher dimensional array using ndim attribute as an argument inside array() method. Note that here the ndmin parameter is used inside the array() function to create the number of dimensions in a given array. For example,

```
import numpy as np
arr = np.array([1, 2, 3], ndmin=5)
print(arr)
print('The number of dimensions are:', arr.ndim)
```

The output of the code is

```
[[[[[1 2 3]]]]]
The number of dimensions are: 5
```

11.1.4 shape Keyword

The shape keyword is used to return a tuple with the length of the dimensions of an array. For example,

```
import numpy as np
np_arr = np.array([[10, 20, 30], [40, 50, 60]])
print(np_arr.shape)
```

The output of the above code is

```
(2, 3)
```

The above example depicts that np_arr has two dimensions with 3 elements in each dimension. Similarly, if we have a NumPy array of 3 dimensions, output will differ accordingly. See the example given below.

```
import numpy as np
new_np_arr = np.array([[[10, 20, 30], [40, 50, 60], [70, 80, 90]],
                       [[1, 2, 3], [4, 5, 6], [7, 8, 9]]])
print(new_np_arr.shape)
```

The output of the code is

```
(2, 3, 3)
```

Here, new_np_arr has 3 dimensions and each dimension consists of 3 rows and 3 columns.

11.1.5 Indexing and Slicing in NumPy Arrays

Indexing

To access an element in a NumPy array, we use indexing. As already known, indexes start with 0 that means the first element will have an index of 0, second will have 1 and so on. Let's see an example.

```
>>>import numpy as np
>>>arr = np.array([1, 2, 3, 4, 5])
>>>print(arr[0])
>>>print(arr[1])
```

The output of the above code is

```
1
2
```

Here, we accessed the first element and second element of the array by referring to its index value. We can access the third, fourth and fifth element in the same manner. If we want to add them, this is also possible using the following code:

```
import numpy as np
arr = np.array([1, 2, 3, 4, 5])
print(arr[2] + arr[3] + arr[4])
```

The output of the above code is

```
12
```

In the above code, the value of `arr[2],arr[3],arr[4]` is 3,4,5 respectively. Let us now understand the indexing in a 2D-array. Suppose, we want to access the element on the first row and second column and second row and third column. Visualize the 2-D array like a table which has rows and columns.

```
import numpy as np
arr = np.array([[1,2,3,4], [5,6,7,8]])
print('The 2nd element on 1st row is: ', arr[0, 1])
print('The 3rd element on 2nd row is: ', arr[1, 2])
```

The output of the above code is

```
The 2nd element on 1st row is: 2
The 3rd element on 2nd row is: 7
```

Negative indexing can also be used to access the elements from an array. Suppose, we want to access the last element of the second dimension using negative indexing. The code will be as follows:

```
import numpy as np
arr = np.array([[1,2,3,4], [5,6,7,8]])
print('Last element from 2nd dim: ', arr[1, -1])
```

The output of the above code is

```
Last element from 2nd dim: 8
```

Array slicing

It is possible to extract elements from one given index to another given index in `NumPy` arrays using the slicing concept. It follows the following syntax:

```
[start:end:step]
```

Here, `start` is the starting index value. Second parameter that is `end` shows the ending index value and `step` is optional and by default it takes 1 as a step value. It determines the step of the slicing. If we do not provide a `start` index, it takes 0 as a default value. And if we do not provide an `end` parameter, it considers the length of the array in that particular dimension.

Let's see some examples on slicing concepts.

```
import numpy as np
arr = np.array([1, 2, 3, 4, 5, 6, 7, 8, 9])
print(arr[1:6])#elements are sliced from index 1 till index 5
print(arr[3:])#elements are sliced from index 3 till the end
print(arr[:5])#elements are sliced from index 0 till index 4
```

The output of the code is

```
[2 3 4 5 6]
[4 5 6 7 8 9]
[1 2 3 4 5]
```

It is important to note that the `end` index value is always excluded in the output. Now, Let's perform slicing in a 2-D array using an example,

```
import numpy as np
arr = np.array([[1, 2, 3, 4], [5, 6, 7, 8]])
print(arr[1, 1:4])
print(arr[0:2, 3])
```

The output of the code is

```
[6 7 8]
[4 8]
```

The above code will slice elements from index 1 to index 4 (not included) in the second element in the first slicing example. In the second slicing example, it will return index 3 from both elements.

Program 11.1: Program to reverse all the elements of a numpy array

```
import numpy as np
arr = np.array([1, 2, 3, 4, 5, 6, 7, 8, 9], dtype=int)
print("The original array: ")
print(arr)
print("The reverse array: ")
arr = arr[::-1]
print(arr)
```

In above Program 11.1, we are reversing the entire `NumPy` array `arr` using slicing approach. Here, `dtype` is an attribute given as a second parameter in `array()` function which shows what kind of values are stored in the given array. It can be `int, float, boolean` or any other data-type. The `dtype` keyword is explained in further sections in this chapter. We have given a step size of `-1` which means it will print all the elements of the array in reverse order starting from the length of the array till index 0, as shown below:

```
The original array:
[1 2 3 4 5 6 7 8 9]
The reverse array:
[9 8 7 6 5 4 3 2 1]
```

11.1.6 Some NumPy Functions

`ones()` and `zeros()`

The `ones()` function creates a `NumPy` array of specified shape, containing all ones (1s). SImilarly thc `zeros()` function creates a `NumPy` array containing all zeros (0s). The following code snippet creates an array, having each element as 1 with dimensions 4 blocks, each having 3 rows and 3 columns.

```
import numpy as np
ones_array = np.ones((4, 3, 3), dtype=int)
print(ones_array)
```

The output of the code is

```
[[[1 1 1]
  [1 1 1]
  [1 1 1]]

 [[1 1 1]
  [1 1 1]
  [1 1 1]]

 [[1 1 1]
  [1 1 1]
  [1 1 1]]

 [[1 1 1]
  [1 1 1]
  [1 1 1]]]
```

Here, we have used another function called `zeros()` that creates an array with all zero elements. The following code creates an array having all elements zero and dimensions 3 blocks, 2 rows and 3 columns.

```
import numpy as np
zeros_array = np.zeros((3, 2, 3), dtype=int)
print(zeros_array)
```

The output of the code is

```
[[[0 0 0]
  [0 0 0]]

 [[0 0 0]
  [0 0 0]]

 [[0 0 0]
  [0 0 0]]]
```

type() function and dtype keyword:

The `type()` function returns the type of the Python object like `int`, `str`, `float`, `boolean`, `lists`, etc. Whereas, the `dtype` keyword gives us information regarding the type of the data such as int, float, etc., size of the data stored in the form of bytes of a `NumPy` array.

Consider the following statements:

```
print(ones_array.dtype)
print(zeros_array.dtype)
print(type(2022))
print(type(3.14))
print(type('Hello'))
print(type([i for i in range(1, 5)]))
```

The output of the code is

```
int32
int32
<class 'int'>
<class 'float'>
<class 'str'>
<class 'list'>
```

The term `int32` refers to a data type that represents integer values within a specific range. This range spans from `-2,147,483,648` to `2,147,483,647`, requiring 32 bits of memory to store. This is why it is called "`int32`". Essentially, `int32` is a shorthand way of saying "a 32-bit integer."

It is important to learn that the `ndim` keyword only finds out the dimension of a given `NumPy` array but the `shape` keyword provides the number of blocks, rows and columns present in each dimension. For example, the `ones_array` and `zeros_array` `NumPy` array are 3-D arrays so `ndim` should return 3 as its dimensional. Let's execute the code,

```
print(ones_array.ndim)
print(zeros_array.ndim)
```

The output of the code is

```
3
3
```

arange() and linspace()

The `arange()` function creates a one dimensional array of numbers within a given range. For example,

```
array_1 = np.arange(2, 11)
print(array_1)
```

The output of the above code is

```
[2 3 4 5 6 7 8 9 10]
```

It has created a 1–D array containing values from 2 to 10. Last number is not included in the `arange()` function. Also, the difference between two consecutive numbers is 1 that is constant.

If we want the difference between the two numbers greater than 1 then we can specify the difference value as an additional parameter to the `arange()` function. For example,

```
array_2 = np.arange(1, 11, 3)
print(array_2)
```

The output of the above code is

```
[1 4 7 10]
```

We can also change the datatype of the elements using `dtype` keyword. For example,

```
array_3 = np.arange(1, 11, 3, dtype=float)
print(array_3)
```

The output of the above code is

```
[1. 4. 7. 10.]
```

The `linspace()` function creates an array of fixed numbers from a given range in such a manner that the difference between every consecutive pair of numbers is constant. Let's understand it using an example given below,

```
array_4 = np.linspace(1, 21, 5)
print(array_4)
```

The output of the above code is

```
[1. 6. 11. 16. 21.]
```

In the above code, the `linspace()` function has created an array containing 5 numbers from 1 to 21 (included) such that the difference between every pair of numbers is constant. Here, 5 is the length of the array to be created.

reshape()

As the name suggests, the `reshape()` function changes the configuration of an existing array. In the following example, `arr1` is a 1D array having 6 elements. The statement `arr1 = arr1.reshape((2,3))` changes the shape of `arr1` to (2,3), i.e., 2 rows and 3 columns, thereby making it a 2D array.

```
>>> arr1 = np.array([1,2,3,4,5,6])
>>> print(arr1) = arr1.reshape((2,3))
>>> arr1
```

The array after reshaping is shown below

```
array([[1, 2, 3],
       [4, 5, 6]])
>>> print(arr1.ndim)
```

The output of the given array `arr1` after using `ndim` keyword is

```
2
```

random.randint()

The `NumPy` module contains a sub-module `random`, which has the `randint()` function. This function generates random numbers from a given range. It takes two input parameters, first is the range specified by two integers—the lower bound and the upper bound; and second is the size parameter which specifies the count of numbers to be generated randomly. It generates numbers in the range which includes the lower bound but excludes the upper bound. For example,

```
random_array1 = np.random.randint(10, 50, size=15)
print(random_array1)
random_array2 = np.random.randint(10, 50, size=(5, 3))
print(random_array2)
random_array3 = np.random.randint(10, 50, size=(3, 2, 4))
print(random_array3)
```

The output of the code is shown below:

```
[22 27 39 13 34 46 36 20 26 49 32 33 33 27 21]
[[19 21 29]
 [41 31 23]
 [33 15 39]
 [28 22 31]
 [26 40 19]]
[[[37 46 30 12]
  [34 42 21 22]]

 [[49 25 17 10]
  [49 26 27 42]]

 [[44 43 49 20]
  [36 38 16 40]]]
```

ndarray()

The ndarray() function is used to create a NumPy array having random numbers as its elements same as of given configuration and data type. It takes two inputs. First input is the configuration of the new array and second input is the data type of the items. For example,

```
any_array = np.ndarray((6, 3), dtype=int)
print(any_array)
```

```
[[       0       0       0]
 [       0       0       0]
 [       0       0       0]
 [       0     700       0]
 [       0 7077988       0]
 [7077996       0       0]]
```

len()

The array length can be determined by the number of elements in a 1-D array, number of rows in a 2-D array and number of blocks in a 3-D array. We use the len() function to calculate the length of an array. For example,

```
import numpy as np
one_dim_arr = np.arange(1, 21)
two_dim_arr = np.arange(1, 29).reshape((4, 7))
three_dim_arr = np.arange(1, 31).reshape((2, 5, 3))
print("Number of items in one dimensional array:", len(one_dim_arr))
print("Number of rows in two dimensional array:", len(two_dim_arr))
print("Number of blocks in three dimensional array:", len(three_dim_arr))
```

The output of the code is shown below:

```
Number of items in one dimensional array: 20
Number of rows in two dimensional array: 4
Number of blocks in three dimensional array: 2
```

size Keyword

The size keyword returns the exact number of items present in a NumPy array, regardless of the given dimensions. It works with NumPy arrays, not with lists. For example,

```
print("Number of items in one dimensional array:", one_dim_arr.size)
print("Number of items in two dimensional array:", two_dim_arr.size)
print("Number of items in three dimensional array:", three_dim_arr.size)
```

The output of the code is shown below:

```
Number of items in one dimensional array: 20
Number of items in two dimensional array: 28
Number of items in three dimensional array: 30
```

As we can observe in the output given above, total number of items in one dimensional array are 20, 28 items in two dimensional array and 20 items in three dimensional array.

Apart from the functions discussed above, the NumPy module also has many statistical functions like sum(), mean(), median(), min() and max() functions. For example, there are some prices mentioned for bags of different brands and we want to compute the sum of the prices of all bags, average or mean price of a bag, price of a cheapest bag, price of the most expensive bag, median price and most frequently occurring price of a bag, the code to perform this is given below:

```
prices=np.array([139, 698, 999, 491, 748, 850, 112, 999, 999, 386])
total_value = np.sum(prices)
print("Total value: ",total_value)
average_price = np.mean(prices)
print("Average Price: " ,average_price)
minimum_price = np.min(prices)
print("Minimum Price: " ,minimum_price)
maximum_price = np.max(prices)
print("Maximum Price: ",maximum_price)
median_price = np.median(prices)
print("Median Price: ",median_price)
```

The output of the code is shown below:

```
Total value: 6421
Average Price: 642.1
Minimum Price: 112
Maximum Price: 999
Median Price: 723.0
```

11.2 PANDAS MODULE

The pandas module helps to examine data. When it comes to managing, manipulating, cleaning and analyzing enormous amounts of data, we use the Pandas module to create Pandas series and Pandas DataFrames. It can clean messy data sets by removing irrelevant or incorrect data and bring them into a readable format. It also provides functions to further manage and manipulate the data. Its powerful functions make it a go-to tool for data scientists, analysts, and researchers alike.

Pandas module provides functions performing the following tasks:

- Handle data easily and efficiently
- Support different file formats such as JSON, CSV, EXCEL, etc.
- Handle missing values in data
- Reshape data into different formats
- Indexing and aligning the data
- Reading and writing data
- Data cleaning
- Data visualization

11.2.1 Installation of Pandas

`Pandas` module, just like `NumPy`, needs to be explicitly installed. To install `Pandas` on a system, we use the popular Python package installer, `pip`. The command is:

```
pip install pandas
```

Once `Pandas` is installed, we need to import it in our program at the very beginning using the keyword `'import'`. Below is the command,

```
import pandas as pd
```

Once it is imported, we can use it in our code. Here `pd` is the alias (or nickname) for `Pandas`. We can also check the version of `Pandas` using the following command:

```
>>>import pandas as pd
>>>print(pd.__version__)
```

The version is

```
1.3.5
```

Data structures in programming are used to store and organize data easily in a computer. In the Pandas module, two types of data structures are commonly used to organize and process data efficiently.

1. Series
2. DataFrame

11.2.2 Pandas Series

The `Pandas Series` is like a one-dimensional array holding data of different data types. Let's create a simple `Pandas Series`.

```
import pandas as pd
x = [1, 2, 3]
y = pd.Series(x)
print(y)
```

The output of the code is

```
0  1
1  2
2  3
dtype: int64
```

We use the `Series()` function to convert any Python list or `NumPy` array into a `Pandas Series`. Note that here 'S' of `Series()` function is in uppercase. Let's write a short program to create a pandas series for generating 20 random numbers between 10 and 50.

```
import random
import pandas as pd
numbers = pd.Series([random.randint(10, 50) for i in range(20)])
print(numbers)
```

The output of the code is shown below:

```
0      41
1      34
2      31
3      41
4      13
5      13
6      50
7      19
8      11
9      45
10     25
11     32
12     17
13     18
14     30
15     50
16     18
17     23
18     50
19     23
dtype: int64
```

In the output, the first column shows the indices and the second column shows the randomly generated numbers within the specified range. We can also verify the type of values stored in `numbers` variable by using `type()` function.

```
>>>type(numbers)
<class 'pandas.core.series.Series'>
```

As the output shows that `type()` function has returned `pandas.core.series.Series` in the output, this confirms that the number is truly a `Pandas Series`. Just like a list, the `Pandas Series` is capable of storing multiple types of values at the same time. Let's see an example of it.

Suppose, we want to store the name of a student, his or her roll number, weight, and whether he or she has paid the fee or not in a Python list. After that, we will convert it into a `Pandas Series`.

```
student_details = pd.Series(['John', 19, 50.7, False])
print(student_details)
print(type(student_details))
```

The output of the code is shown below:

```
0     John
1       19
2     50.7
3    False
dtype: object
<class 'pandas.core:series.Series'>
```

Here, the `dtype` associated with the `Series` is shown as: `object` as all items belong to different data types. However, the next statement : `print(type(student_details))` gives output as `Pandas Series`.

We can also create `Pandas Series` from `key:value` objects, just like a dictionary. For example,

```
import pandas as pd
months = {"January": 1, "February": 2, "March": 3}
my_series = pd.Series(months)
print(my_series)
```

The output of the code is shown below:

```
January    1
February   2
March      3
dtype: int64
```

Here, column 1 (also called as labels) in the output represents the *keys* and column 2 represents the *values* corresponding to each key.

`size` Keyword

The `size` keyword is also used with `Pandas Series`. It returns the number of items present in a `Pandas Series`. We use dot `(.)` operator to apply this keyword on a `Series`. For example,

```
print(numbers.size)
```

The output of the code is

```
20
```

Here, the `numbers` pandas series has 20 items so the output is 20.

`shape` Keyword

The `shape` keyword determines the number of rows and columns in a given `Pandas Series`. For example,

```
print(numbers.shape)
```

The output of the code is

```
(20,)
```

`min()` and `max()` Functions

The `min()` and `max()` functions help in retrieving the lowest and highest values from a given `Pandas Series` respectively. For example,

`print(min(numbers))` gives the output

```
13
```

`print(max(numbers))` gives the output

```
46
```

If we try to apply `min()` and `max()` functions on a heterogeneous `Pandas Series`, it gives an exception `TypeError`. Let's understand this concept using the example given below.

```
>>>import pandas as pd
>>>student_details = pd.Series(['John', 19, 50.7, False])
>>>print(max(student_details))
```

It gives an error as shown below:

```
Traceback (most recent call last):
  File "C:\Users\AKANSHA\Desktop\pythondemo.py", line 3, in <module>
  print(max(student_details))
TypeError: '>' not supported between instances of 'int' and 'str'
```

mean(), mode() and median() Functions

All the three `mean()`, `mode()` and `median()` functions are used on numerical data. The `mean()` function finds out the average of the numbers in a pandas series. The `mode()` function returns the frequently occurring value from the series. And `median()` finds out the median value. Let's use them in the code. The output is also given.

```
print(numbers.mean())
26.15
print(numbers.mode())
0    36
dtype: int64
print(number.median())
29.0
```

Program 11.2 Program to perform addition, subtraction, multiplication, and division on two pandas series

```
import pandas as pd
series1 = pd.Series([6, 5, 9, 3, 8])
series2 = pd.Series([3, 2, 5, 1, 4])
add_result = series1 + series2
print("Adding series1 and series2: ")
print(add_result)
sub_result = series1 - series2
print("Subtracting series2 by series1: ")
print(sub_result)
mul_result = series1 * series2
print("Multiplying series1 and series2: ")
print(mul_result)
div_result = series1 / series2
print("Dividing series1 by series2: ")
print(div_result)
```

The output of the code is shown below:

```
Adding series1 and series2:
0     9
1     7
2    14
3     4
4    12
dtype: int64
Subtracting series2 by series1:
0     3
1     3
2     4
3     2
4     4
deype: int64
Multiplying series1 and series2:
0    18
1    10
2    45
3     3
4    32
deype: int64
Dividing series1 by series2:
0   2.0
1   2.5
2   1.8
3   3.0
4   2.0
dtype: float64
```

In the above Program 11.2, we have created two pandas series `series1` and `series2`. On these two `Pandas Series`, we have performed basic arithmetic operations such as addition, subtraction, multiplication and division using operators `'+'`, `'-'`, `'*'`, `'/'` respectively.

Indexing in Pandas Series

The concept of indexing is the same in `Pandas Series` as we learnt in list or `NumPy` array. The syntax for indexing a pandas series is as follows:

```
pandas_series[start_index:end_index]
```

For example,

```
print(numbers[5:10])
print(number[13:18])
```

```
5      44
6      14
7      22
8      41
9      22
dtype: int64
13     21
14     18
15     12
16     11
17     17
dtype: int64
```

sort_values()

The `sort_values()` function sorts the numbers in a `Pandas Series` either in ascending order or descending order. This function takes one input which is `ascending = True` if we want to order the range of numbers in ascending order else `ascending = False` if numbers should be arranged in decreasing order. For example,

```
print(numbers.sort_values(ascending=True))
```

```
16      10
2       10
9       15
15      15
19      16
17      19
4       19
3       20
0       24
8       28
5       35
11      36
10      37
14      37
18      38
12      40
7       41
13      41
1       41
6       45
dtype: int64
```

```
print(numbers.sort_values(ascending=False))
```

```
9       50
12      46
4       45
11      45
0       41
16      36
2       33
5       32
18      32
17      31
3       30
6       29
13      27
19      23
15      20
8       17
14      16
7       16
10      15
1       13
dtype: int64
```

value_counts()

This function counts the number of times an element has occurred in a Pandas Series. It cannot be applied on Python lists or NumPy arrays. For example,

```
print(numbers.value_counts())
```

```
28      2
13      2
50      2
45      2
17      1
37      1
30      1
12      1
18      1
34      1
14      1
39      1
48      1
42      1
33      1
16      1
dtype: int64
```

`head()` and `tail()`

If we do not want to see the entire dataset and just want to see the first few rows or the last few rows from the dataset then we use `head()` and `tail()` functions respectively. The `head()` function specifically shows the first five rows of our dataset and `tail()` function shows the last five rows from our dataset. For example,

```
print(numbers.head())
```

```
0     36
1     45
2     10
3     23
4     35
dtype: int64
```

```
print(numbers.tail())
```

```
15    38
16    31
17    21
18    31
19    23
dtype: int64
```

If we want to show rows more than five then we have to pass that number as an argument inside the `head()` and `tail()` function. For example,

```
print(numbers.head(10))
```

```
0     46
1     11
2     22
3     29
4     28
5     33
6     35
7     17
8     48
9     47
dtype: int64
```

```
print(numbers.tail(10))
```

```
10    17
11    17
12    40
13    46
14    41
15    38
16    14
17    28
18    33
19    10
dtype: int64
```

11.2.3 Pandas DataFrames

The DataFrame in Pandas is a two dimensional array just like a table having rows and columns. It is used to store data, where the columns are the various fields and each row is a separate record. Let's create a simple DataFrame.

```
import pandas as pd
data = {
  "maximum_marks": [100, 150, 200, 250],
  "obtained_marks": [80, 120, 155, 210]
   }
df = pd.DataFrame(data)
print(df)
```

The output of the code is shown below:

```
   maximum_marks  obtained_marks
0            100              80
1            150             120
2            200             155
3            250             210
```

The loc Attribute

To return one or more specified rows from the Pandas DataFrame, we use loc attribute. For example,

```
print(df.loc[0])
```

```
maximum_marks      100
obtained_marks      80
Name: 0, dtype: int64
```

In the above code, the output is a Pandas Series that returns the very first row from the given DataFrame. Let's see another example for better understanding,

```
print(df.loc[[1, 2]])
```

```
   maximum_marks  obtained_marks
1            150             120
2            200             155
```

Here, it returns the values present in row 1 and row 2.

Naming Indexes in Pandas DataFrame

Row indexes in a DataFrame can be named using the index parameter. For example,

```
import pandas as pd
data = {
  "maximum_marks": [100, 150, 200, 250],
  "obtained_marks": [80, 120, 155, 210]
  }
```

```
index_lables=["subject1", "subject2", "subject3", "subject3"]
df = pd.DataFrame(data, index=index_lables)
print(df)
```

The output of the code is shown below:

```
         maximum_marks  obtained_marks
subject1           100              80
subject2           150             120
subject3           200             155
subject3           250             210
```

Now we can use the named index in `loc` attribute to retrieve the specified row. For example,

```
print(df.loc["subject3"])
```

```
         maximum_marks  obtained_marks
subject3           200             155
subject3           250             210
```

Program 11.3: Program to display the first four rows of the DataFrame

```
import pandas as pd
import numpy as np
result_data  = {'Name': ['Akshit', 'Neha', 'Riya', 'Jatin',
'Nikhil', 'Saumya'],
     'Marks': [52.5, 26, 80, 75.5, 32, 60],
     'Remarks': ['Pass', 'Fail', 'Pass', 'Pass', 'Fail', 'Pass']}
labels = ['a', 'b', 'c', 'd', 'e', 'f']
df = pd.DataFrame(result_data , index=labels)
print("The first four rows of the data frame are: ")
print(df.iloc[:4])
```

The output of the code is shown below:

```
The first four rows of the data frame are:
     Name    Marks   Remarks
a   Akshit    52.5     Pass
b     Neha    26.0     Fail
c     Riya    80.0     Pass
d    Jatin    75.5     Pass
```

In the above Program 11.3, we have created a dictionary `result_data` storing information for six students. Also, we have created a list `labels` which will be used to label the rows of the `DataFrame`. We have further converted this dictionary to a DataFrame `df` using index parameter. In order to print the first four rows of the DataFrame, we have used the `iloc` attribute which will return row 1 till row 4.

Joining of DataFrames

One way to combine two DataFrames is by using the `pandas.DataFrame.append()` method. This function adds the rows of the second DataFrame to the end of the first DataFrame.

Additionally, any columns that are not present in the first DataFrame will be added as new columns. This is a useful method for merging data and creating a more comprehensive dataset. Program 11.4 given below illustrates this concept.

Program 11.4: Program to combine two DataFrames using append()

```
import pandas as pd

# First dictionary having student data
dataset1 = {'Name':['Ram', 'Riya', 'Amit'],
            'Age':[30, 19, 25],
            'Sex':['Male', 'Female', 'Male'],
            'State':['Kerala', 'Delhi', 'Kolkata']}

# Second dictionary having student data
dataset2 = {'Name':['Gaurvit', 'Rekha', 'Seeta'],
            'Age':[27, 45, 16],
            'Sex':['Male', 'Female', 'Female'],
            'State':['Punjab', 'Orissa', 'Haryana']}

# Converting first dictionary into DataFrame df1
df1 = pd.DataFrame(dataset1,index=[0, 1, 2])

# Converting second dictionary into DataFrame df2
df2 = pd.DataFrame(dataset2, index=[3, 4, 5])

print(df1, "\n\n", df2)
# using append function
print()
result = df1.append(df2)
print(result)
```

The output of the code is shown below:

```
      Name   Age     Sex     State
0      Ram    30    Male    Kerala
1     Riya    19  Female     Delhi
2     Amit    25    Male   Kolkata

      Name   Age     Sex     State
3  Gaurvit    27    Male    Punjab
4    Rekha    45  Female    Orissa
5    Seeta    16  Female   Haryana

      Name   Age     Sex     State
0      Ram    30    Male    Kerala
1     Riya    19  Female     Delhi
2     Amit    25    Male   Kolkata
3  Gaurvit    27    Male    Punjab
4    Rekha    45  Female    Orissa
5    Seeta    16  Female   Haryana
```

The aforementioned Program 11.4 involves the creation of two dictionaries, `dataset1` and `dataset2`, which are subsequently converted into DataFrames, `df1` and `df2`, using the `pd.DataFrame()` function. To merge these DataFrames, we have utilized the `append()` function to append `df2` to `df1`.

Alternatively, if we append `df1` to `df2`, the rows of `df2` will come before the rows of `df1`.

The `append()` function is a powerful tool in pandas that allows combining data from multiple sources. Table 11.1 shows several parameters which can be used with the `append()` function that one should be aware of.

Table 11.1 Parameters used with `append()` Function

Parameter	Description
other	This parameter can be a DataFrame, Series, dict-like object, or a list of these. It represents the data that you want to append to your existing DataFrame.
ignore_index	If set to `True`, this parameter will ignore the index labels of the data you are appending. This can be useful if you want to create a new index for the combined data.
verify_integrity	If set to `True`, this parameter will raise a exception `ValueError` if there are any duplicates in the index of the combined data. This can be helpful in ensuring data integrity.
sort	By default, this parameter will sort the columns of the combined data if they are not aligned. To ensure that the column labels appear in a sorted order, we can set the parameter `sort=True`. Conversely, if we set the parameter `sort=False`, the column labels will appear in an unsorted order.

By understanding these parameters, we can use the `append()` function to efficiently combine data and perform powerful data analysis.

Loading CSV File into DataFrame

The CSV (comma-separated value) file format is widely used for storing data in text files, as well as in tab-separated value (TSV) and other formats. In Chapter 9, we explored one method for utilizing CSV files. Specifically, we employed the `pandas.read_csv()` function to import the contents of the file. This function requires the full file path or location as an argument. To load a CSV file using Pandas, the following syntax must be followed:

```
pd.read_csv(r'Location or path of the file\File_name.csv')
```

For example, let's create a csv file having data of three persons in the form of a table. While saving this csv file, it should be saved with the `.csv` extension. Here, `'r'` is necessary to use before the path because it helps to encounter any special characters like `'\'` present in the path.

```
Name,  Age, Sex,    City
Ram,   18,  Male,   Delhi
Geeta, 20,  Female, Mumbai
Shyam, 23,  Male,   Orissa
Niti,  22,  Female, Kolkata
```

```
import pandas as pd
df = pd.read_csv(r'C:\SAMPLE\file.csv')
print(df)
```

```
     Name   Aqe     Sex     City
0     Ram    18    Male    Delhi
1   Geeta    20  Female   Mumbai
2   Shyam    23    Male  Orissa
3    Niti    22  Female  Kolkata
```

Missing Data in Pandas DataFrame

Missing data can appear in a dataset when information is not provided for one or more items. This can be a significant issue in real-life scenarios, as it can lead to inaccurate analyses and flawed conclusions. In the context of pandas, missing data is often referred to as NA (Not Available) values. It is not uncommon for datasets to arrive with missing data, either because it was not collected or because it never existed in the first place. Addressing missing data is crucial for ensuring the validity and reliability of data-driven insights. Missing data can be represented in two ways: `NaN` (Not a Number) or `None` values.

To detect, remove, replace the missing data, there are various functions available. However, we will focus on two specific functions, `null()` and `notnull()`, which are used to detect the presence of missing data in a DataFrame. These functions return a DataFrame of boolean values as a result, indicating whether the data is missing or not. It is crucial to identify and handle missing data appropriately to ensure accurate analysis and decision-making. Program 11.5 demonstrates this concept using a sample DataFrame.

Program 11.5: Program to check the presence of missing values in a DataFrame

```
import pandas as pd
import numpy as np

# storing data in dictionary consisting lists
sample_dict = {'Student1 marks':[80, 75, np.nan, 90],
         'Student2 marks': [40, np.nan, 52, 60],
         'Student3 marks':[92, 67, 77, np.nan]}

# converting list to DataFrame
df = pd.DataFrame(sample_dict)

# using isnull() function
df.isnull()
```

The output of the code is shown below:

	Student1 marks	Student2 marks	Student3 marks
0	False	False	False
1	False	True	False
2	True	False	False
3	False	False	True

The output of the Program 11.5 shown above illustrates that `isnull()` has returned `True` where missing data is present in the form of `NaN` values. Similarly, we can use the `notnull()` function that returns `False` for all `NaN` values present in the pandas DataFrame.

Data Cleaning and Data Visualization

Data cleaning is the process of identifying and correcting erroneous or inaccurate data in your dataset. This can include empty cells, data in the wrong format, incorrect data, and duplicates.

It is crucial to ensure that your data is accurate and of high quality, as bad data can negatively impact processes and analysis. By cleaning your data, we can increase overall productivity and ensure that the information used in decision-making is of the highest quality.

In summary, data cleaning is an essential step in data management that should not be overlooked. By taking the time to clean the data, we can ensure that our analysis is accurate and reliable, ultimately leading to better decision-making and improved outcomes.

Additionally, Data visualization is a crucial aspect of presenting extensive datasets in a visual format. In Chapter 12, we have provided an in-depth analysis of this feature. It enables us to comprehend complex data quickly and efficiently. By utilizing various graphical representations, such as charts, graphs, and maps, data visualization can transform raw data into meaningful insights.

11.3 DIFFERENCE BETWEEN PYTHON LIST, NUMPY ARRAY AND PANDAS SERIES/DATAFRAME

It is important to understand the basic difference between Python list, NumPy array and Pandas Series. When it comes to data storage and manipulation in Python, it's essential to know the differences between Python list, NumPy array, and Pandas Series. While there are no strict rules for when to use each one, there are some key considerations to keep in mind.

Firstly, Python lists are ideal for storing, fetching, adding, and manipulating data. They're versatile and can handle a wide range of data types, making them a popular choice for many Python developers.

On the other hand, NumPy arrays are specifically designed for storing numeric data in an array-based format. Whether it's one-dimensional or multidimensional, NumPy arrays are perfect for performing various mathematical operations on your data.

Finally, Pandas Series are best suited for importing data from external files such as CSV, TXT, or XML. If your data is available in a table format, then Pandas DataFrame is the way to go.

By understanding the differences between these three data structures, you can choose the right one for your specific needs and ensure that your Python code is efficient, effective, and easy to maintain.

SUMMARY

- Python is considered as one of the powerful languages as it has many inbuilt functions, modules, libraries and packages that makes it effortless to write the programs in it.
- A module in Python is a set of functions that consists of functions definition, classes, variables and other various statements written in Python language.
- The file containing code for a module has an extension of *.py*.
- These modules can be imported inside other programs to make the code convenient and to obtain desirable output.

- The `NumPy` module is used to deal with arrays. It basically stands for Numeric (or Numerical) Python.
- It consists of multidimensional array objects and assemblage of different tools that helps in working with arrays. `NumPy` has the capability to perform major mathematical computations and logical operations efficiently.
- To handle and decipher data, Python provides a `Pandas` module.
- Using the `Pandas` module, we can easily and effectively process, manipulate and analyze the data using various tools.
- It is one of the open-source Python libraries. The `Pandas` is one of the modules available in Python programming language which majorly helps to clean, process, manipulate and examine data.

EXERCISES

11.1 Explain the difference between `arange()` and `linspace()` in the `NumPy` array using an appropriate example.

11.2 Write a program to convert a numeric list into a 1D `NumPy` array. Take input list from the user.

11.3 Create a 3D array having values from 1 to 9 range.

11.4 Suppose you have a `NumPy` array [16 10 20 42 65]. Write a program to convert it into a `Pandas Series`.

11.5 Given below is a sample `Pandas Series`. Write a program to sort it.

```
Sample Pandas Series:
0 50
1 20
2 pandas
3 10.12
4 40
```

11.6 Write a program to convert an array to float type array.

11.7 Write a program to append values to a given `NumPy` array using `append()` function.

Sample arrays: `arr1 = [5, 10, 15]` and `arr2 =[[20, 25], [30, 35, 40]]`
Output `arr3 = [5, 10, 15, 20, 25, 30, 25, 40]`

11.8 Write a `NumPy` program to create a 4 × 4 matrix. The values of the matrix should range from 5 to 20.

11.9 Write a program to convert the given dictionary to `Pandas Series`.
Sample dictionary:

```
dict1 = {'item1': 10, 'item2': 30, 'item3':50, 'item4':70, 'item5':90}
```

11.10 Write a program using `Pandas` that uses the given sample dictionary. Create and display a DataFrame from it.

Sample Dictionary:

```
{'A':[22,41,26,18], 'B':[34,56,43,29], 'C':[27,89,76,48]}
```

12

Data Visualization

In the previous chapters, we have learnt various constructs in Python which produce textual or numerical output. In this chapter, we will learn how to represent data graphically. We will learn to represent data in the form of graphs, charts, etc.

Data visualization is the graphical representation of data, which is vital to the field of data analysis. Graphs and charts give us a visual summary of the data and help the user get a better understanding. Visualization becomes important when the data is huge and complex, it becomes impossible to interpret any patterns in the data in spreadsheets, this is where graphs and plots become handy.

Python provides various libraries to plot 2D and 3D graphics, namely Matplotlib, Seaborn, VisPy, etc. These libraries have various functions for plotting graphs and customizing them. We will be using the library `Matplotlib` to create various plots and 2D objects. Further, this chapter details the plotting of 3D objects using VPython, and gives a brief introduction to another Python library, names— `plotly`.

12.1 MATPLOTLIB

`Matplotlib` is the Python library to create 2D graphs and charts. It is robust, free and easy to use for data visualization. It supports interactive and noninteractive plotting and the graphs/plots can be saved in different output formats PNG, PS, etc. It can be used on all the Python platforms Jupyter, Spyder, Google Colab, etc.

It has the `pyplot` module, which supports a variety of graphs/charts, histogram, pie chart, bar charts, line plots, scatter plots, etc. `matplotlib.pyplot` module can be used in Python scripts, shell, web application servers.

Before we start plotting, the `matplotlib` library needs to be installed. In order to install any library, we have to run the `pip` command in the command window. For Python versions above 4, `pip` comes pre-installed; but for lower versions, it has to be installed manually. So, let's first see how to first install Python `pip`.

1. Download `get-pip.py` from `https://bootstrap.pypa.io/get-pip.py` and store it in the same directory as Python.
2. Change the current path to the directory where `get-pip.py` is present.
3. Run the script `get-pip.py`, in the command prompt as follows:

```
python get-pip.py
```

Once `pip` is installed on the system, the next step is to install `matplotlib`. In the command prompt, run the following command:

```
pip install matplotlib
```

or

```
py -m pip install matplotlib
```

This completes the installation of `matplotlib` and now we can begin plotting graphs and charts.

12.2 STARTING WITH MATPLOTLIB

Let's start by plotting a simple graph as shown in Program 12.1.

Program 12.1: Program to plot a simple graph

```
import matplotlib.pyplot as plt

# initializing the data
x = [10, 20, 30, 40]
y = [20, 30, 40, 50]

# plotting the data
plt.plot(x, y)

# Adding the title
plt.title("Simple Plot")

# Adding the labels
plt.ylabel("y-axis")
plt.xlabel("x-axis")
plt.show()
```

The Program 12.1 plots the graph on the basis of the X and Y coordinates provided in two separate lists. The chart title, x-axis label and y-axis labels are also provided.

We will make use of the `pyplot` module of matplotlib for plotting graphs, charts, etc. This module also has functions for adding chart titles, axis labels and modifying layouts. The output of Program 12.1 is shown below:

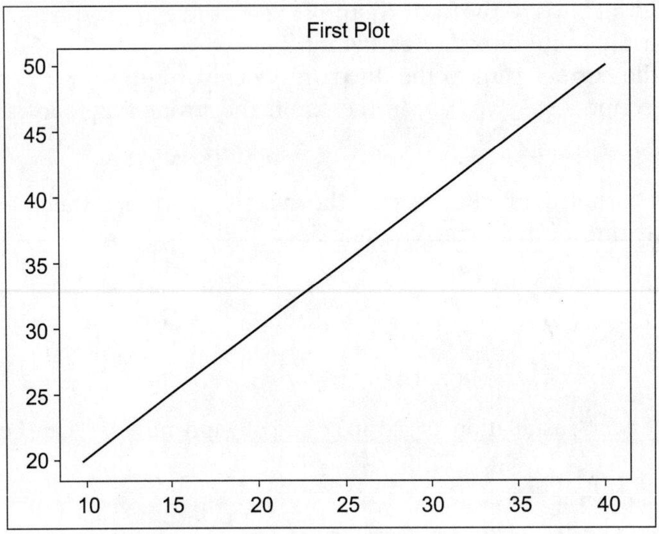

12.3 PYPLOT MODULE

`Matplotlib.pyplot` is a collection of functions related to setting the environment for plotting 2-D graphics. We have to first import the `pyplot` module as given below:

```
import matplotlib.pyplot as plt
```

Some important functions of `matplotlib.pyplot` are explained in Table 12.1.

Table 12.1 Some Functions in `pyplot` Module

Function name	Description
`show()`	This function will display the currently active figure(s) in a window. The `show()` function should be used only once per Python session.
`figure()`	This function creates an instance of `pyplot.figure()` class and it is like a single container for all objects representing axes, graphics, text, labels, etc.
`axes()`	This function creates an instance of `pyplot.axes()` class. It will create the bounding area which will contain all the plot elements.
`plot()`	This function is used to plot the data. The `plot()` function takes some parameters, which are explained below: ♦ Color — specifies the line colour ♦ Linestyle — can take values '-','--','-.',':'
`xlim() & ylim()`	These functions specify the limits on x-axis and y-axis respectively.
`axis()`	This function allows specifying the x and y limit together in one call.
`title()`	This function is used to display the title to the plot.
`xlabel()` `ylabel()`	This function is used to specify titles for x-axis and y-axis respectively.
`legend()`	This function is used to display a legend for the plot.

All the above functions have been used in Program 12.2.

Program 12.2: Program to demonstrate use of functions of pyplot module

```
import matplotlib.pyplot as plt
import numpy as np
x=[0,1,2,3,4,5,6,7,8,9]
plt.plot(x, np.sin(x),color='blue',linestyle='--')
plt.plot(x, np.cos(x),color='red',linestyle='-.')
plt.xlim(-1, 11)
plt.ylim(-1.5, 1.5)
plt.axis('Scaled')
plt.xlabel('X-axis')
plt.ylabel('Y-axis')
plt.title('Sine and Cosine curve')
plt.show()
```

The output of Program 12.2 is shown below:

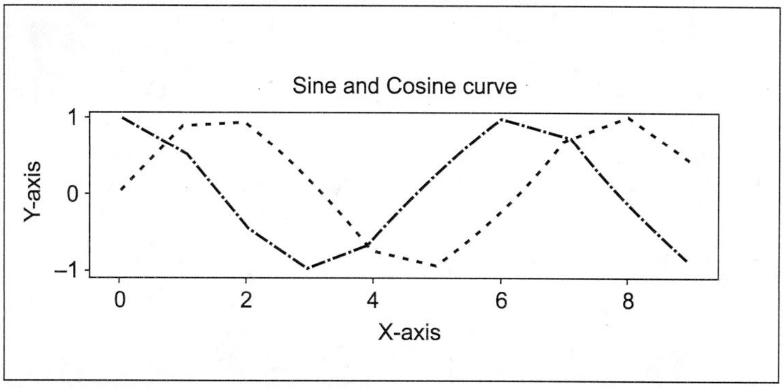

12.4 CREATING DIFFERENT TYPES OF CHARTS

12.4.1 Line Charts

Line charts are created using `plot()` function. The line charts are used to plot lines for a set of given coordinates.

Program 12.3: Program to plot a line chart

```
import matplotlib.pyplot as plt
# data to be plotted
x = [13, 10, 3]
y = [10, 12, 11]
```

```
# The plot function is used to plot a line
plt.plot(x, y)
plt.title("Line Chart")
# X and Y axis labels
plt.ylabel("y-axis")
plt.xlabel("x-axis")
# Adding the legends
plt.legend(["Line"])
plt.show()
```

The output of Program 12.3 is shown below:

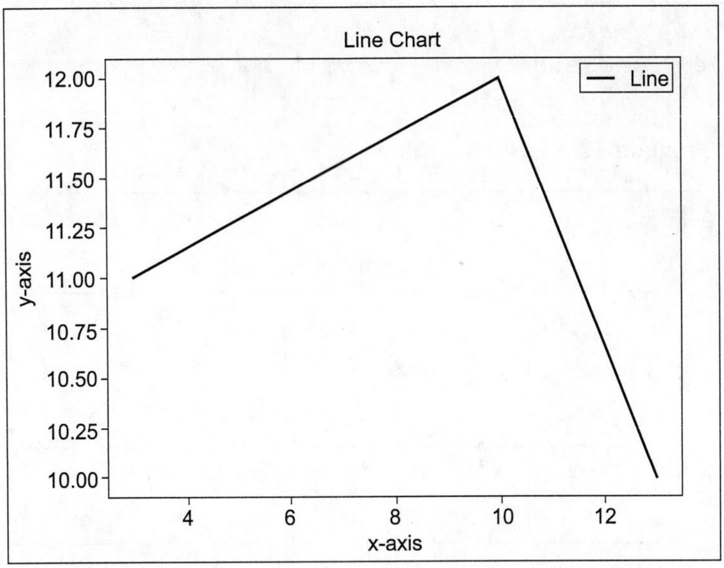

The syntax of the `plot()` function is given below:

```
matplotlib.pyplot.plot(*args, scalex=True, scaley=True, data=None,
**kwargs)
```

Or

```
plot([x], y, [fmt], *, data=None, **kwargs)
```

Or

```
plot([x], y, [fmt], [x2], y2, [fmt2], ..., **kwargs)
```

Parameters:

`x and y` : Coordinates of the point to be plotted.

`fmt` : Optional parameter, used for providing the format information like the line colour, marker style, line style, etc. For example: 'ro','bo', 'r+', etc. The format string is written as: `fmt = '[marker][line][color]'`, all three of them are optional.

Some **marker** notations:

'.'	Point marker
'o'	Circle marker
'*'	Star marker
'+'	Plus marker
'x'	X marker
's'	Square marker

Some **line** notations:

'-'	Solid line style
'--'	Dashed line style
'-.'	Dash-dot line style
':'	Dotted line style

Color notations:

'r'	red
'g'	green
'b'	blue
'c'	cyan
'm'	magenta
'y'	yellow
'k'	black
'w'	white

Some examples of format strings are:

'*b' # blue star markers
'B' # blue markers with default shape
'or' # red circles
'–y' # yellow solid lines
'–' # dashed lines with default color
'sk' # black square markers connected by a dotted line

`data` : provides label names of x and y coordinates to be plotted.
`**kwargs` : Specifies properties like line label, line width, marker color, etc.

```
>>> plot([6, 12, 30], [8, 15, 22], 'go-', label='line 1', linewidth=2)
>>> plot([2, 4, 6], [1, 3, 8], 'rs', label='line 2')
```

Plotting more line charts

Program 12.4 gives another example of plotting a line chart.

Program 12.4: Plotting line chart

```
import matplotlib.pyplot as plt
# data to be plotted
x = [13, 10, 3]
y = [10, 12, 11]
# The plot function is used to plot a line
plot(x, y, 'go--', linewidth=2, markersize=12)
plt.title("Line Chart")
plt.show()
```

The output of Program 12.4 is given below:

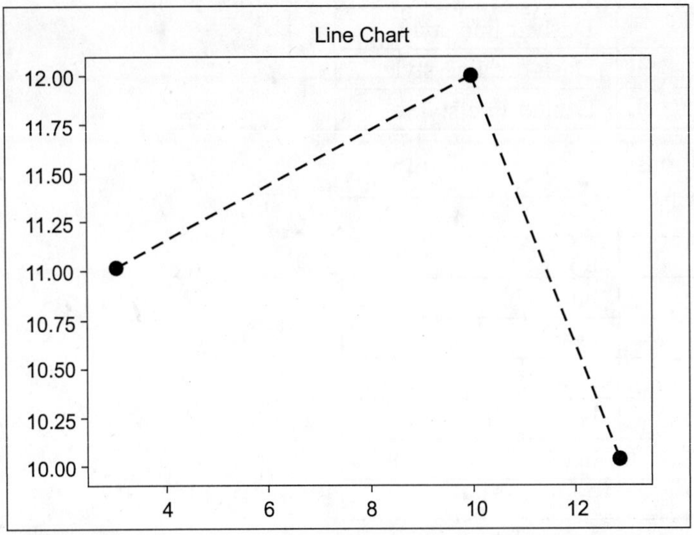

Replacing the plot function with `plt.plot(x, y, 'bo:')` in Program 12.4, will yield the line chart below:

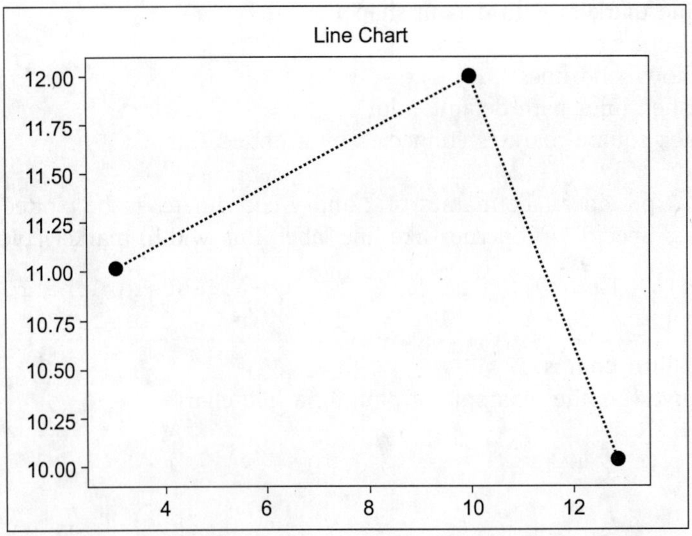

Plotting multiple lines

The plot function has to be called multiple times in order to plot multiple lines as shown in Program 12.5.

Program 12.5: Program to plot multiple lines

```
import matplotlib.pyplot as plt
# The plot function is used multiple times to lines
plt.plot([1, 2, 3], [1, 2, 3], 'go-', label='line 1', linewidth=2)
plt.plot([1, 2, 3], [1, 4, 9], 'rs-.', label='line 2')
plt.title("Multiple Line Plotting")
plt.show()
```

The output of Program 12.5 is shown below:

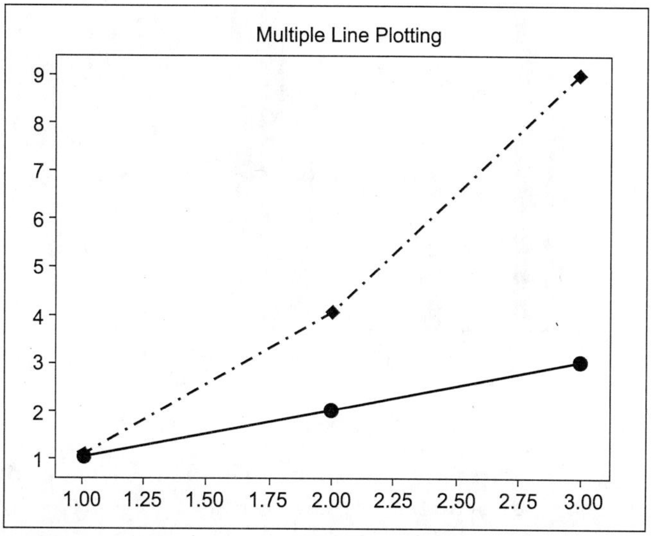

12.4.2 Bar Chart

In Python, a bar chart represents the data with rectangular bars with length/ height proportional to the value that is to be represented. The bar charts can be plotted horizontally and vertically. The bar chart can be plotted in Python using the bar() function of matplotlib.pyplot module. The Program 12.6 shows how to plot a bar chart.

Program 12.6: Program to plot a bar chart

```
import matplotlib.pyplot as plt
# data to display on bar charts
x = [5, 8, 13, 12, 20, 14, 4]
y = [9, 2, 10, 4, 3, 8, 6]

# This will plot a simple bar chart
plt.bar(x, y)
```

```
# Title to the plot
plt.title("Bar Chart")

# Adding the legends
plt.legend(["bar"])
plt.show()
```

The output of Program 12.6 is shown below:

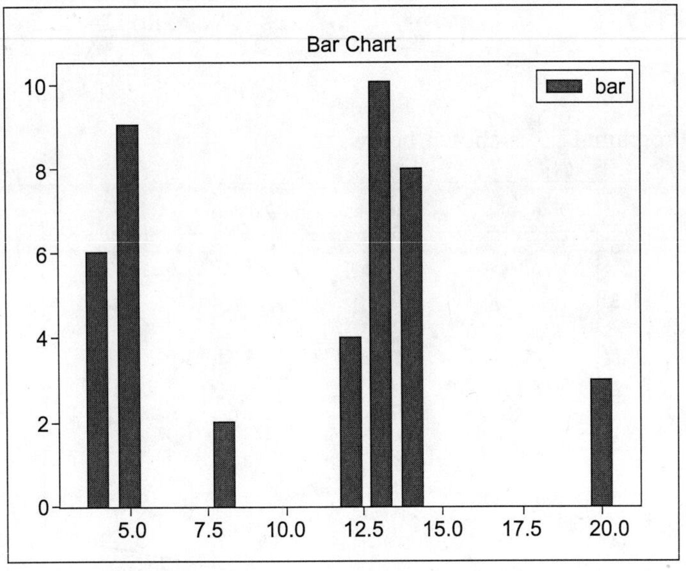

The syntax of the `bar()` function is given below:

```
matplotlib.pyplot.bar(x, height, width=0.8, bottom=None, *,
align='center', data=None, **kwargs)
```

Or

```
bar(x, height, width, bottom, align)
```

Parameters:

`x`	:	specifies x coordinates of the bars. It can have a single float value or an array having float x values for each bar.
`height`	:	specifies the height of the bars. It can have a single float value or an array having float height values for each bar.
`width`	:	specifies the width of the bars. It can have a single float value or an array having float width values for each bar.
`bottom`	:	specifies the y coordinate of the bottom side of the bars. It can be a single float value or an array having float width values for each bar. The default value is 0.
`align`	:	specifies the alignment of the bars. The possible values for alignment are {'center', 'edge'} and the default value is 'center'. In order to align the bars on the right edge, `width` should have a negative value.

Other Parameters:

`color`	:	specifies the colors of the bar faces
`edgecolor`	:	specifies the colors of the bar edges
`linewidth`	:	specifies the width of the bar edges. If the value is 0, edges are not drawn.
`tick_label`	:	specifies the tick labels of the bars. It is a string value. The default value is none.

Program 12.7: Program to plot more bar charts

```
import matplotlib.pyplot as plt
# data to display on bar charts
x = [5, 8, 13, 12, 20, 14, 4]
y = [9, 2, 10, 4, 3, 8, 6]

# This will plot a simple bar chart
plt.bar(x, y,color="blue",align="edge",edgecolor="red")

# Title to the plot
plt.title("Bar Chart")

# Adding the legends
plt.legend(["bar"])
plt.show()
```

In the Program 12.7, the `color, align` and `edgecolor` parameters have been used. The output of this program is shown below.

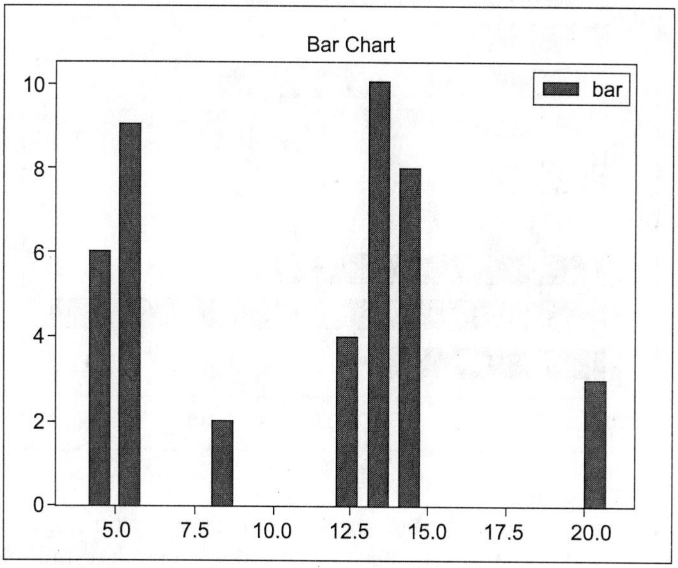

It is possible to plot a horizontal bar chart by using a `barh()` function instead of `bar()` function. We would also have to exchange the positions of x and y parameters as the graph will be plotted horizontally, y coordinates would serve as x coordinate and vice versa. In the Program 12.7, we have to replace the `bar()` function with `barh()` as shown below:

Program 12.8: Program to plot bar chart horizontally

```
import matplotlib.pyplot as plt
# data to display on bar charts
x = [5, 8, 13, 12, 20, 14, 4]
y = [9, 2, 10, 4, 3, 8, 6]

# This will plot a bar chart horizontally
plt.barh(y,x,color="blue",align="edge",edgecolor="red")

# Title to the plot
plt.title("Bar Chart")

# Adding the legends
plt.legend(["bar"])
plt.show()
```

The output of Program 12.8 is shown below:

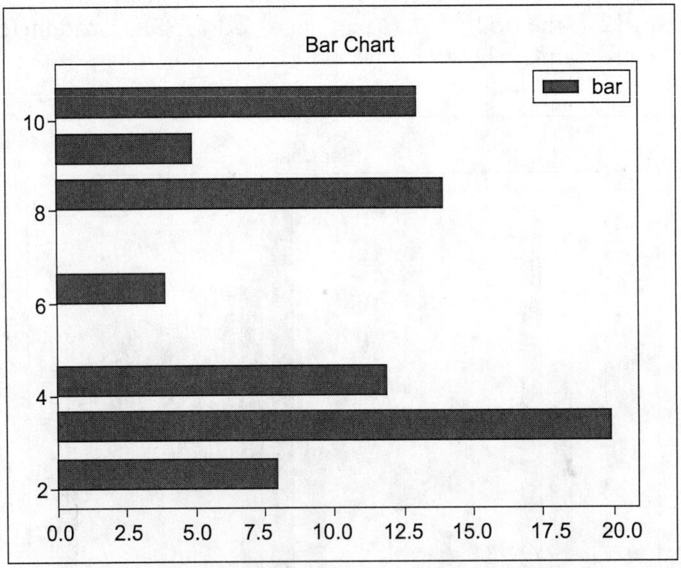

Plotting multiple bar charts

Multiple bar charts need to be plotted when we want to compare the data. In this case, the data in the form of x and y coordinates need to be provided so that multiple bar charts can be plotted. The program below shows the number of admissions in Commerce, Arts and Science over 5 years.

Program 12.9: Program to plot multiple bar charts

```
import numpy as np
import matplotlib.pyplot as plt

barWidth=0.25
# set height of bar
Commerce = [92, 100, 91, 98, 102]
Arts = [88, 86, 76, 85, 90]
Science = [79, 73, 74, 75, 87]

# Set position of bar on X axis
br1 = np.arange(len(Commerce))
br2 = [x + barWidth for x in br1]
br3 = [x + barWidth for x in br2]

# Make the plot
plt.bar(br1, Commerce, color='r', width=barWidth, label='Commerce', hatch='x')
plt.bar(br2, Arts, color ='g', width = barWidth, label ='Arts', hatch='/')
plt.bar(br3, Science, color='b', width=barWidth, label='Science', hatch='+')

# Adding Xticks
plt.xlabel('Stream')
plt.ylabel('Admissions')
plt.xticks([r + barWidth for r in range(len(Commerce))],
           ['2018', '2019', '2020', '2021', '2022'])

plt.legend()
plt.title("Admissions (2018-22)")
plt.show()
```

The output of the Program 12.9 is shown below:

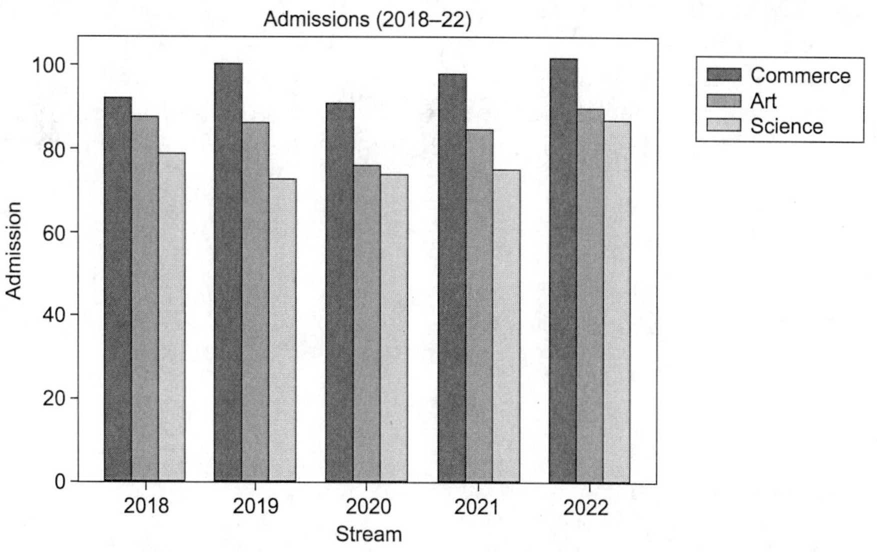

Stacked bar chart

A stacked bar chart is one which shows the bar charts for another group on one top of another. In order to do this, we need to set the bottom parameter. The bottom parameter for the bar charts for all groups except the first one has to be set to the combined height of all the previous groups. In Program 12.10, we have modified Program 12.9 and stacked the values of two groups Commerce and Arts. So, the bottom parameter for the bar chart of Arts is set to the y values of Commerce.

Program 12.10: Program to demonstrate stacked bar chart

```
import numpy as np
import matplotlib.pyplot as plt

barWidth=0.25
# set height of bar
Commerce = [92, 100, 91, 98, 102]
Arts = [88, 86, 76, 85, 90]

# Set position of bar on X axis
br1 = np.arange(len(Commerce))

# Make the plot
plt.bar(br1, Commerce, color ='r', width = barWidth,label
='Commerce', hatch='+')
plt.bar(br1, Arts, color='g',bottom=Commerce, width=barWidth,label
='Arts',hatch='-')
#The bottom of the bar is set to y coordinate of Commerce


# Adding Xticks
plt.xlabel('Stream')
plt.ylabel('Admissions')
plt.xticks([r + barWidth for r in range(len(Commerce))],
        ['2018', '2019', '2020', '2021', '2022'])

plt.legend()
plt.title("Admissions (2018-22)")
plt.show()
```

The output of Program 12.10 is shown below:

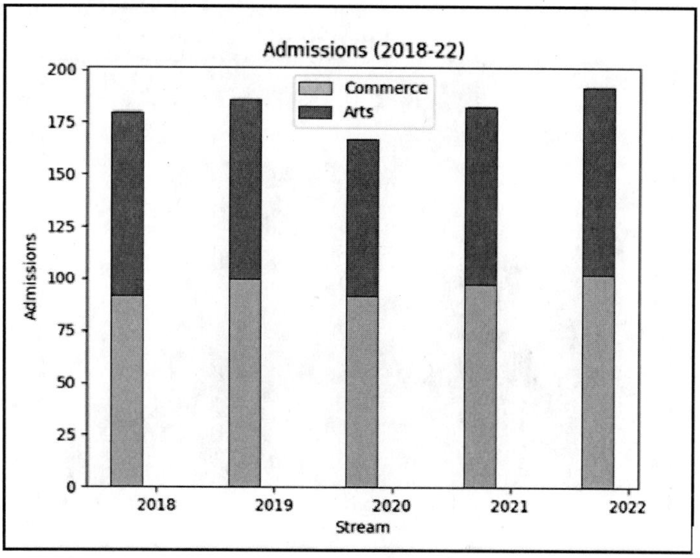

12.4.3 Histogram

A histogram is a graph representing the frequency distribution of values. It is a type of bar chart where the X-axis represents the bin ranges or the class intervals while the Y-axis represents the frequency distribution. The `matplotlib.pyplot.hist()` function is used to plot a histogram.

In Program 12.11, `numpy` is used to provide the data in the form of an array. The class intervals `[0, 20, 40, 60, 80, 100]` are set as `bins`.

Program 12.11: Program to demonstrate histogram

```
import matplotlib.pyplot as plt
import numpy as np

# Creating dataset
a = np.array([66,45,23,12,1,8,76,89,56,34,27,70,61,43,29,38,44])
# Creating histogram
plt.hist(a, bins = [0, 20, 40, 60, 80, 100])

# Show plot
plt.title("Histogram")
plt.show()
```

The output of the Program 12.11 is shown below:

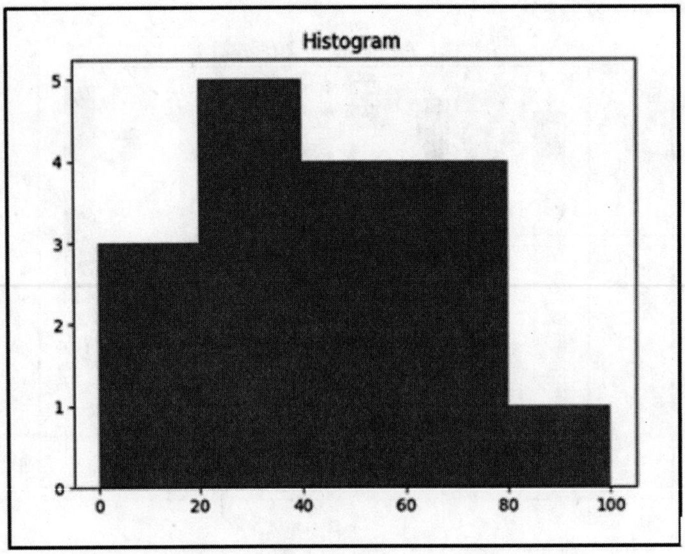

The syntax of the `hist()` function is given below:

```
matplotlib.pyplot.hist(x, bins=None, range=None, density=False,
bottom=None, histtype='bar', align='mid', orientation='vertical',
rwidth=None, color=None, label=None, **kwargs)
```

Parameters

`x`	:	specifies the data in the form of array or sequence of arrays
`bins`	:	specifies the class intervals as *int or sequence or string*
`range`	:	specifies the upper and lower range of bins
`density`	:	is a boolean value which specifies the probability density.
`bottom`	:	specifies the baseline of each bin
`histtype`	:	specifies the type of histogram ['bar', 'barstacked', 'step', 'stepfilled'], default is 'bar'
`align`	:	specifies the alignment ['left', 'mid', 'right']
`orientation`	:	specifies the plot direction ['vertical','horizontal']
`rwidth`	:	specifies the relative width of the bars with respect to bin width

Program 12.12: Program to plot another histogram

```
import matplotlib.pyplot as plt
import numpy as np

# Creating dataset
a = np.array([66,45,23,12,1,8,76,89,56,34,27,70,61,43,29,38,44])
# Creating histogram
plt.hist(a, bins = [0, 20, 40, 60, 80, 100], color='b',
histtype='step', orientation='horizontal')
```

```
# Show plot
plt.xlabel("x-axis")
plt.ylabel("y-axis")
plt.title("Histogram")
plt.show()
```

The output of Program 12.12 is shown below:

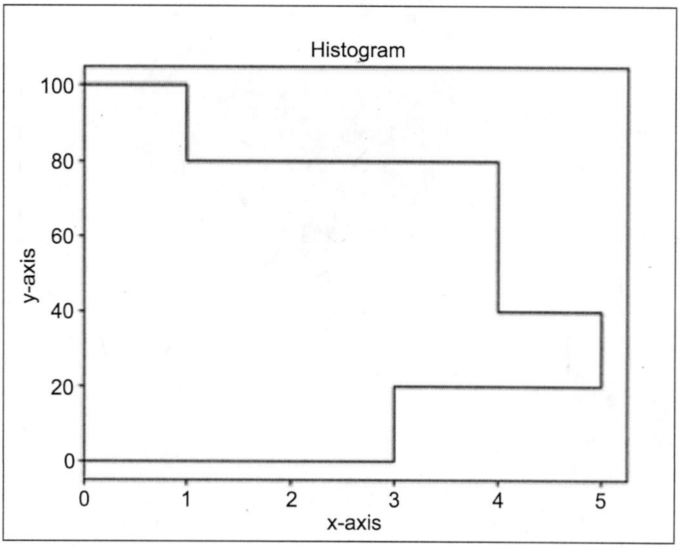

12.4.4 Pie Charts

Pie charts are commonly used in business presentations to provide a quick summary. A pie chart is a circular representation of data. The pie chart is divided into several slices called *wedges*, the area of these wedges is proportional to the data to be plotted. The data is represented as the percentage of the total data to be represented. The pie chart can be plotted by the `pie()` function in `matplotlib.pyplot`.

Program 12.13: Program to plot pie chart

```
import matplotlib.pyplot as plt

# Creating dataset
states = ['Rajasthan', 'Jharkhand', 'West Bengal', 'H.P.', 'Bihar', 'Karnataka']
data = [500, 170, 350, 200, 120, 410]

# Creating plot
plt.title("Area of states")
plt.pie(data, labels = states)
# show plot
plt.show()
```

The output of the Program 12.13 is shown below:

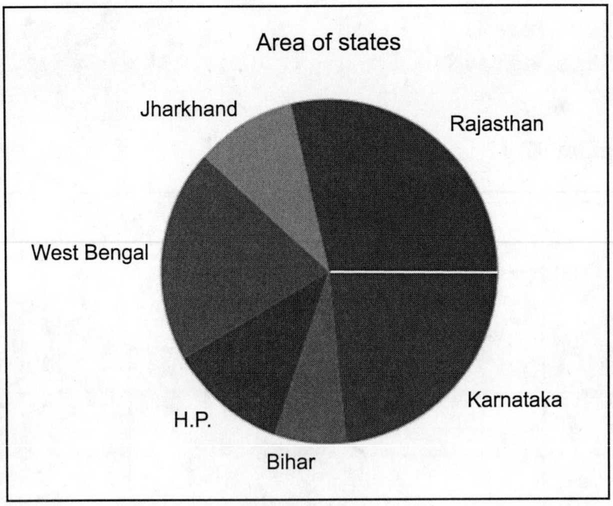

The syntax of the `pie()` function is given below:

matplotlib.pyplot.pie(x, labels=None,colors=None,autopct=None, shadow=False)

Parameters

`x`	:	specifies the array of data values
`labels`	:	specifies the labels of the wedges
`colors`	:	specifies the colors for the wedges
`autopct`	:	specifies the string to label the wedges with the numeric values
`shadow`	:	is a boolean value, specifies if a shadow of the wedges is to be created

The pie chart shown above has been customized in the Program 12.14.

Program 12.14: Program to customize a pie chart

```
import matplotlib.pyplot as plt

# Creating dataset
states = ['Rajasthan', 'Jharkhand', 'West Bengal','H.P.', 'Bihar',
'Karnataka']
data = [500, 170, 350, 200, 120, 410]

# Creating plot
explode = (0.1, 0.0, 0.2, 0.3, 0.0, 0.0)
plt.title("Areas of states")
plt.pie(data, labels = states, autopct="%.2f", explode=explode,
shadow=True)

# show plot
plt.show()
```

The output of Program 12.14 is shown below:

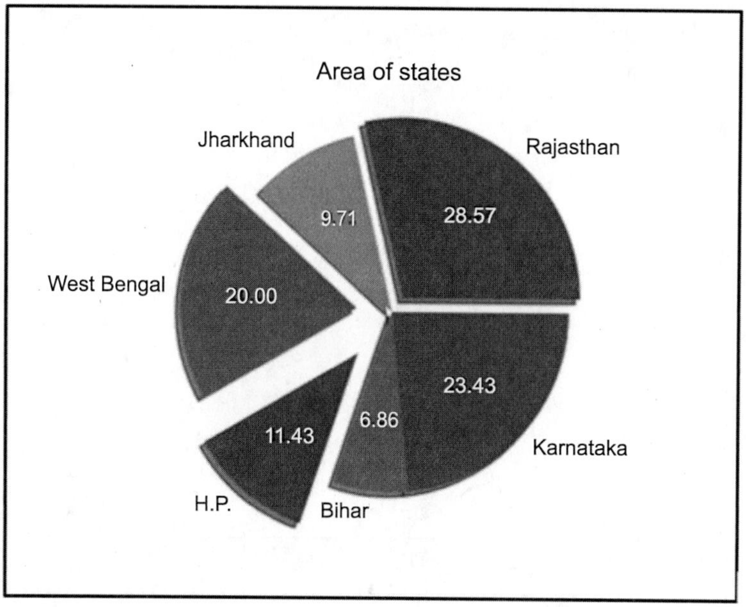

12.4.5 Scatter Plot

Scatter plot is a diagram where each value is represented by a dot in the plot area. The `matplotlib.pyplot` has a `scatter()` function for plotting the scatter plot. In order to plot a scatter plot, the user should provide x and y coordinates in the form of arrays of the same length. A sample scatter plot is plotted in Program 12.15.

Program 12.15: Program to plot a scatter plot

```
import matplotlib.pyplot as plt

x = [15,17,18,17,20,7,12,19,14,10]
y = [80,85,84,83,91,82,93,78,92,87]

plt.scatter(x, y)
plt.title("Scatter Plot")
plt.show()
```

The output of Program 12.15 is shown below:

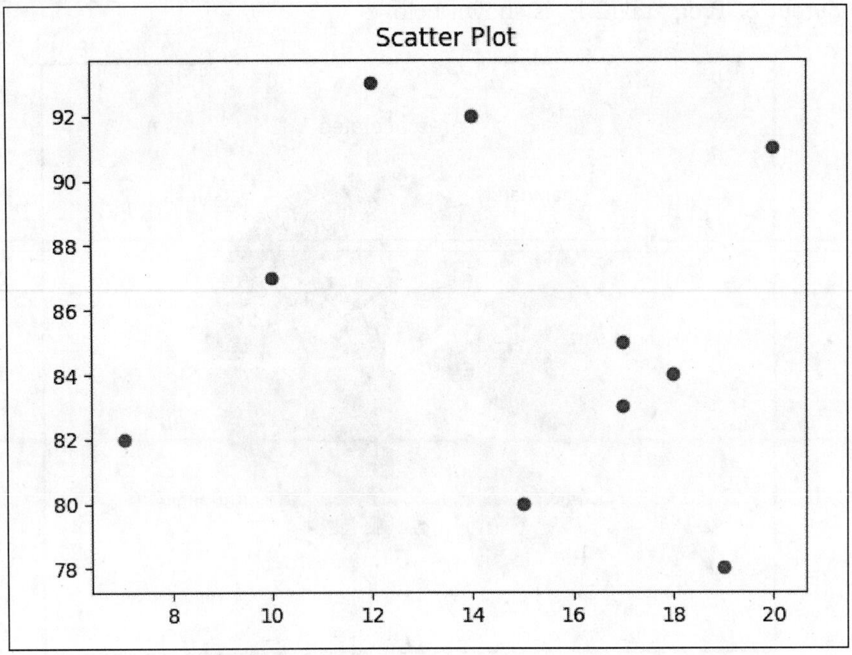

Plotting multiple scatter plots

When we wish to compare the data, multiple scatter plots can be drawn. In this case there will be multiple instances of data x and y and the scatter plots will be plotted in two different colors. Program 12.16 demonstrates to plot multiple scatter plots.

Program 12.16: Program to plot multiple scatter plots

```
import matplotlib.pyplot as plt

#scatter plot 1
x = [15,17,18,17,20,7,12,19,14,10]
y = [80,85,84,83,91,82,93,78,92,87]
plt.scatter(x, y, marker="*")

#scatter plot2
x = [35,37,28, 22,24,27,22,29,34,40]
y = [90,95,94,93,90,92,93,88,92,87]
plt.scatter(x, y,marker="+")

plt.title("Scatter Plot")
plt.show()
```

In the Program 12.16, 2 data sets are given, hence the scatter plot is plotted in two colors 'blue' and 'orange'. The output of Program 12.16 is shown below:

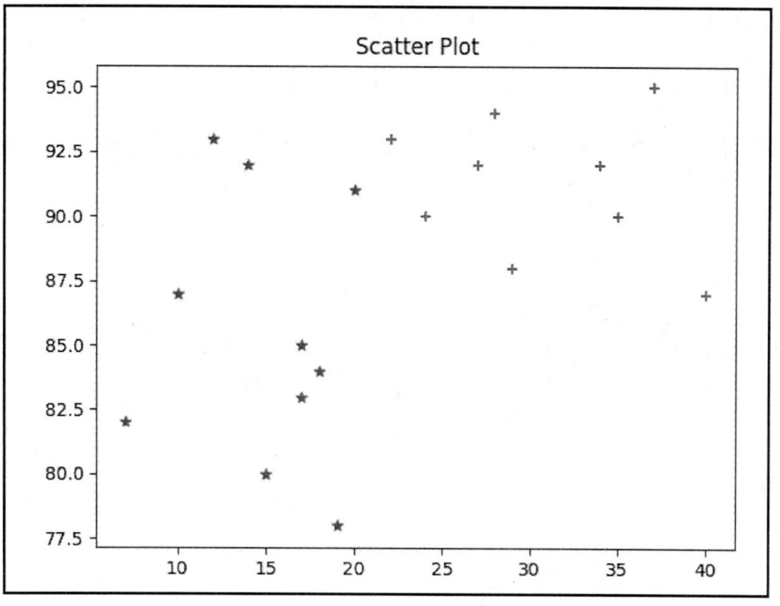

The syntax of the `scatter()` function is given below:

*matplotlib.pyplot.scatter(x, y, s=None, c=None, marker=None, cmap=None, alpha=None, **kwargs)*

Parameters

`x and y`	:	specifies the array of data values
`s`	:	specifies the array of dot sizes in point. The size of this array has to be the same as that of x and y.
`c`	:	specifies the array of color of each dot.
`marker`	:	specifies the marker style
`cmap`	:	specifies the color map
`alpha`	:	specifies the transparency factor for the dots. It can be in the range of 0 to 1.

Program 12.17: Program to plot a scatter plot with transparent color dots using random points

```
import matplotlib.pyplot as plt
import numpy as np

x = np.random.randint(50, size=(50))
y = np.random.randint(50, size=(50))
cs = np.random.randint(50, size=(50))
ss = 10 * np.random.randint(50, size=(50))

plt.scatter(x, y, c=cs, s=ss, alpha=0.5, cmap='nipy_spectral')
plt.colorbar()
plt.title("Scatter plot")
plt.show()
```

The output of Program 12.17 is shown below:

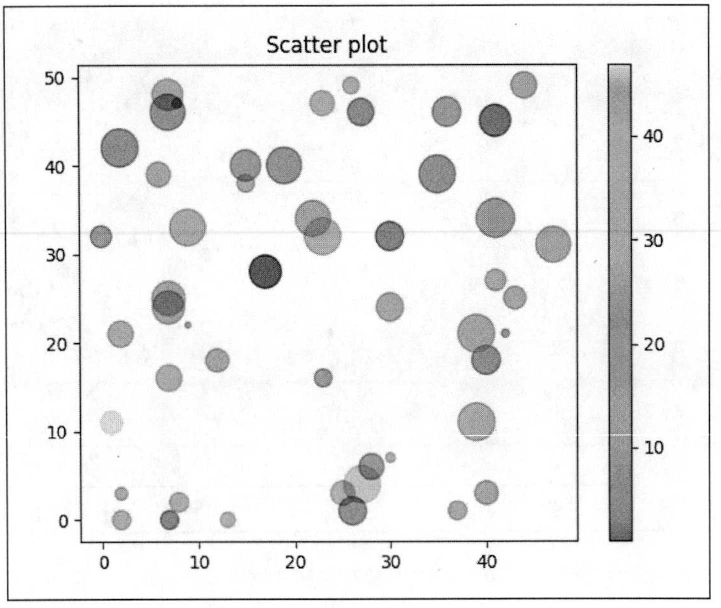

12.4.6 Sub-Plots

Python supports the `subplot()` function which can plot multiple graphs but in the same figure. The function `subplot()` is written as `matplotlib.pyplot.subplot(row,col,index)` where

Parameters

`row` : specifies the number of rows
`col` : specifies the number of columns
`index` : specifies the position of the graph

The `subplot()` function allows to specify the dimension of the figure in terms of rows and columns and the position of the graph inside the figure.

Program 12.18: Program to demonstrate sub-plots

```
import matplotlib.pyplot as plt
import numpy as np

#graph 1:
x1 = [10, 11, 12, 13]
y1 = [14, 17, 10, 20]

plt.subplot(1, 2, 1)
plt.plot(x1,y1)
```

```
#graph 2:
x2 = [0, 1, 2, 3]
y2 = [10, 20, 30, 40]

plt.subplot(1, 2, 2)
plt.plot(x2,y2)
plt.show()
```

The output of Program 12.18 is shown below:

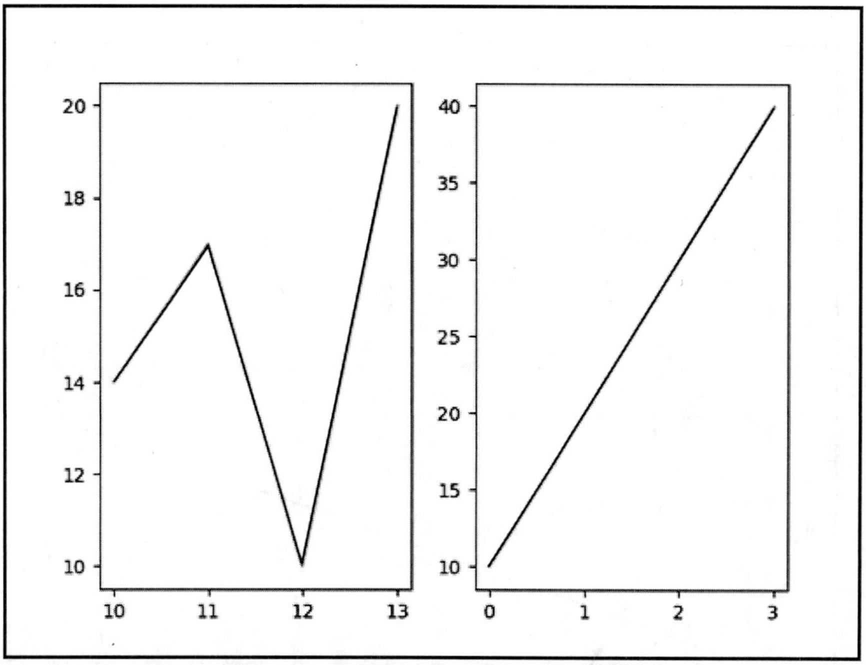

In Program 12.18, statement `plt.subplot(1, 2, 1)` specifies that there is 1 row and 2 columns in the figure and the position of the graph is 1, similarly `plt.subplot(1, 2, 2)` specifies that the graph position is 2. Hence, the graphs are arranged horizontally side by side.

Let us consider another example, where we can arrange the graphs vertically, in order to do so the `col` parameter should be specified as 1 as shown in Program 12.19.

Program 12.19: Program to demonstrate sub-plot, arranging the graphs vertically

```
import matplotlib.pyplot as plt
import numpy as np

#graph 1:
x1 = [10, 11, 12, 13]
y1 = [14, 17, 10, 20]

plt.subplot(2, 1, 1)
plt.plot(x1,y1)
```

```
#graph 2:
x2 = [0, 1, 2, 3]
y2 = [10, 20, 30, 40]

plt.subplot(2, 1, 2)
plt.plot(x2,y2)

plt.show()
```

The output of Program 12.19, shows 2 graphs arranged vertically.

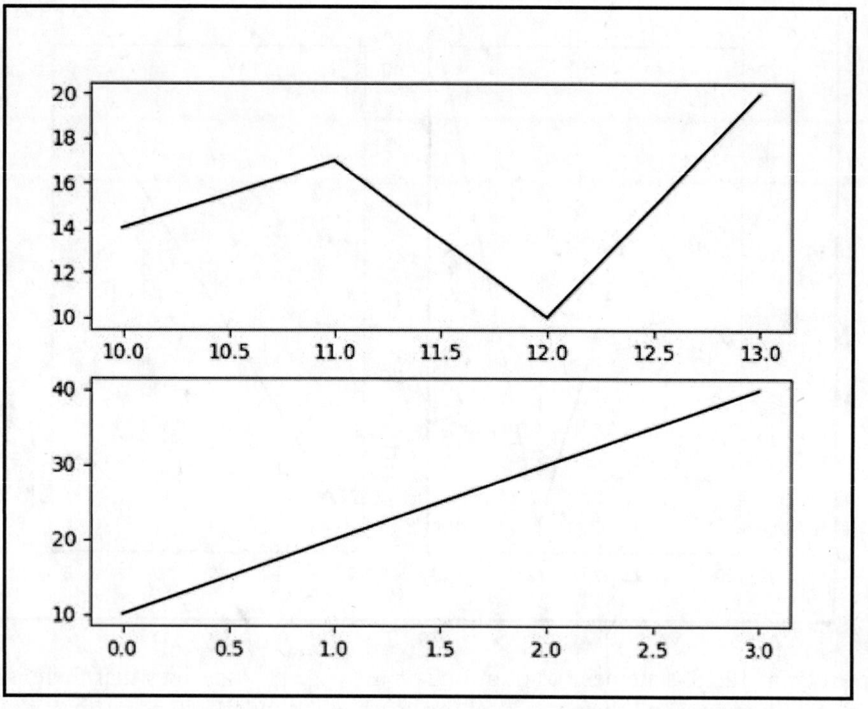

Similarly, multiple graphs can be plotted in the same figure by giving appropriate values for row and col parameters. Program 12.20 below shows plotting 4 separate graphs in a figure.

Program 12.20: Plotting multiple graphs

```
import matplotlib.pyplot as plt
#graph 1:
x1 = [1,2,3,4,5,6,7,8,9,10]
y1 = [x**2 for x in x1]

plt.subplot(2, 2, 1)
plt.title("Plot X - X**2")
plt.plot(x1,y1)
```

```
#graph 2:
y2 = [x**3 for x in x1]

plt.subplot(2, 2, 2)
plt.title("Plot X - X**3")
plt.plot(x1,y2)

#graph 3:
y3 = [x**4 for x in x1]

plt.subplot(2, 2, 3)
plt.title("Plot X - X**4")
plt.plot(x1,y3)

#graph 4:
y4 = [x**5 for x in x1]

plt.subplot(2, 2, 4)
plt.title("Plot X - X**5")
plt.plot(x1,y4)

plt.suptitle("Multiple Graphs using Subplots")
plt.show()
```

The output of Program 12.20 is shown below:

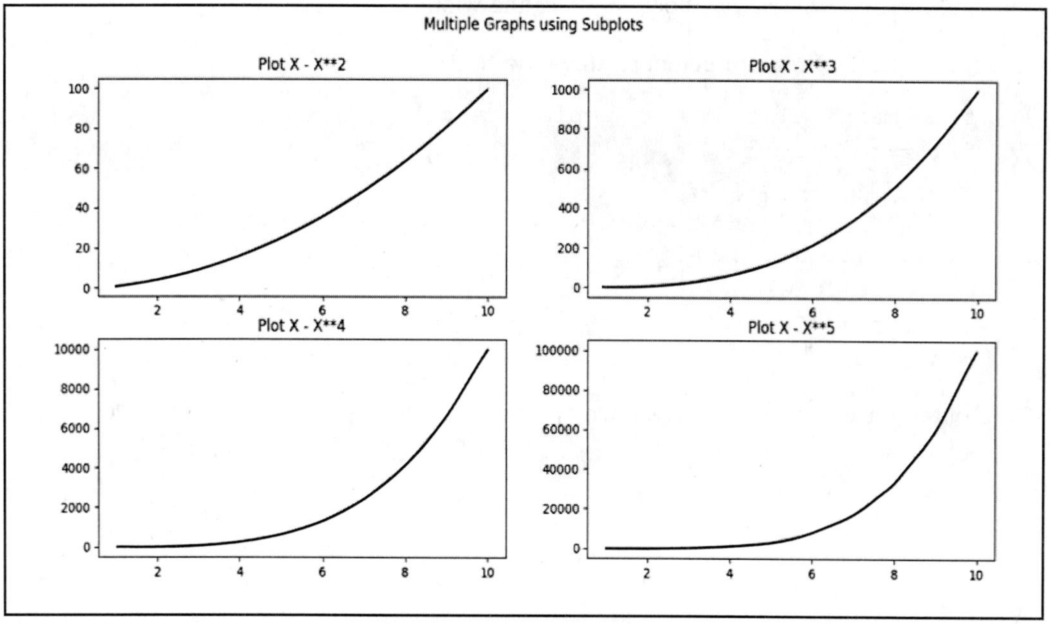

12.5 2-D GRAPHICAL OBJECTS

The `matplotlib` library in Python has a `patches` module which provides many built-in functions for plotting 2-D objects like circle, rectangle, ellipse, etc. in the form of classes. The `patches` module has classes `Circle`, `Rectangle`, `Ellipse`, `Polygon`, `Regular Polygon` and `Arrow` to draw these shapes. These classes are called patches. In order to draw a 2-D object, we have to create an object of that class and provide the parameters for it. The object then needs to be added to the patch using the `add_patch()` function. Setting the axis to `Scaled` allows the system to automatically select a suitable scale for the figure.

12.5.1 Circle

In order to draw a circle, an object of the class `Circle` is created. The syntax is as below:

```
matplotlib.patches.Circle(xy, radius=5, **kwargs)
```

The parameters in the `Circle` object are:

`xy`	:	coordinates of the center in the form of tuple
`radius`	:	radius of the circle. Default value is 5.
`color`	:	fill color
`edgecolor or ec`	:	color of the edge of the circle
`facecolor or fc`	:	color of the face
`fill`	:	`True` or `False`, whether the shape has to be filled with color
`linestyle`	:	'-','--','-.',':'
`linewidth or lw`	:	float, specifies the width of the edge

Program 12.21: Program demonstrates how to draw a circle

```
from matplotlib import pyplot as plt, patches
fig = plt.figure()
ax = fig.add_subplot()
circle1 = patches.Circle((0.2, 0.2), radius=0.5, color='green')
ax.add_patch(circle1)
plt.axis('Scaled')
plt.title('Circle')
plt.show()
```

The output of Program 12.21 is shown below:

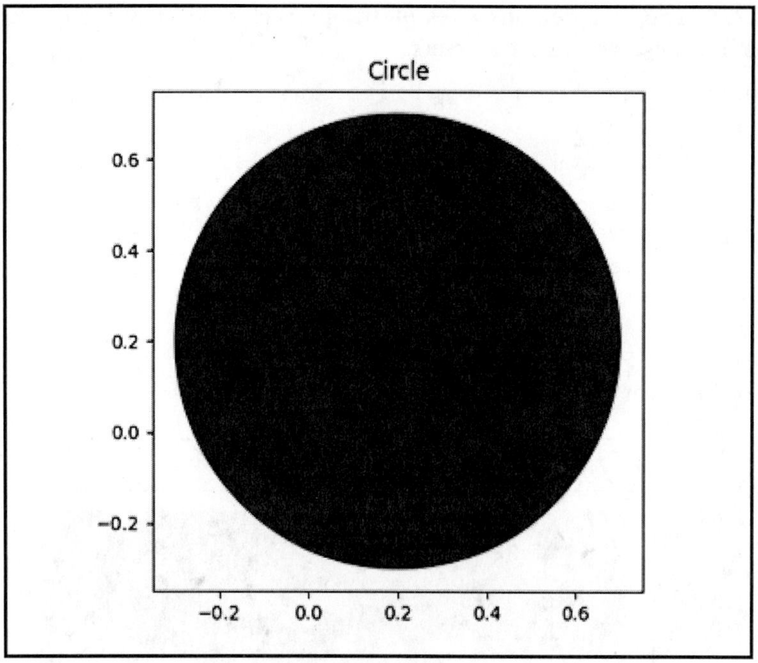

12.5.2 Rectangle

A rectangle can be plotted by creating an instance of the class `Rectangle`. The syntax is as follows:

```
matplotlib.patches.Rectangle(xy, width, height, *, angle=0.0,
rotation_point='xy', **kwargs)
```

The parameters in the `Rectangle` object are:

`xy`	:	coordinates of the anchor point in the form of tuple
`width`	:	width of the rectangle
`height`	:	height of the rectangle
`rotation_point`	:	coordinates of the center of rotation in the form of tuple
`angle`	:	rotation of the rectangle in degrees in anti-clockwise direction about the rotation point.
`edgecolor or ec`	:	color of the edge of the shape
`facecolor or fc`	:	color of the face
`fill`	:	`True` or `False`, whether the shape has to be filled with color
`linestyle`	:	'-','--','-.',':'
`linewidth or lw`	:	float, specifies the width of the edge

Program 12.22: Program demonstrates plotting a rectangle, here the center, width, height and color have been given as parameters

```
from matplotlib import pyplot as plt, patches
fig = plt.figure()
ax = fig.add_subplot()
rect1 = patches.Rectangle((0.2, 0.2), 6,4, color='green')
ax.add_patch(rect1)
plt.axis('Scaled')
plt.title('Rectangle')
plt.show()
```

The output of Program 12.22 is shown below:

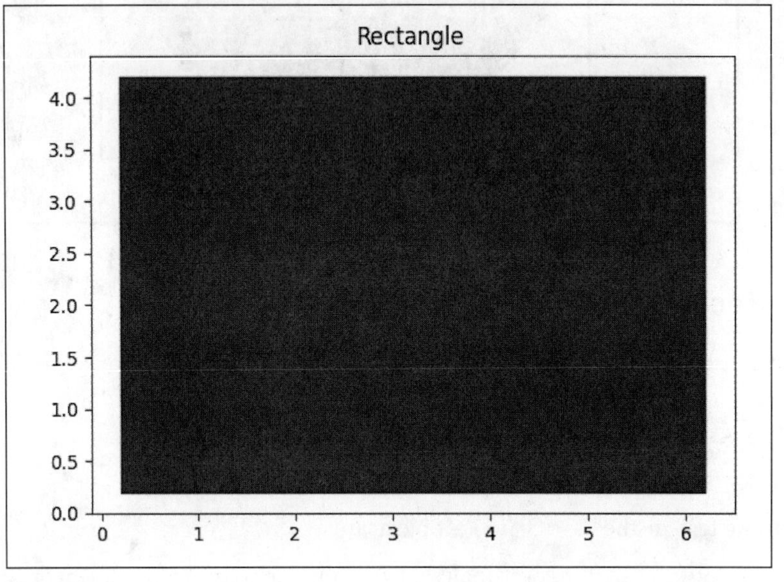

12.5.3 Ellipse

The ellipse can be drawn by creating an object of the class `Ellipse`.The syntax as below:

```
matplotlib.patches.Ellipse(xy, width, height, *, angle=0, **kwargs)
```

The parameters in the `Ellipse` object are:

`xy`	:	coordinates of the center in the form of tuple
`width`	:	width of the ellipse
`height`	:	height of the ellipse
`angle`	:	rotation of the ellipse in degrees in anti-clockwise direction
`edgecolor or ec`	:	color of the edge of the ellipse
`facecolor or fc`	:	color of the face

```
fill              : True or False, whether the shape has to be filled with color
linestyle         : '-','--','-.',':'
linewidth or lw   : float, specifies the width of the edge
```

Program 12.23: Program shows plotting an ellipse, here the parameters are center, width, height and color and edge color

```
from matplotlib import pyplot as plt, patches
fig = plt.figure()
ax = fig.add_subplot()
ell1=patches.Ellipse((0.2, 0.2), 6,4, angle=30, color='green',ec='red')
ax.add_patch(ell1)
plt.axis('Scaled')
plt.title('Ellipse')
plt.show()
```

The output of Program 12.23 is shown below:

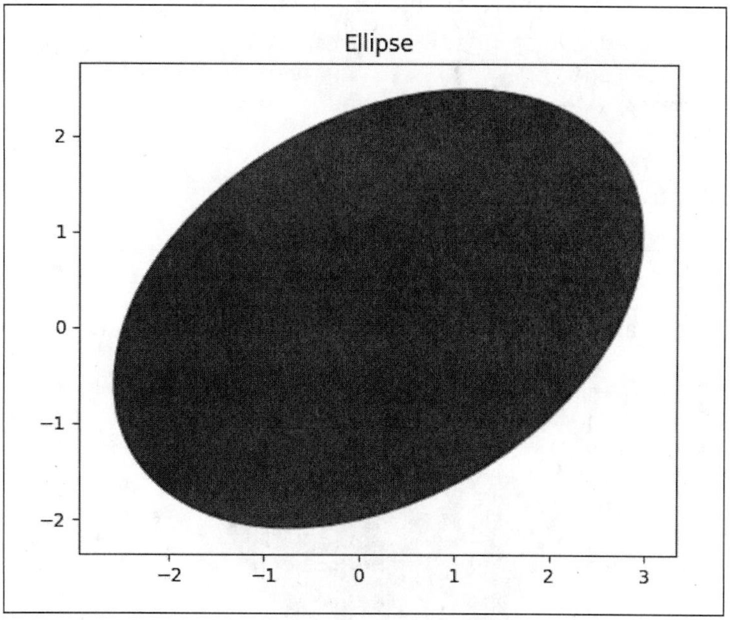

12.5.4 Polygon

A polygon can be created by instantiating an object of the class `Polygon` or `RegularPolygon`. The syntax is given below:

```
matplotlib.patches.Polygon(xy, *, closed=True, **kwargs)
or
matplotlib.patches.RegularPolygon(xy, numVertices, *, radius=5,
orientation=0, **kwargs)
```

The parameters in the `Polygon` object are:

`xy`	:	provides the coordinates of the polygon vertices in the form of a list
`closed`	:	`True`, which implies that the first point and the last point are the same.

The parameters in the `RegularPolygon` object are:

`xy`	:	coordinates of the center point of the polygon
`numVertices`	:	number of vertices of the polygon
`radius`	:	distance of the vertices from the center point, default is 5
`orientation`	:	the angle of the polygon

Program 12.24: Program demonstrates plotting a pentagon

```
from matplotlib import pyplot as plt, patches
fig = plt.figure()
ax = fig.add_subplot()
points=[[2,4],[1,6.5],[4,8],[5,8],[3,5]]
poly=patches.Polygon(points,color='green',ec='red', linestyle='dashed')
ax.add_patch(poly)
plt.axis('Scaled')
plt.title('Polygon')
plt.show()
```

The output of Program 12.24 is shown below:

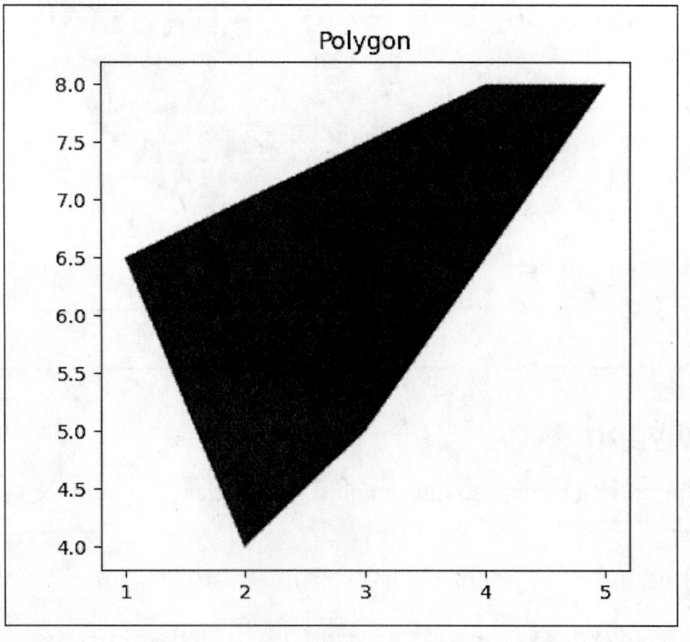

12.5.5 Arrow

Graphical object Arrow can be plotted by creating an object of the class `Arrow`. The syntax is as follows:

```
matplotlib.patches.Arrow(x, y, dx, dy, *, width=1.0, **kwargs)
```

The parameters in the `Arrow` object are:

`x`	: x coordinate of the tail of the arrow
`y`	: y coordinate of the tail of the arrow
`dx`	: length of arrow in x direction
`dy`	: length of the arrow in y direction

Program 12.25 Program demonstrates plotting arrow

```
from matplotlib import pyplot as plt, patches
fig = plt.figure()
ax = fig.add_subplot()
arr = patches.Arrow(0,0,5,5, color='green',ec='red',linestyle='dashed')
ax.add_patch(arr)
plt.axis('Scaled')
plt.title('Arrow')
plt.show()
```

The output of Program 12.25 is shown below:

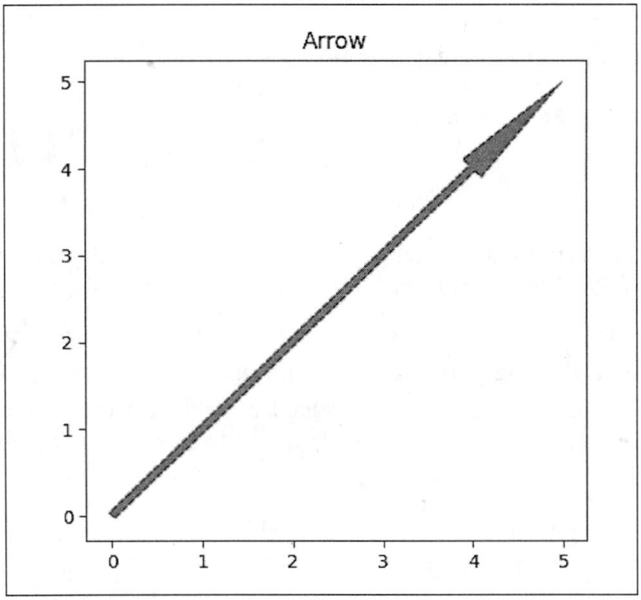

12.6 3-D GRAPHICAL OBJECTS

Many applications use three-dimensional objects for better visualization. Three-dimensional objects also find their use in animation. In this section, we cover some basic concepts of 3D visualization in Python. It aims to cover two aspects—3D objects, such as sphere, cone, etc.; and 3D plots, which involve using one more axis in the 2D plots covered in the previous section.

12.6.1 3D Objects using VPython

VPython is a Python based library used for basic plotting and animation. It is convenient to use even with little knowledge of programming. This is why it is extensively used in several scientific and educational applications.

VPython needs to be installed, like any other Python module, in order to be used. However, VPython has some compatibility constraints. The latest VPython version works with Python 3.8, 3.9 and 3.10. There are certain versions of VPython that work with an older version of Python. There also exist some constraints on the version of VPython compatible with a particular type of operating system. Hence, it is recommended that the reader goes through the download guidelines for VPython available on *vpython.org*. We have used the recommended setting for a 64-bit Windows system—Python v2.7.9 and VPython v6.11. Once installed, an icon titled **VIDLE for VPython** should be visible on the desktop or on the start menu. This is where we will create Python programs to create 3D objects. In this book, we cover objects—sphere, arrow, cone and text. However, VPython also offers support to create some other 3D objects such as cylinder, ring, etc.

Sphere

Let us see a simple program to create a sphere.

Program 12.26: Program to create a sphere in VPython

```
from visual import *
sphere(pos=(2,4,-3), radius=2.5, color=color.yellow)
```

The first statement imports the components of the **visual** module. Next, we call the sphere function with the following parameters:

- `pos` — a tuple specifying the (x,y,z) coordinates of the center of the sphere.
- `radius` — a floating point value denoting the radius of the sphere
- `color` — This can either be a 3 valued tuple that specifies the RGB values of the color, or we can use the specified colors - `color.yellow`, `color.red`, `color.blue`, `color.green`, `color.cyan`, `color.magenta`, etc.

Upon execution, it results in the output which is a sphere in a separate window as shown below:

There are some other parameters to the sphere function. Program 12.27 shows their usage.

Program 12.27: To display 3 spheres using VPython

```
from visual import *

#1
sphere(radius=1.5, color=color.cyan, opacity=0.25)
#2
sphere(pos=(3,-4,0),color=color.red, shininess=0.6)
#3
sphere(pos=(-3,4,0), size=(2,5,1), color=color.magenta, shininess=0.3)
```

The first call to the sphere function generates a cyan colored sphere centered at $(0,0,0)$ by default, having `radius` 1.5 units. The `opacity` parameter controls the transparency/opacity of the object. A value of 1 makes the object opaque, and 0 makes it transparent.

The second sphere is in red color and centered at $(3,-4,0)$. Its `radius` is 1 unit by default. Shininess of the object can be controlled by providing a value between 0 (least shiny) and 1 (most shiny) to the `shininess` parameter.

The magenta sphere created by the third statement is centered at $(-3,4,0)$. Instead of the radius parameter, we have used the `size` parameter. It takes a tuple of 3 values denoting (length, height, width). If all 3 values are identical, the object is a sphere. In case different values are specified, the resulting object is an *ellipsoid*. The output of Program 12.27 is shown below:

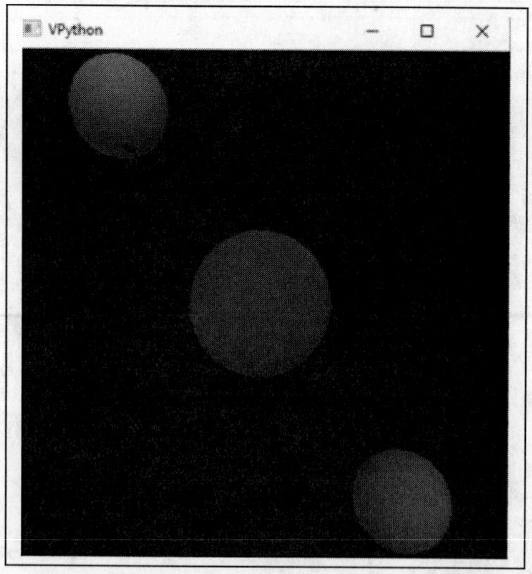

Note that all parameters are optional. If no arguments are passed, a white sphere centered at origin with radius = 1 unit is displayed.

Arrow

Similar to the `sphere()` function, there exists an `arrow()` function to plot a 3D arrow. Let us understand its usage with some programs.

Program 12.28: Program to create a simple arrow

```
from visual import *
arrow(length=5, opacity=0.4, color=color.green)
```

This call to `arrow()` generates an arrow of `length` 5, with its base at the origin, pointing in the direction of the positive x-axis.

The `arrow()` function has some other parameters as well, the color, shininess, opacity, etc. parameters have the same purpose as described with a sphere. Similar to sphere, all parameters in `arrow()` are optional. Let us see some more parameters.

Program 12.29: Program to create 3D arrows of varied sizes

```
from visual import *

#1
arrow(pos=(0,-8,0), axis=(9,5,-3))
#2
arrow(axis=(-6,8,3), shaftwidth=0.4, length=5, color=color.yellow,
shininess=0.6)
#3
arrow(axis=(5,7,0), headwidth=0.7, headlength=1.25, shaftwidth=0.25,
color=color.blue, opacity=0.6)
```

The first arrow will have its shaft at the point $(0,-8,0)$ and will head in the direction of the vector specified by the axis parameter. Since no color is provided, it will be white.

The second statement displays a yellow arrow with its shaft at the origin, as the `pos` parameter is not given. It will grow in the direction of the vector specified by the `axis` parameter. The `shaftwidth` parameter controls the width of the shaft of the arrow, it takes a floating point number as its value. Its `length` will be 5 units.

The third arrow, blue in `color`, will start at origin and head in the direction of the vector $(5,7,0)$. In this we specified the width and length of the arrow head. The difference in 3 arrows can be seen in the output.

The output of Program 12.29 is shown below:

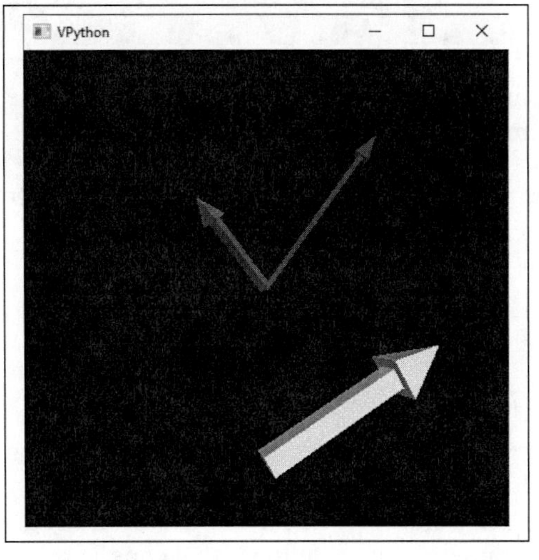

Cone

The VPython library also provides the `cone()` function to plot a three-dimensional cone. Several of its parameters are similar to those defined for sphere and arrow. Let us create a simple cone.

Program 12.30: Program to plot a cone

```
from visual import *

cone(pos=(-4,4,0), axis=(5,-5,0))
```

The `pos` parameter is a 3D vector specifying the x, y, and z coordinates of the center of the base of the cone. The `axis` parameter is a vector that controls the direction of the cone. In Program 12.30 since no color is specified, the output is a white colored cone with its base centered at $(-4, 4, 0)$ pointing in the direction specified by $(5, -5, 0)$. The output of Program 12.30 is shown below:

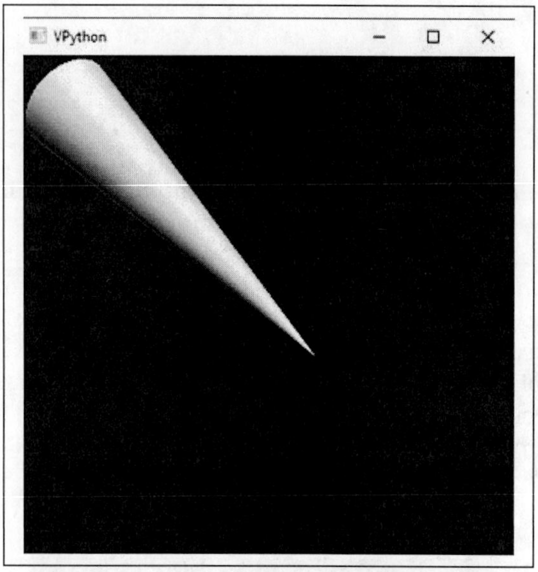

Even though all parameters of the `cone()` function are optional, Program 12.31 demonstrates other parameters.

Program 12.31: Program to demonstrate use of other parameters in cone() function

```
from visual import *

cone(pos=(-4,-4,-1), axis=(0,3,-2), radius=1.5, color=color.yellow)
cone(axis=(2,4,2), length=5, radius=0.75, color=color.red, opacity=0.7)
cone(pos=(0,7,3), radius=2, length=7)
```

The first statement generates a yellow cone with a base having `radius` 1.5 units centered at $(-4, -4, -1)$, growing in the direction of $(0, 3, -2)$.

The second one is a red colored cone having a base `radius` of 0.75 units and `length` 5 units. Since the `pos` parameter is not defined, this cone is by default centered at the origin. It grows in the direction specified by the axis parameter. The `opacity` parameter is used in the same context as explained with sphere and arrow.

The third cone has its base as specified by the `pos` parameter, and by default grows in the direction of the x-axis. Its `radius` is 2 units and `length` is 7 units. The output of Program 12.31 is shown below:

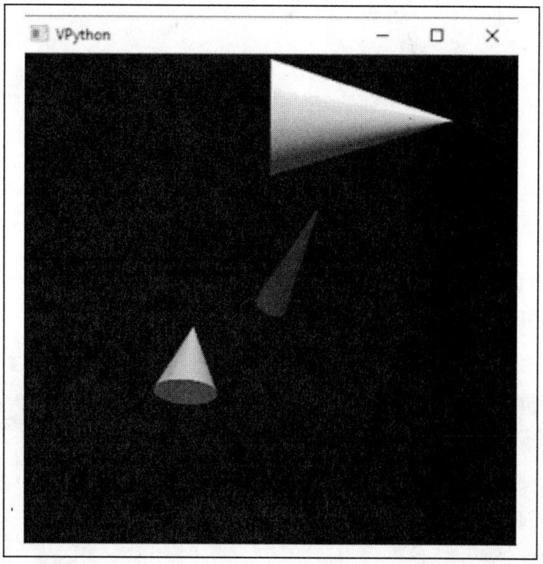

Text

VPython also allows the user to create graphical text objects using the `text()` function. These functionalities are very commonly used in basic animations created using VPython. Programs below demonstrate a graphical text object with some basic parameters.

Program 12.32: Program to create text object with some basic formatting

```
from visual import *

text(pos=(-8,-2,0), text='Hello!', align='center',color=color.
yellow, length=20, height=30, depth=4)
```

In Program 12.32 the text begins at the point specified by the pos parameter. It's yellow in color and is centrally aligned. The output is shown below:

Program 12.33: Program to display multiple text objects

```
from visual import *

text(text='Hello!', pos=(-5,2,2), axis=(5,3,-3), height=7, depth=4,
shininess=1, font='sans')
```

```
text(text='People', pos=(-8,-10,-2), color=color.cyan, axis=(5,
-3,0), height=6, depth=3)

text(text='Visual Python', pos=(-20,-3,0), color=color.yellow,
opacity=0.3, height=3, length=20, depth=3)
```

The text *Hello!* begins at (–5, 2, 2) and is aligned in the direction specified by axis parameter. The `height` of this text is 7 units, and `depth` is 4 units. The `font` parameter describes the font face to be applied. It can either be "sans" or "serif". Similarly, the text *People* is adjusted to the window. The text *Visual Python* begins at `pos` and since no axis is defined, it is aligned with the x-axis. The output of Program 12.33 is given below:

12.6.2 3D Visualization using Plotly

The 3D objects created using VPython work well for basic applications and animations. There are, however, limited features in some aspects. This section covers usage of another popular visualization library—`plotly`. It helps to create interactive visualizations and plots. Similar to `matplotlib`, `plotly` needs to be installed first, using the `pip` command as illustrated in section 12.1. Figure 12.1 demonstrates the installation process of `plotly`.

`Plotly` is a library used for advanced visualization. Instead of producing static image-like outputs, `plotly` generates its outputs in a tree structure, similar to what is constructed in an XML or HTML page. This implies that `plotly` needs a renderer application to generate outputs. This is one of the many reasons `plotly` works well with platforms such as Jupyter notebook, etc. However, in this book, we have been working with IDLE, which does not provide an output rendering system on its own. Hence, we will direct all outputs to an HTML file for rendering and viewing. Let us now see some visualizations that can be achieved using `plotly`.

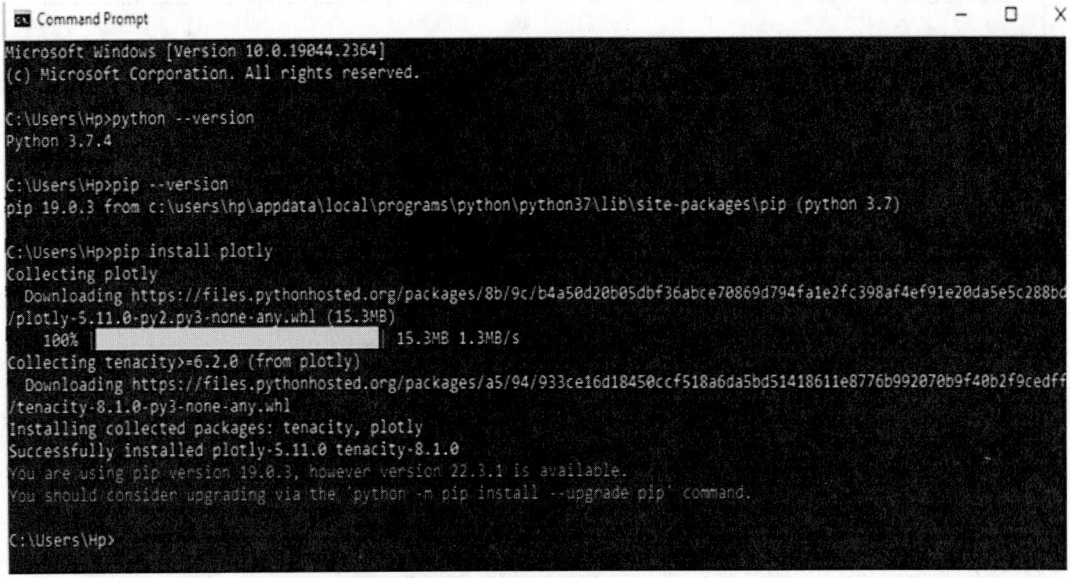

Figure 12.1 Installation of `plotly`.

Cone

We use the `graph_objects` module from `plotly` here. The `Figure()` function is used to get a figure or plot object. There are numerous types of plots or objects that the `graph_objects` module provides. We use the `Cone()` constructor. Coordinates of the center of the base of the cone are passed to x, y and z. And, coordinates of the direction or alignment or norm of the cone are passed to u, v and w.

Program 12.34: Program to display a cone using plotly

```
import plotly.graph_objects as go

fig = go.Figure(data=go.Cone(
    x=[5, 0],
    y=[7, 0],
    z=[-1, 0],
    u=[1, 0],
    v=[0, 5],
    w=[-2, 0]))

fig.write_html(r'C:\Users\Hp\Desktop\Samples\cone.html')
```

In Program 12.34, we have given a list of 2 values to these parameters as we are plotting 2 cones. The first cone is centered at (5,7,–1) and has direction of the vector (1,0,–2). The second cone is centered at origin (0,0,0) and has norm (0,5,0), i.e., moves in the y-direction. Lastly, we use the `write_html()` function associated with the `fig` object, and direct it to the specified path. The output of Program 12.34 is shown from 2 different perspectives.

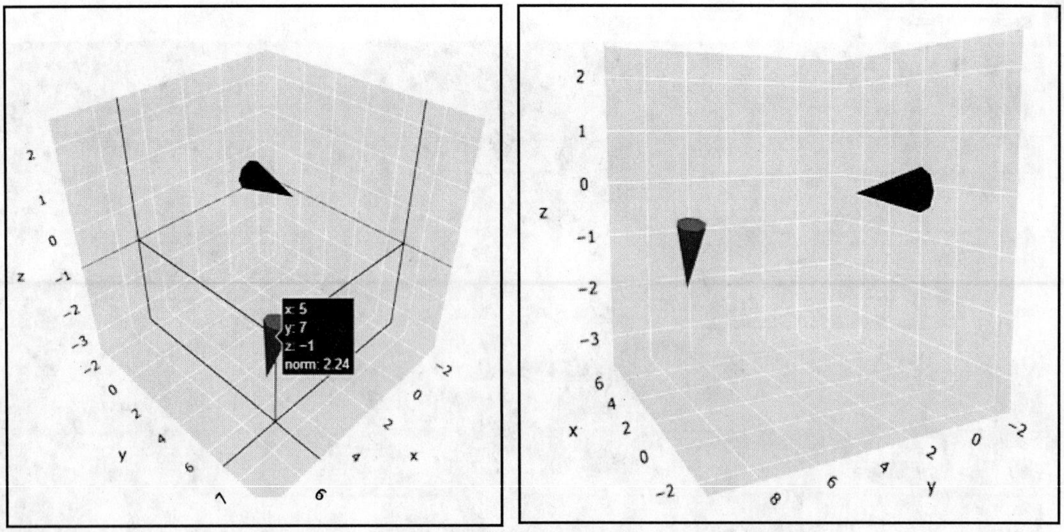

While the Cone object is provided directly by the graph_objects, not all 3D objects can be plotted in a similar way. It can be done by interpolating points on the plane according to the equation of the surface of the object to be created.

Scatter Plots

As already stated, plotly generates interactive plots. In terms of scatter plots, we can create both 2D and 3D Scatter plots in plotly. Let us understand it using Program 12.35.

Program 12.35: Program to plot a scatter plot

```
import plotly.graph_objects as go
import random

x=random.sample(range(6,600), 100)
y=random.sample(range(3,900), 100)
z=random.sample(range(2,500), 100)
#2d plot
fig = go.Figure(data = [go.Scatter(x=x,y=y, mode='markers',
                        marker=dict(color='magenta', size=15,
                        line=dict(color='blue', width=1)))])
fig.write_html(r'C:\Users\Hp\Desktop\Samples\scatterplotly.html')

#3d plot
fig = go.Figure(data = [go.Scatter3d(x=x,y=y,z=z, mode='markers',
                       marker=dict(color='yellow', size=8,
                       line=dict(color='red', width=2)))])
fig.write_html(r'C:\Users\Hp\Desktop\Samples\scatterplotly3d.html')
```

First this code generates 100 random points to be plotted in three dimensional space. Next, we use the `Figure()` function of the `graph_objects` module. As data, we pass an instance of the `graph_objects.Scatter` object which accepts the x and y coordinates of the 100 points as argument. We also define the `mode` of this scatter plot as 'markers'. It could also be 'lines' or 'lines+markers'. The `marker` argument specifies the marker style. Here, we have used magenta colored circular markers of size 15 units, having a blue colored border of width 1 unit.

This generates a 2D scatter plot as shown below. Upon hovering on a point, its coordinates are displayed.

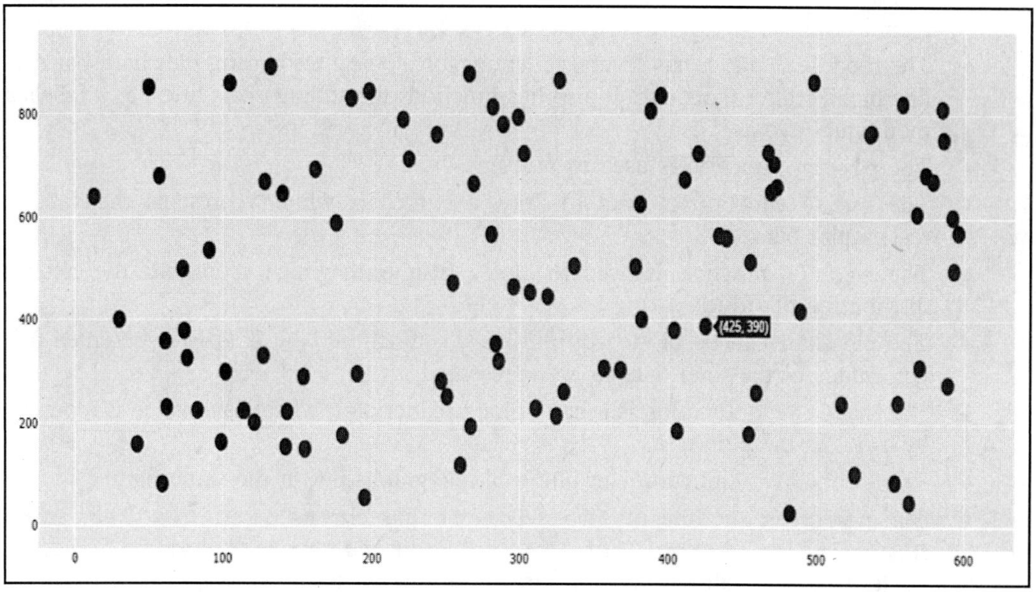

The next statement uses the `graph_objects.Scatter3d` object to plot the points in three dimensions, hence all x, y and z parameters are specified. Upon hovering, the coordinates of the point are displayed, the output of this statement is shown below:

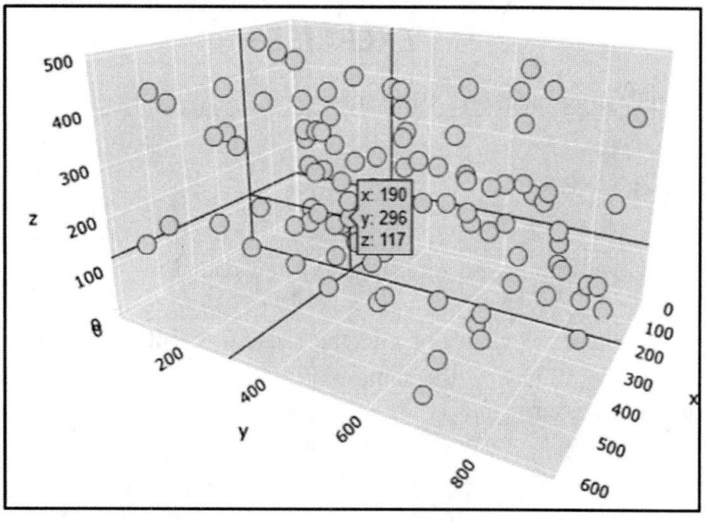

It must be noted that merely a preface to the plethora of functionalities offered by `plotly` have been covered within the limits of this book. Having gained the basic working knowledge of Python, the reader is encouraged to explore more about the visualization features offered by `plotly`.

SUMMARY

- `Matplotlib` is a python library which has a collection of functions for plotting 2-D graphics.
- The module `pyplot` has several functions for plotting histogram, pie chart, bar charts, line plots, scatter plots, etc. It also has functions for adding chart titles, axis labels and modifying layouts.
- The `plot()` function is used to plot lines.
- The `bar()` function is used to draw a bar chart which represents the data with rectangular bars.
- The `hist()` function is used to plot a histogram which represents the frequency distribution of values.
- The pie chart can be plotted by the `pie()` function. The data is represented as the percentage of the total data to be represented.
- The `scatter()` function is used to plot a scatter plot, where each value is represented by a dot in the plot area.
- The `subplot()` function can plot multiple graphs but in the same figure.
- The `patches` module of `matplotlib` has classes `Circle`, `Rectangle`, `Ellipse`, `Polygon`, `Regular Polygon` and `Arrow` to draw 2-D objects like circle, rectangle, ellipse, polygon, arrow, etc. in the form of classes.
- `VPython` is a Python based library used for plotting 3-D objects and animation.
- The functions `sphere()`, `arrow()`, `cone()`, `text()` are used for creating 3-D sphere, arrow, cone and text respectively.

EXERCISES

12.1 Plot the following functions using subplots.

$x^2 + 2x + 1$

$x * \sin(x) + \cos(x)$

$z^3 + 4z^2 - 15z - 90$

12.2 Plot the following function tan(x), sec(x) and cot(x) for the values of x in the range 10 to 20.

12.3 Plot a scatter plot for values of x in the range 0 to 360 and y=Sin(x).

12.4 Plot two or more lines on the same plot with suitable legends of each line and each with different colour.

12.5 Plot lines with different styles for the following sales data for the following years:

2019	30	67	90	45	59	41	78	88	49
2020	84	56	78	92	93	89	78	80	81
2021	67	70	80	90	77	88	43	99	56

12.6 Plot the pie chart for the number of admissions in different departments in a college:

Botany	Chemistry	Physics	Maths	Zoology	Economics	History	Hindi
89	108	56	73	78	98	59	35

12.7 Plot a bar chart in horizontal and vertical direction using the data given in question 12.5.

12.8 Plot separate histograms for the data given in question 12.5.

12.9 Plot the text "HELLO WORLD" in 3D space.

12.10 Plot a 3-D scatter plot of 50 random points.

Index